THE DATE OF
CHRIST'S RETURN

THE DATE OF CHRIST'S RETURN

Biblical prophecy for the Final Generation

Arnold V Page

BOOKS FOR LIFE TODAY
86a Totteridge Lane, High Wycombe, HP13 7PN, England
Email: sales@booksforlife.today
Website: www.booksforlife.today

What people have said

A fascinating and remarkable portrayal of the world's entire timeline in one cohesive, panoramic form, from a Biblical perspective. There's little doubt left about the soundness of the author's claims. The right audience for this book is anyone concerned about the world's future... I recommend it to futurists, scientists, the religious, seers, prophets, and heads of government. Regardless of your religion/value system, I would urge you to read this book.

From a review by Raju Chacko for Reedsy.com

Current events have all of us wondering what's happening with the world. In this book, Page gives us a comprehensive analysis of biblical and historical writings that show us the signs that Jesus will return and encourages us to prepare for a day that is coming closer every time the Earth turns. The facts presented give us a clear understanding of what to expect when the time comes and, more importantly, admonish us to be prepared. Arnold V Page explains many points that had me confused, especially in the prophecies of Daniel and the Book of Revelation. His writing is excellent, clear and concise, with examples from his personal experiences and other people he has known or heard of. *The Date of Christ Return* isn't a "scare tactic", but rather an encouraging reminder of the power of our faith that will sustain us for all of eternity.

From a review by Sherri Fulmer Moorer for
ReadersFavorite.com

I appreciated the references to Judaism, Muslim texts, and even science. I especially enjoyed the description of the Jewish feasts and how Christ's ministry was and will be the fulfilment of these prototypes. The appendices include all sorts of fascinating data.

From a review by Cecelia Hopkins for ReadersFavorite.com

The Date of Christ's Return

First edition. Copyright © Arnold V Page 2022

The right of Arnold V Page to be identified as the author of this work has been asserted by him in accordance with The Copyright, Designs and Patents Act 1988.

British Library Cataloguing-in-Publication Data
A catalogue record for this book is available from the British Library.

ISBN: 978-1-91612-132-4 (Paperback)
ISBN: 978-1-91612-137-9 (Epub)
ASIN: B09QRRTBKK (Kindle)

Figures 1 to 6: © Arnold V Page, 2022
Figure A1: © 2003-2022 by Stephen Tam. 3dbibleproject.com. All rights reserved. Modified with permission.

NOTE ABOUT SPELLING

British spelling (e.g. prophecy, centre, defence, favourite, judgement, sceptical), and 'for ever' as in the RSV translation of the Bible, has been used throughout.

DISCLAIMER

The Date of Christ's Return is an updated and expanded version of the second half of the author's book, *Z: The Final Generation*, published by Westbow Press in 2018. It is a work of non-fiction, based on the author's interpretation of the prophecies in the Holy Bible. Neither the author nor the publisher can accept responsibility for any actions taken as a result of reading this book.

Print information is available on the last page.

BOOKS FOR LIFE TODAY
86a Totteridge Lane, High Wycombe, HP13 7PN, England
Website: www.booksforlife.today

ACKNOWLEDGEMENTS

As I look back over my eighty years of life to date, I realize that I owe an enormous debt to those who helped me to know and love God as they did.

In particular I thank God for my mother, Ivy Stella Page, who taught me to believe in God from my earliest years; for Rev Dr John Ogden, who persuaded me as a young teenager to join a Christian Endeavour group, and through a sermon at Kentwood Methodist Church inspired me with a vision for evangelism; to Rev Peter Morley, the Methodist chaplain at Bristol University, who with his wife Mary blessed me and my fellow students with genuine love; to Rev David Watkins, my support and mentor in the Holy Spirit during my first difficult years as a probationary Methodist minister; to the evangelist Don Double, for his Good News Crusade family camps which meant so much to me and my young family in the 1970s, and for his partnership with me in various evangelistic crusades in Chile during the 1980s; and to Rev José and Carris Pulgar, for their unsurpassable love and support for me and my family during our brief but seminal ministry in Punta Arenas.

I cannot thank God enough for bringing me and my late wife Ann together. She dedicated her life to me and our four children, and she set the course of much of our life together through her genuine prophetic gifting. She was especially enthusiastic about the original version of this book, believing in its message even more firmly than I did.

Looking further back, I give thanks for the sermons of Rev. John Wesley, who taught me about salvation by faith and the hope of Christian perfection; and for all God's servants and martyrs who from the time of the Lord Jesus himself have preserved and propagated the knowledge of God and his promise of everlasting life through faith in Jesus Christ.

I believe this book to be the most important one I shall ever write, and I commend it to you as the fruit of the life and ministries of many, many people.

Preface

EVEN PROFESSIONAL FUTURISTS agree that no human being can foretell the future with certainty. The year I started to write the original version of this book, the British people voted to leave the European Union. Before the referendum nobody seriously thought the vote would go that way, not the government, nor the pollsters, nor even the leaders of the so-called Brexit campaign. Yet they were all mistaken. The majority of us felt like a galactic hitchhiker who decides he's being driven in the wrong direction. We tapped the EU on the shoulder, said, "So long, and thanks for giving back our fish," and got out of the car.

Here in the UK we still can't forecast the weather reliably more than a day or two ahead. We can't predict a volcanic eruption or an earthquake, nor can we always predict a devastating flash flood with sufficient time to move everyone to safety. So how impossible it must be to predict how the world as we know it will end, or when Jesus of Nazareth will keep his promise to return. Jesus himself said, *"But of that day or that hour no one knows, not even the angels in heaven, nor the Son, but only the Father."* (Mark 13:32)

But it's those words of Jesus which give us the clue we need. If anyone knows with certainty what is going to happen it can only be someone who has more than human knowledge, someone who can genuinely see into the future, someone who even has the power to determine what is going to happen and when. In other words, it can only be a supernatural being like the person Jesus called 'Father', the all-knowing, all-powerful being whom most people call 'God', at least in the English language.

If God does exist, if there really is a being with more than human knowledge and power, who is in some way shaping the future and who knows what the future is, then there is at least a possibility that he has told us what he is going to do and perhaps even when. The ancient Jewish prophets believed in such a God.

"...I am God, and there is none like me, declaring the end from the beginning and from ancient times things not yet done, saying, 'My counsel shall stand, and I will accomplish all my purpose.'"

Isaiah 46:9,10

Surely the Lord God does nothing without revealing his secret to his servants the prophets.

Amos 3:7

The revelation of Jesus Christ, which God gave him to show to his servants what must soon take place... Blessed is he who reads aloud the words of the prophecy, and blessed are those who hear, and who keep what is written therein; for the time is near.

Revelation 1:1,3

Those remarkable prophets predicted amazing details about the birth, life, death and even the resurrection of the Messiah, centuries before Jesus came. Their words have been preserved, and we can read them today. But they also spoke of a time when he would return, not as a humble preacher to die on a cross, but in power and glory to reign as a king; a time when he would take control of this suffering world and finally establish God's kingdom of peace and righteousness on the earth.

Hidden among their prophecies was the date of Christ's return, a secret God promised he would reveal at the time of the end. I began to study the Bible's teaching on this subject some fifty years ago, but it is only in recent years that all the dust has been removed, and the full, consistent and thrilling message of the word of God has sparkled with crystal clarity in my understanding. Generation Z, the current generation of children and young people, will be the last generation to be born before Christ returns.

I completely understand your scepticism. Christians have been prophesying Christ's imminent return ever since he left the earth. And didn't Jesus say, "No one knows"? It's true no one knew the date of his return when he said those words. But he also said that just as men know that summer is near when the fig tree comes into leaf, so we shall know that his coming again is at least imminent when all the signs he spoke of have been fulfilled. And the final and most definite sign that Jesus mentioned will be fulfilled in the next few years.

At the end of the book of Daniel, an angel gave the prophet a detailed outline of the events which would take place up to the end of this age. Daniel asked when they would all occur. The angel twice replied, *"The words are shut up and sealed until the time of the end."* (Daniel 12:9) The only sensible interpretation of this is that the meaning of the angel's prophecies would become comprehensible when it was time for this age to come to a close. And as you are about to read, there is overwhelming evidence that the end of this age is almost upon us.

For the first time in history, the Bible's unambiguous teaching about the date of the Messiah's return can now be understood in its totality.

Contents

LIST OF FIGURES

LIST OF TABLES

First of all you must understand this, that scoffers will come in the last days with scoffing, following their own passions and saying, "Where is the promise of his coming? For ever since the fathers fell asleep, all things have continued as they were from the beginning of creation."

Peter, in 2 Peter 3:3,4

Introduction

IT WAS THE EVENING of Wednesday February 18th 1981 at the end of the earth. I was living with my wife Ann and three of our four young children in Punta Arenas, the most southerly city on the mainland of South America, and earlier that day I had received news from England that my father had died.

I'd just been asked to say a closing prayer in the Methodist chapel in Fitzroy. Fitzroy is a district of Punta Arenas named after the British admiral, Robert Fitzroy, who explored that part of the world. (He had been the captain of HMS Beagle on Darwin's famous voyage.) I found myself praying, "Father, we know we need not fear anything, not even an earthquake or a fire, for whatever happens to us we are secure in your hands, and you are ordering all things in love for our good." I had never prayed such a prayer before in English, let alone in Spanish.

I wanted to return to England immediately to help my mother with arrangements for my father's funeral. This involved a visit the following afternoon to the International Police in the city centre to ask about recovering my passport from Santiago. It had been there for several months while our applications for permanent residence were being processed. The police assured me that I could collect it on my way back to England, which meant I could go the following day.

I was about to return to our house and start packing when I realized I needed to visit a travel agent to book a flight. But after a few steps in the new direction, something stopped me. For two days a phrase from the Bible had been swimming through my mind and it raised its head above the surface again: 'My times are in your hands'. So I stood still on the pavement

1

with traffic and people passing by me, and once more I prayed to God.

"Lord, my times are in your hands. Shall I go straight home or shall I go to the travel agent first to arrange a flight back to England?"

And somehow the Lord's answer came into my head: "Go home. Ann needs you."

I sometimes wonder how many disasters we might be saved from if we took more time to listen to God. Forty years before the terrible siege of Jerusalem in AD 70, Jesus warned his followers to flee to the hills when they saw the Roman armies approaching. Instead of that, most of the population rushed into the city, seeking refuge behind its walls. In the ensuing siege 1,100,000 people died of starvation, and when Jerusalem finally surrendered and the soldiers entered, they found only 97,000 people still alive.

A black collective taxi displaying my bus route number drove towards the bus stop where I was waiting for a bus. In those days collective taxis were large old saloon cars, which sagged into the ground like punch-drunk boxers longing for a knockout to bring their fight to an end. Deciding to save time rather than money, I accepted the driver's invitation to get in. For once, I was the only passenger. When you are crushed together in a back seat with two complete strangers bumping up and down in unison over potholed roads, you do sometimes wonder whether you've made the right choice of transport.

"You're going to Fitzroy?" the driver asked, as though he knew the answer already.

The drivers of 'colectivos' had to keep to their designated route, and they normally drove quite slowly because passengers, at least in those days, could flag them down anywhere, not just at bus stops. But my driver was different. Disobeying orders, he took the shortest route possible to our house, driving as though his life depended on it. He was in such a hurry that when I got out of the car at the end of our street, he was off again even before I'd closed the door. I thought I had annoyed him by taking too long to get out. It was only when I reached our house that I learned the reason for all the haste: the open doorway was filled with smoke.

My first thought was that everyone must have got out, but I stuck my head inside and called out several times, "Is anyone there?" There was no response. I retreated into the front yard and put my bag down in what seemed to be a safe place. There were no mobile phones in those days to summon a fire brigade, and I wouldn't have known the number anyway. So I shouted, "Help me, Jesus!", and went back into the house. I had to be sure it was empty.

Already there was so much smoke I couldn't see anything. This time I heard my daughter's voice upstairs. Putting a handkerchief over my mouth, I ran up the stairs and found her on the landing. I more or less carried her down. As we reached the ground floor, flames from the open-plan dining room singed her eyebrows. We made it outside to safety.

"Is anyone else in the house?" I asked.

"Nathanael is. We were playing in our bedroom. I told him to follow me."

The internal hardboard walls of the house were insulated with slabs of polystyrene, which by now was fully on fire. Whatever remained of the staircase was completely hidden from view by a curtain of oily black chemical smoke. I began climbing again and bumped into Nathanael in the pitch darkness. Our five-year-old had come nearly all the way down on his own! I tucked him under my arm like a rugby ball and turned to face the flames. I didn't know if the lowest stairs could still support us or whether they were even there any more. But in rugby there is only one way to score a try. You go for the touchline, regardless of whoever is or is not in the way. Somehow, I touched down with my small son in the open air.

Ann was now shouting for help from the first-floor bedroom window. She had been fast asleep, taking a siesta after a morning of teaching at the British School. The smell of smoke had woken her up.

3

"What shall I do?" she called.

"Come down the stairs!"

"I can't. They are all in flames."

"Then you must jump. I'll try to catch you."

"I can't do that!"

I remembered there was a short wooden ladder in the yard. A neighbour appeared and together we lifted it up to the level of the bedroom window. Ann was able to clamber down it to safety, although she did twist her ankle on the final jump. By now other neighbours were on the scene.

"Where's Jonathan?" I asked the world at large.

Jonathan was our three-year-old, the only one in the family still unaccounted for. Mary, a teacher from England, also lived with us, but someone reported she had jumped from her bedroom window and had been taken to hospital. That was good, but why had no one mentioned little Jonathan? Was he unconscious somewhere in the house? Or worse – had he burned to death? Where was he? Somebody said he might be with his 'granny' across the street. The widow, Carmen Barria, had become a dear friend to all our children, and especially to our youngest son. Perhaps he had gone over to her house for some reason. I knocked on her front door and Jonathan himself opened it, safe and sound!

By this time there was an enormous crowd of onlookers in the street. Two or three fire engines arrived, along with policemen and some marines trained in fire fighting. Then some reporters and photographers turned up. Next day there was a front page report in the principal local newspaper claiming that all six of the city's fire brigades had come to rescue us! The firemen who did turn up put out the fire and saved our most precious possessions, but we believe it was the Lord who rescued my family by bringing me back to the house in time.

The following day I returned to the scene of devastation, and looked around the kitchen where the fire had evidently started. The floor was black with smoke and the remains of burnt lino. All that was left of the two internal walls were charred wooden frameworks with gaping holes through them. On the outer two walls the wallpaper and part of the hardboard panelling had burned away. Everything had burned, except for one small corner of the kitchen. By the floor two small areas of patterned wallpaper were still intact. Between them on the smoke-blackened floor there were two light-coloured rectangular patches where two objects must have been standing during the blaze. Whatever were they?

Our next-door neighbours told me that the day before, they had removed as much as possible from the house for safe keeping after everyone left, including Ann's small stock of jewellery. So they must also have taken whatever had stood in that one unburnt part of the entire ground floor. And then I remembered what it was. Two 5-litre plastic cans filled with paraffin for our paraffin stove had been standing there. Miraculously the inferno had bypassed that one small explosive corner in the very room where the fire had started. "Not even an earthquake or a fire…"

The house fire in 1981 totally changed the direction of our lives, and eventually many people came to believe in the God revealed by Jesus Christ as a result of it. But I'll tell you about that later.

Why did I begin this book by telling you about the fire in Fitzroy? It's because it was just one of many events in our family's life through which my heavenly Father has demonstrated his reality, his care, and his power to act within the world he has created. Telling you this story will help you to understand why I believe there is a God who speaks to us, who can warn us of the things to come, and who is able to rescue us even when the world disintegrates around us.

'Generation Z' comprises people born between about 1995 and 2015. These young people are facing a future which is perhaps more uncertain than it has been for at least a century. But there is no uncertainty about the future in the mind and purposes of God. Z is the final letter of the alphabet and, as you will learn if you read on to the end, there are convincing reasons to believe that Z is the final generation who will grow to adulthood before Christ returns.

1. The world today

Doom predictions through the ages

'There are signs that the world is speedily coming to an end.' [1] Whether or not these words really were inscribed on an Assyrian clay tablet around 2800 BC,[2] there have since been hundreds of published predictions of the imminent end of the world, or at least of this current age. Here are a few examples.

In September 1666 London was beginning to recover from the Great Plague. This bubonic plague had slaughtered some 100,000 of London's estimated 400,000 inhabitants during the preceding year. Life had almost returned to normal when the old City of London caught fire. St Paul's Cathedral and most of the buildings in the city were consumed, including 87 parish churches and 13,200 houses. Bearing in mind that the year was 1666 and that the last book of the Bible says the 'beast' who will appear at the end of this age will be characterized by the number 666, most of London's inhabitants believed the end of the age had come and that Christ's return was imminent.

The Prophecy of the Popes was attributed to Saint Malachy in AD 1140, but was more probably written in 1590. It describes with surprising accuracy the characteristics of successive popes, with the current pope as the final one, during

---

[1] The first known reference to this version of an Assyrian inscription was in 1922: *Librarian's Report, 1920-22*. Report of the State Librarian to The Governor, State of Connecticut: Public Document No. 13, p.93, State of Connecticut, Hartford, Connecticut.

[2] As a Christian I prefer the traditional 'BC' and 'AD' for year dates. BC stands for 'before Christ' and AD stands for 'the year of our Lord' in Latin. Whichever letters we use, we still date our years from the year in which it was thought that Jesus Christ was born.

whose reign Rome was destined to be destroyed. Unfortunately for Malachy, Pope Francis is not called 'Peter the Roman' as he predicted.[3]

When I began writing this, someone was confidently predicting on YouTube that the USA would be wiped out by an electromagnetic pulse bomb from Russia by the end of the year. The bomb was going to disable everything electrical in the United States, even refrigerators. Consequently, no one would be able to survive, unless they bought a remarkable survival kit from this gentleman for the bargain price of $39. His sales spiel, that Bible prophecies about the destruction of Babylon actually referred to the USA, was surprisingly persuasive. This only goes to show how careful we have to be to balance faith and reason, and not twist the Bible to suit our personal agendas or bank balances.

In spite of the increasingly frequent predictions concerning the return of Christ and the imminent end of the world, the promised dates have so far all come and gone. The Messiah hasn't yet come, neither has Armageddon, the Rapture, the Antichrist, or even an invasion from Mars. So why am I adding yet another prediction about the end of the world as we know it, when history suggests that mine too will be proved wrong when the predicted date has gone by? You'll have to read on to discover the answer!

The Holy Bible

The basis of any serious belief that Christ will return, and of what will happen when he does, must come from the Bible. The Bible, above all other books, is about Jesus Christ. 'The

---

[3] *The Prophecy of the Popes* describes the final pope as 'Peter the Roman', and Pope Francis does not fit that description. However, at the time of his election there was an eligible African cardinal who was called Peter the Roman, and some have said that the election of Pope Francis did not comply with the laws for papal elections, because some cardinals were lobbied to vote for him.

Holy Bible', to give it its proper title, is a remarkable compilation of history, laws, poetry, songs, prophecies, biography and teaching. Although it was written by many hands in Hebrew, Aramaic and Greek over some 1500 years, it is consistent in its overall teaching from beginning to end. It is in two main parts, commonly termed the Old Testament and the New Testament.

The books in the Old Testament were written before the birth of Jesus by various Jewish prophets, priests, kings and historians. The first five books are often called the 'Torah', i.e. 'the Law' or 'the Teaching'. They include the accounts of creation, the flood, the origin of the Jewish and Arab races, the exodus of the Jews from Egypt, and the giving of the Ten Commandments and its associated laws.

The Old Testament also makes repeated promises about a saviour or 'Messiah' who was to come. Orthodox Jews and Christians (and Muslims for that matter[4]) believe that its history, teaching, prophecies and songs were inspired by God and tell us the truth about our Creator. This was a belief that Jesus Christ unquestionably shared.[5]

The books in the New Testament were written during the forty years that followed Jesus's death and resurrection. The authors were also Jews, people who had either known him personally and had travelled around with him, or who came to believe, after he had gone, that he was the promised Messiah and saviour of the world. The contents were eventually selected by the church on the basis that their authors were acknowledged to be men whom God had chosen and inspired

---

[4] Because the historical passages in the Muslim Qur'an don't agree with the corresponding passages in the Old Testament, Muslims claim that the Old Testament must have been changed since God gave it. This argument is difficult to sustain historically.

[5] In the Gospel of John, chapter 10, verse 35, Jesus (referring to a Psalm) said, *"...scripture cannot be broken."* Referring to the Torah he said in Matthew 5.18, *"...not a dot, will pass from the law until all is accomplished"*, and he repeatedly said that the Old Testament prophecies must be fulfilled.

to be his trustworthy messengers and teachers. They included at least two of Jesus's original disciples and two of his own brothers, James and Jude.

The New Testament begins with four 'Gospels'. These four short books are accounts of the life, teachings, miracles, death and resurrection of Jesus Christ. They are followed by the story of the early believers and the teachings of their leaders, and finally the book of Revelation deals mainly with the events leading up to Christ's return to set up the kingdom of God on earth.

The Qur'an, to which I shall also briefly refer, is the holy book of Islam. It was written soon after the death of the Arab leader Muhammad in AD 632. Muhammad believed that Allah, the name he gave to God, had given him the words via the angel Gabriel. He received and memorized these words over a period of 23 years and taught them to his followers. For Muslims, the Qur'an is the foundational book of their religion. It always speaks positively of 'the Torah' and 'the Gospel' as being teaching revealed by Allah to Jews and to Christians respectively.

Jesus promised his first disciples, *"When the Spirit of truth comes, he will guide you into all the truth; for he will not speak on his own authority, but whatever he hears he will speak, and he will declare to you the things that are to come."* (John 16:13)

You might not believe in the concept of absolute truth, preferring to define truth as whatever you choose to believe or 'what works for you'. But the main point in this verse is that Jesus promised that the Holy Spirit would tell his disciples what was going to happen in the future. I believe that if the Bible does tell us when this immediate age will end – and I do say *if* it does – then the end will almost certainly come around AD 2030. And I'm pretty sure I'll get you to agree with me on that if you keep reading.

My reason for thinking that the Bible leads us to a date around AD 2030 is not based on dubious interpretations of the meanings of symbolic beasts, nor on complicated codes assigning numbers to letters, nor even on some of the more traditional signs the Bible associates with the end times, such as wars, earthquakes, or blood-red moons. For the record, neither volcanic eruptions, earthquakes nor deaths from warfare appear to have increased in frequency during the last 50 or 100 years. They may do closer to Christ's return, but at present they do not provide any evidence that he is near.

My principal reason for believing that Jesus Christ's return is near is actually based on some rather simple deductions from what is plainly written in the Bible.

My plan

So here is my plan. According to the Guinness Book of Records, the Holy Bible is the best-selling book of all time. I hope to persuade you that it tells us, at least in outline, what is going to happen in the years immediately preceding Christ's return, and that it tells us when all this will take place.

I am not an astrologer, psychic, UFO hunter or mystic, nor am I a member of any religious cult. I am naturally rather rational and sceptical. This means I don't readily believe what other people say unless it is supported by convincing evidence based on facts. I am accustomed to dealing with facts, having been engaged in engineering research and development for 20 years. I consider that I have a sound understanding of the Bible, having been a full-time minister and Bible teacher for a further 20 years. And I have university degrees in both engineering and theology.

Furthermore, I am not trying to sell you anything apart from this book, and very few books make a profit for their authors. So I haven't produced an 'Armageddon Survival Kit for only US$39', and I won't be inviting you to buy a small plot of land on the Pitcairn Islands, far away from the coming nuclear war.

I've written this book simply because I believe the Lord wants me to share with you what he has shown me, and to convince you of its truth. He wants you to know what's going to happen and to realize how important it is to be ready for it. Then you will not only survive beyond the year 2030, but will live for ever! Yes, I did say that. God has told us what's to come so that you and I will live for ever. What the Bible describes as 'eternal salvation' is available to you, whoever you are, if you first believe it and then you accept it on God's terms. If this book helps you to do that, it will make me very, very happy.

And I'll be happier still if you will encourage all your friends to read *The Date of Christ's Return* and be saved too!

In this first main chapter, I simply want to survey some world trends which suggest the age we are living in is truly and objectively distinct from any preceding age in history. Something awe-inspiringly significant is coming to a head! Let's start with the world's population.

World population

Figure 1 shows the total human population from 10,000 BC to AD 2021, according to a study[6] published in 2019 and more recent information. Around AD 1600 it began to increase rapidly, and since 1900 it has exploded. It is true that the *rate* of population growth has recently plateaued, but no one knows if this trend will be maintained. In any case, the world's population will continue to grow at an alarming and unprecedented rate for the foreseeable future. By the time you

---

[6] *World Population Growth*. E.Ortiz-Ospina & M.Roser, revised in May 2019, published online at OurWorldInData.org. Retrieved from: https://ourworldindata.org/world-population-growth/ [Online Resource] Reproduction is authorized under a CC BY-SA licence. The data come from three sources:
  (i) before 1900: History Database of the Global Environment
  (ii) 1900 to 1940: The World at Six Billion, a UN publication
  (iii) 1950 to 2015: World Population Prospects: the 2015 revision, a UN publication.

read this it will be at least 8 billion. In the days of Jesus Christ, it was only about 170 million.

Figure 1: World population from 10,000 BC to AD 2021

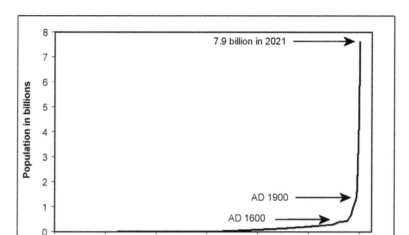

Food security

The world's swiftly rising population inevitably raises the question, will there be enough to feed everybody?

In general, the wealthier countries produce all the food they need, although soil erosion and depleting mineral content in the soil are beginning to take a toll. The indigenous populations of these countries are no longer growing fast and some are even projected to fall, so for many of us food security does not seem to be an issue.

It is in the world's poorer countries that there is cause for real alarm. Many of them are already suffering from food shortages. This is partly due to corrupt government and an unjust global economy, but in general it is because they have little scope for producing much more. Their lands are often semi-arid with little potential for irrigation, and they have limited natural resources to sell in exchange for food from other countries.

Centuries ago, North Africa was the bread basket of the Roman Empire, yet now even parts of southern Spain are turning into desert. Lake Chad in west central Africa used to supply fresh water to three west African countries, but between 1963 and 2001 its surface area decreased from approximately 25,000km^2 to a mere 1,350km^2, and it has now almost disappeared. The freshwater Aral Sea in central Asia, once the fourth largest lake in the world, has practically dried up. Other major sources of fresh water are heading in the same direction. The World Wildlife Fund predicts that by 2025 two-thirds of the world's population will be facing water shortages.

Yet it is in the poorest countries, where soil and water are vanishing, that the population is really exploding. The population of Niger, for example, is projected by the UN to grow from 14 million in 2006 to 58 million in 2050; Yemen's population from 22 million to 54 million in the same period; and Uganda's from 30 to 91 million. Even with all the resulting added manpower, when their lands will probably have become still drier and less fertile, will they really be able to grow three times as much food as they did in 2006?

It's likely that in the coming few years there will be either mass starvation or mass emigration. If the latter happens it will lead to increased social conflict in the receiving countries and perhaps even the erection of physical barriers to keep out hordes of hunger refugees. These things have already begun.

Rainforests and wildlife

About 80% of the world's known biodiversity is found in tropical rainforests. These forests provide the only habitats for countless kinds of plants, animals and insects, irreplaceable sources of new drugs, and genetic variations which can be used in developing disease- and insect-resistant crops. And they are disappearing. It has been estimated that between 1947 and 2006 about 50% of the Earth's remaining mature tropical forests disappeared, and that unless current trends change significantly only 10% will remain in 2030.[7]

About 137 plant, animal and insect species are being lost every single day as a result of tropical rainforest deforestation, equating to 50,000 species a year.[8] The World Wide Fund for Nature's Living Planet Report 2020 reported that over two-thirds of the world's wildlife had disappeared in the previous 50 years.

Loss of mineral resources

We depend on all kinds of minerals, for everything from heating and power to the manufacture of motor vehicles, smart phones and heart pacemakers, but some of these essential resources are being used up.

In the year I wrote this, the price of gas rose by 250% due to a worldwide shortage. Oil is the all-important mineral which currently powers road vehicles, ships and aeroplanes, and is vital for the production of plastics, synthetic fibres and a multitude of other things. Oil supplies seem to be reasonably safe for the predictable future,[9] but metals and chemical elements known as rare earths are fast disappearing. The latter are essential for the manufacture of smart phones, hybrid cars, wind turbines, computers and other things. China, which produces around 90% of the world's supply, claims that its mines will run out some time between 2030 and 2035. Some say that on current estimates silver will be gone by 2035, platinum by 2030, and copper – vital for electrical wiring – by the same year.

---

[7] *The Little Green Handbook: Seven Trends Shaping the Future of Our Planet.* R.Nielsen, Picador, New York, 2006.

[8] *Rainforest Facts.* Rain-tree.com., viewed 1 October 2016.

[9] *Why the world isn't running out of oil.* Detailed article by Brian Viner in the Daily Telegraph, 19 February 2013.

The increasing scarcity of finite mineral resources is the inevitable consequence of a seemingly infinite growth in the number of people who want to use them. Perhaps that's one reason why, according to the Bible, God is going to make a new earth when this present one finally wears out.

Rather than completely run out, what is more likely to happen is that vital raw materials will become more and more expensive as there is less and less of them in a usable form, so the demand for them will inevitably dry up. Where possible, generally less efficient alternatives will be found to replace them. Where that's not possible, we shall just have to learn to live without things we now take for granted. As Einstein said during an interview in 1949, *"I know not with what weapons World War III will be fought, but World War IV will be fought with sticks and stones."*[10]

If the world continues much beyond 2030, sticks and stones may be all we have left.

Global warming

In the 1960s, long before most people began to ascribe the cause of global warming to human activity, a British professor, Stafford Beer, predicted a potential problem with the polar ice. The polar ice caps help to keep the earth cool by reflecting a significant portion of sunshine back to the sun. Without the ice caps the earth would be far hotter. If for some reason the earth were to warm up just a little, some of this ice would melt, leaving less ice to reflect the sunlight, with the result that the earth would become warmer still, so the ice caps would melt still further. And this cycle of further warming and melting would probably continue until no ice was left.

What Professor Beer foresaw has started to happen. The massive Greenland Ice Sheet is shedding 300 gigatons of ice

---

[10] Einstein's quotation was recorded by A.Werner in *Liberal Judaism 16* (April-May 1949), Einstein Archive 30-1104.

into the ocean each year, while the sea ice around the North Pole is melting away so fast that it may be possible to kayak to the North Pole itself by 2030. The total area covered by ice in September (when it is at its minimum) decreased from 6.5 million km^2 in around 1985 to only 4 million km^2 in 2021.[11]

In the south, an article in *Science Advances*[12] has reported on the condition of the West Antarctic Ice Sheet. The authors wrote, '*There is evidence that a self-sustaining ice discharge from the West Antarctic Ice Sheet (WAIS) has started, potentially leading to its disintegration. The associated sea level rise of more than 3 m would pose a serious challenge to highly populated areas, including metropolises such as Calcutta, Shanghai, New York City, and Tokyo.*' They continued, '*The potential long-term sea level rise due to the instability of the marine ice sheet is estimated to be 1.2 m from the Amundsen Sea sector or 3.3 m if the entire marine part of West Antarctica is affected. This scenario is independent of whether natural oceanic variability or human activity caused the initiation of the instability.*'

Even the authors' lower calculation of a permanent 1.2 m rise in sea-level is far, far greater than any potential rise being mentioned by politicians and most news commentators. Once the West Antarctic Ice Sheet has melted into seawater, Antarctica's protective shield against the sun will be reduced, so the global temperature will rise still further, whatever success we may have in reducing carbon dioxide emissions. Putting our faith in offshore wind power to save the world is like trying to avert a nuclear attack by building more anti-aircraft guns. Human activity may well have triggered Stafford Beer's cycle of polar disintegration, but now that it's started it is very unlikely that we can stop it.

---

[11] *Current State of Sea Ice Cover.* Comiso J C, Parkinson C L, Markus T, Cavalieri D J and Gersten R, NASA Earth Sciences, October 2021. earth.gsfc.nasa.gov/cryo/data/current-state-sea-ice-cover (This web page is continually updated from satellite imagery.)

[12] *Stabilizing the West Antarctic Ice Sheet by surface mass deposition.* Feldmann J, Levermann A and Mengel M, "Science Advances", 03 Jul 2019. Vol. 5, no. 7.

Money

How we pay for goods and services has also been changing more and more rapidly, as Table 1 shows. The dates shown are very approximate, particularly for the early years, since different civilizations adopted different methods of payment at different times.

Table 1: Currency through the ages

Date	Method of payment
-4000	Barter
-1000	Barley, salt, etc.
-700	Metal coinage
1000	Tally sticks
1500	Bills of exchange
1700	Banknotes
1750	Cheques
1950	Credit cards
1987	Debit cards
1994	Online banking
2003	Chip and PIN cards – no signature required
2005	First online only banks
2007	Contactless cards
2008	Faster payments electronic fund transfers (EFT) introduced
2009	Digital cryptocurrency, especially bitcoin
2012	Contactless payments introduced on London buses
2012	'Swish' mobile phone app system for person-to-person payments introduced in Sweden
2014	Payment of friends and small businesses by mobile phone (PAYM) introduced in the UK (www.paym.co.uk) and other countries
2016	The city of Zug in Switzerland allows payment of small bills in bitcoin digital currency

Methods of payment are moving away from physical forms of currency to digital transactions, even if they still represent pounds, dollars or euros, etc. Sweden is leading the way towards a cashless society, with most bank branches no longer accepting or issuing cash at all. Since 2012 Swedes have been able to pay each other using their mobile phones, and since 2014 a similar system supported by seventeen banks and building societies in the UK has allowed payments by mobile phone to be made to both individuals and small businesses who register for it. There are apps for paying friends by phone, and others to pay for goods and services from both online and high street stores.

According to the market research website CoinMarketCap.com, more than 10,000 different cryptocurrencies were being traded publicly in 2021, with a total value of around 2 trillion US dollars.

Physical money in every form may become a thing of the past within the lifetime of many of us.

All these enormous changes have taken place since 1950, and most within the last 25 years only.

Weaponry

Throughout most of human history, weapons such as sticks, stones, spears, arrows and even guns, could kill only one person at a time. In the ninth century the Chinese discovered gunpowder and put it to limited use in warfare, and by the fourteenth century gunpowder was being used to fire cannonballs, which could sometimes sink a ship with all its crew. In the twentieth century, weaponry became increasingly destructive. Machine guns and shells using TNT were employed in the First World War, and during the Second World War powerful bombs were dropped. In 1945, a single atomic bomb was enough to kill about 90,000 people in Hiroshima.[13]

In 1994 the UK deployed a small fleet of nuclear submarines equipped with American Trident missiles. A single thermonuclear warhead on a Trident missile is eight times more powerful than the bomb dropped on Hiroshima, and each missile can carry four warheads, so by one calculation a single missile could kill $32 \times 90,000 = 2.88$ million people.

In July 2016 the UK parliament voted by a large majority to proceed with the building of a new 'Dreadnought' class of submarine to replace the current Vanguards. These will be operational from about 2028 with similar or yet more sophisticated weaponry. Russian president Vladimir Putin must have thought it was the funniest news he had heard for ages. His 40 megaton RS-28 Sarmat missile is two thousand times as powerful as the bombs dropped on Hiroshima and Nagasaki. A single missile with sixteen warheads could wipe out England and Wales, or France, or Texas, i.e. nearly 60 million people. With a top speed of 7 km/sec (4.3 miles per second) it can outfox any existing anti-missile shield systems, and with a range of 10,000 km or 6,213 miles it can reach not only Europe but both the east and west coasts of the USA.[14]

As Figure 2 shows, the killing power of missiles has exploded in more than one sense within the lifetime of many of us.

---

[13] *How many died at Hiroshima?* Dan Ford, http://www.warbirdforum.com/hirodead.htm, viewed 16 August 2016.

[14] *Putin's greatest warning to the West yet.* Daily Mail, 26 October 2016.

Figure 2: Deaths per missile

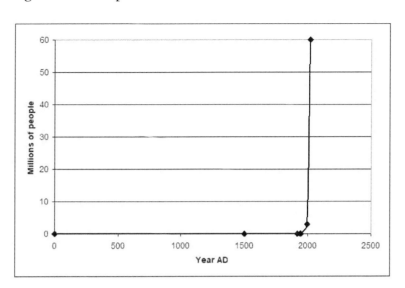

At the opposite end of the scale, but potentially even more deadly, are lethal autonomous weapons systems controlled by artificial intelligence.[15] These are tiny weapons that can seek out and select human targets without further human intervention. They could be programmed to kill, for example, all males in a region aged between sixteen and sixty. A single shipping container could carry a million such weapons, which could be made for a few dollars each. At the time of writing, their development has not been banned under any internationally accepted treaty. Autonomous AI-powered weapons systems are already on sale and may in fact have been used.

Equally terrifying is the possible deployment of biological weapons. These could be used, for example, to poison drinking water reservoirs. Only 15gm of the bacillus botulinus Type H, if injected, is sufficient to kill everybody in the world.[16]

---

[15] Described by Professor Stuart Russell in the BBC's 2021 Reith Lecture.

[16] *A novel strain of Clostridium botulinum that produces Type B and Type H botulinum toxins.* J.Barash & S.Arnon, Journal of Infectious Diseases, 2013.

Speed of transportation

The speed at which humans can travel has accelerated in a similar way to the increase in population. Ignoring the 17,500 mph that the space shuttle Columbia reached under manual control when it returned to earth in 1981, the speed at which normal people can travel has clearly increased geometrically and is continuing to do so. Table 2 gives an approximate summary of these speeds on land and in the air:

Table 2: Speeds of transport through the ages

Dates	Method	Approximate speeds in mph
Speeds on land		
10,000 BC to 3000 BC	Foot	7.5 jogging, 15 running
3000 BC to 1850	Horseback	10 trotting, 50 galloping
1850	Train	25
1950	Train	125
1970 to present	Train ('Bullet', TGV, maglev)	200
2027 (planned)	Chuo Shinkansen maglev (Japan)	315
2027 (possibly)	Intercity ETT or vac-trains	1000
Speeds in the air		
1925	Imperial Airways and others	100
1935	Imperial Airways and others	170
1940 to 1950	Commercial airlines	300
1950 to present day	Jet airlines	600

1976 to 2003	Supersonic airlines (Concorde)	1350
2023	SpaceShipTwo	2600

ETT or Evacuated Tube Transport, also known as vac-trains or Hyperloops, are transportation systems in which magnetically levitated capsules in evacuated tubes obviate the speed limitations of both friction and air resistance. Such tubes can be located either on land or under the land or sea. In the USA four companies are developing the idea.[17] Elon Musk, head of the Boring Company, estimated that the 350-mile journey between Los Angeles and San Francisco could be made in 30 minutes at a speed of over 700 mph. Richard Branson's Virgin Hyperloop One carried out a successful full-scale test in July 2017. Branson claimed that passengers would be able to travel from London to Scotland in 45 minutes at a similar speed. Other protagonists have projected that by the year 2025, passengers could be travelling at 1000 mph in intercity tubes.

In 2021 four 'amateur astronauts', the first real space tourists, spent three days circling the earth in Elon Musk's SpaceX vehicle at a speed of 17,000 mph.[18]

Figures 3 and 4 illustrate how the speed of transport on land and in the air has increased over time. As you can see, both figures look remarkably similar to the population graph in Figure 1. A further graph for travel by sea, ranging from human swimming to hydrofoils, would exhibit another similar trend.

Two modes of transport I chose not to consider were skiing down steep snowy slopes, which at one time was the fastest method of travel on land; and jumping off a high cliff, which for millennia must have been the quickest means of travel through the air!

---

[17] *Closing the loop.* K.T.Lee, Materials World, Institute of Materials, Minerals and Mining, December 2017.

[18] https://metro.co.uk/2021/09/16/spacex-launches-worlds-first-amateur-astronaut-crew-into-orbit-15266707/

Figure 3: Speed of transport by land through the ages

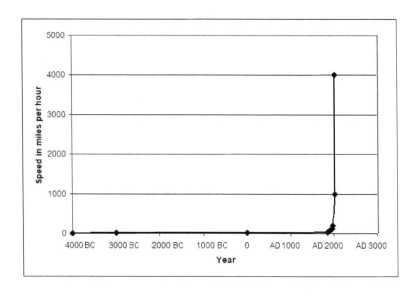

Figure 4: Speed of transport by air through the ages

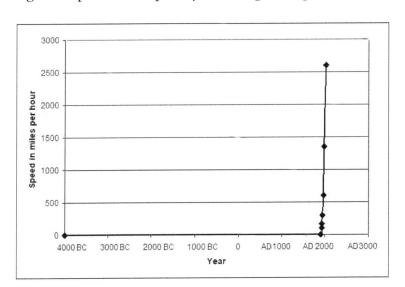

Distances travelled

Closely related to the speed of transport are the distances people travel. Before the Industrial Revolution, most people worked at home or close to their home, either in a cottage industry, in domestic service, or locally on the land. Almost throughout history the average 'commute' distance has probably been well under a mile. Only 80 years ago relatively few families owned a car, and people relied on bicycles or local buses to travel to work within the UK and similar countries.

Nowadays however most people travel by car, train or bus, and the distances they travel are continuing to increase. In 2016 the average regular one-way commuting distance reached 10 miles in the UK and around 14 miles in the USA.[19]

---

[19] The 2016 UK commute distance is extrapolated from the 2001 and 2011 national censuses. The 2016 US average commute distance is taken from http://www.statisticbrain.com/commute-statistics, viewed September 2016.

With the advent of cheap air flights, people are also travelling further and further for their holidays, even for short breaks. One can fly around the entire world for £1200, which is a mere month's rent of a one-bedroom flat in London. And while few people are likely to travel much beyond the earth in the very near future, Elon Musk has announced that he hopes to fly the first astronauts to Mars by 2026.

Strangely enough, there is a prediction about such travelling in the Bible. Around 590 BC a devout Jew named Daniel and a number of other bright young men from Jerusalem were taken captive to Babylon by Nebuchadnezzar's invading army. Daniel yearned to return to his homeland, and he spent long periods in fasting and praying to God for some clue as to what the future might hold for the nations of the world and for his own people in particular. Finally, after three weeks of semi-fasting, he was granted an extraordinary vision. An angel granted him an extended preview of the future, concluding with this message: *"But you, Daniel, shut up the words, and seal the book, until the time of the end. Many shall run to and fro, and knowledge shall increase."* (Daniel 12:4)

'Many shall run to and fro' must have seemed an odd thing to predict, but if Daniel could have been transported to London or New York in the rush hour today, what he saw would exactly explain to him what the angel meant. Not only the frenetic haste of the commuters, but their vast numbers ('many') would have taken his breath away.

Knowledge

'…and knowledge shall increase.' A rough guide to how human knowledge is increasing is to look at the number of books printed per annum. Between 1454 and 1800 the total number of copies of books printed in Europe per annum increased fairly steadily from 0.25 million to 12.58 million.[20] In the period 1990 to 2014 around 587,900 new titles were published per annum in Europe.[21] I don't know how many books are printed per title[22], but if it is 500 then we are talking about nearly 300 million new books per annum, a huge increase on the 12.58 million estimated to have been printed in 1800.

From moon landings to materials only one molecule thick; from the eradication of smallpox to heart transplants; from mapping the human genome to artificial kidneys; from ultra-high-rise buildings to robotics; from miniaturization to Bluetooth technology; and from spreadsheets to the World Wide Web – all these represent an extraordinary and historically unprecedented increase in knowledge within the lifetime of many readers of this book!

It is said that Thomas Aquinas, who died in 1274, was the last person to possess the total sum of human knowledge, at least as it existed within European civilization in the thirteenth century. However, the poor saint would have found it difficult to live up to this claim in August 2010, when Google calculated there were 129,864,880 different books in the world![23]

The reason Google wanted to know how many books there were is that the company aims to digitize them all.[24] If and

---

[20] *Charting the "Rise of the West": Manuscripts and Printed Books in Europe, a long-term perspective from the sixth through eighteenth centuries.* E.Buringh & J.Luiten van Zanden, The Journal of Economic History 69(02):409-445, June 2009.

[21] *Books published per country per year.* Wikipedia – data from UNESCO sources – 1990 to 2014.

[22] In 2010 the average number of copies per title sold in the USA was 500 according to T.Ward and J.Hunt in *The Author's Guide to Publishing and Marketing*, 2010. The number printed was considerably more.

[23] *Books of the world, stand up and be counted! All 129,864,880 of you.* L.Taycher, Google software engineer, 5 August 2010. Google's booksearch.blogspot.co.uk, accessed 16 August 2016.

[24] Taycher's post in the previous reference began, '*When you are part of a company that is trying to digitize all the books in the world, the first question you often get is: "Just how many books are out there?"*'

when it succeeds in that goal it will be possible to locate anything that has been committed to print simply by conducting an online search. No doubt by then Google will have combined its search algorithms with its improving translation programs, so a search for 'diseases of cats' ears', for example, will produce information on the subject in every language which has something to say about it in print. In other words, it will be possible for anyone to become an Aquinas and to know everything in the world, at least as and when needed.

This will be an extraordinary and almost frightening fulfilment of the revelation made to Daniel, that knowledge would increase at the time of the end.

Premonitions

The weekend I wrote this section there were three different films about the end of the world shown on terrestrial and Freeview television channels in the UK. *2012* visualized the destabilization of the Earth's core, *The Day After Tomorrow* predicted the near extinction of the human race by a new ice age, and *End of the World* saw the world burnt up by a solar flare.

If the production of apocalyptic films is any indication of a widespread sense that life as we know it is nearing its end, the Wikipedia article 'List of apocalyptic films' proves that more and more people are sharing this feeling. Figure 5 plots the number of apocalyptic films produced in each decade from the pre-1950s onwards.

Figure 5: Number of apocalyptic films released per decade

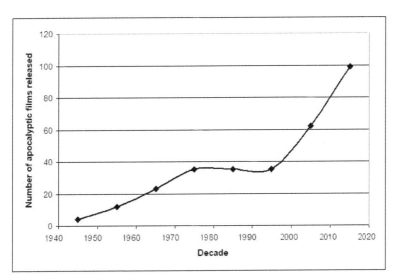

The figure of 99 for the decade 2010-2019 is extrapolated from a figure of 66 films listed for 2015.

Film titles listed for the previous decade include *4:44 Last Day on Earth, After Earth, Extinction, Goodbye World, The Last Survivors, Oblivion, These Final Hours, This is the End, World War Z,* and *The World's End.*

The assumption generally shared by futurists is that '*we are in the midst of a historical transformation. Current times are not just part of normal history.*'[25] Anyone who reads this chapter can see that the times we are living in are historically unique. Something extraordinary is happening to the world in our generation, and it is evident that many people sense it.

---

[25] *The Views of Futurists. Volume 4, The Knowledge Base of Futures Studies.* Edited by S.Inayatullah, Foresight International, Brisbane, 2001. Quoted on Wikipedia: 'Futurist', November 2017.

2. God's seven thousand-year plan

A model world

Figure 6: Brickplayer Kit 3

I think I was 11 years old when I was given a Brickplayer Kit 3. Brickplayer was a toy building construction kit popular before and after World War II. It consisted of building plans; small bricks, which were 10, 15 or 20 mm long and about 4 mm thick; metal doors and windows; sheets of tiled and concreted cardboard roofing; a 'cement' made from flour and chalk; and of course a small metal trowel. The cement set hard when mixed with cold water, but it could later be dissolved in warm water so that the bricks could be reused.

31

I made a bus shelter, a railway siding office, a small railway station and a signal box. I gave up on the bungalow and the 1½ storey house, so it's just as well it wasn't a Kit 4. Kit 4 comprised an entire village!

Whether it was this that gave my mother the idea, or whether her birthday present to me was actually part of a cunning plan to teach me bricklaying, all I know is that the following year she presented me with a pile of real bricks and some bags of sand and cement, and told me to build a coal bunker!

It is fascinating how often the historical events recorded in the Old Testament were models of much more important events which were to occur later in the life and teaching of Jesus.

Brickplayer models in the Old Testament

(i) The Flood (Genesis 6:1-9,18)

As we shall see in the next chapter, Jesus taught that at the time of the end there will be a period of such trouble on earth that few will survive it. To rescue those who love him, he will take them out of the world, taking everyone else by surprise. He likened this coming event to the occasion when God rescued Noah and his family from the flood.

> *"As were the days of Noah, so will be the coming of the Son of man. For as in those days before the flood they were eating and drinking, marrying and giving in marriage, until the day when Noah entered the ark, and they did not know until the flood came and swept them all away, so will be the coming of the Son of man."*
> Matthew 24:37-39

(ii) Abraham (Genesis 22:1-19)

God tested Abraham by telling him to sacrifice his son Isaac as a burnt offering, on what is believed to have been one of the hills on which Jerusalem was later built. When they arrived, Isaac asked his father where the lamb was, and Abraham replied, *"God will provide himself the lamb for a burnt offering, my son."*

As Abraham was about to slay his son, an angel appeared and told him to stop because he had passed the test. Abraham turned and found a ram behind him caught by its horns in a thicket, and he sacrificed this instead. This event clearly prefigured God's provision of his own son, Jesus Christ, to die as a sacrifice in our place. John the Baptist called Jesus 'the Lamb of God'.

(iii) Moses and the serpent (Numbers 21:4-9)

Towards the end of their 40 years in the wilderness, many of the Israelites died after being bitten by snakes. Moses prayed for them and God told him to cast a model snake in bronze, erect it on a pole, and tell anyone who had been bitten to look at it. When they did this, they didn't die.

Years later Jesus was speaking to his disciples about his forthcoming death by crucifixion. He said, *"As Moses lifted up the serpent in the wilderness, so must the Son of man be lifted up, that whoever believes in him may have eternal life."* (John 3:14,15)

(iv) Jonah (Jonah 1:1-4,11)

Most people have heard how the prophet Jonah was swallowed by an enormous fish which later coughed him up alive on the seashore, presumably as near as possible to the great city of Nineveh, where God had told him to go.[26] (Jonah, chapters 1 and 2) Nineveh was in what is now northern Iraq. Jesus linked this story to his own forthcoming visit to the underworld and his subsequent resurrection.[27]

> *"An evil and adulterous generation seeks for a sign; but no sign shall be given to it except the sign of the prophet Jonah. For as Jonah was three days and three nights in the belly of the whale, so will the Son of man be three days and three nights in the heart of the earth."*
>
> Matthew 12:39,40

The godless people of Nineveh believed Jonah's preaching. They repented and turned to God, with the result that they and their city were saved from destruction. They believed Jonah because they had heard about the storm and God's miraculous deliverance of him. In the same way, the people who listened to Peter's first Christian sermon believed him, repented and turned to God for eternal salvation, because they had got to know about Christ's death and his miraculous resurrection from the dead.

(v) The Exodus, the wilderness and the promised land

The escape of the Hebrew people from Egypt is the most famous event in Israel's history. (Exodus chapters 11 to 14) The full story of their deliverance from 400 years of slavery to their entry 40 years later into Canaan so closely parallels the

---

[26] Dozens of fossils of giant megalodon sharks (*Carcharocles megalodon*) have been found. Some of these are 18 metres (60 feet) long. A fish that size, whether a shark or not, could have swallowed Jonah almost without noticing him!

[27] In Matthew 12:40 Jesus said he would spend three days and nights in the realm of the dead. Job 3:19-21 and 17:16 describe this realm, while 1 Peter 3:18,19 and Ephesians 4:8-10 describe Christ's visit there to preach the gospel.

Christian gospel that one can only conclude God stage-managed the whole thing!

Table 3: Comparison of the salvation stories in the two
       Testaments

Old Testament	New Testament
Slavery to the Pharaohs and their taskmasters	Slavery to Satan and sin
Deliverance from the angel of death through the blood of a lamb	Deliverance from death by 'the Lamb of God, who takes away the sin of the world' (John 1:29)
Entry into a new life under the leadership of Moses through the waters of the Red Sea	Entry into a new life under the lordship of Jesus, through baptism in water
Learning God's will through the Ten Commandments and the Law	Learning God's will through the commandments and teachings of Christ
Guidance on their journey by a pillar of cloud and fire	Guidance by the Holy Spirit in various ways
Leaving the wilderness by crossing the River Jordan	Leaving mortal life by crossing the river of death
Beginning life in 'a land of milk and honey' under the rule of God	Beginning eternal life in a new world under the delegated rule of the Lord Jesus Christ

All the major events described in the Old Testament, at least until Jerusalem's destruction, were models of something yet more important, which God would fulfil later through his Son Jesus Christ. They all predicted events that were to happen, even though no one could have understood it at the time.

However, there is one major event in Old Testament history which I haven't yet mentioned, an event so important that you and I wouldn't be here if it hadn't happened. Can you guess what it is? I am talking about the creation of the world! Thinking about this, I asked myself whether that too could have been a model of something significant which God intends to do, perhaps something so significant that it rivals the death and resurrection of Jesus Christ in its importance!

A clockwise creator

Anyone who reads the Old Testament will discover that God is very concerned about time and timing. Being all-powerful he could have created everything in an instant, yet he deliberately took six days over the task. Later, he told Noah to start building an ark, but he waited another 75 years[28] until Noah was exactly 600 years old before he sent the flood. God promised Abraham a son, but delayed fulfilling his promise for years until Abraham was exactly 100 years old. He told him that his descendants would be enslaved in a foreign land for 400 years. (Genesis 15:13) He could have rescued them at any time, but he waited exactly 400 years before he called on Moses to do it.

After the people left Egypt, God made them wait in the wilderness 40 years before telling them it was time to conquer Canaan. He told the prophet Jeremiah that the nation would go into exile in Babylon for 70 years. And in Babylon he told the prophet Daniel about the coming four empires, the Neo-Babylonian, the Medo-Persian, the Greco-Macedonian and the Roman empire, each with a timescale on them.[29]

Then for 500 years after the Persian ruler Cyrus allowed a remnant of Jews to return to Jerusalem, there were no more angelic visitations, no prophets, no miracles, and no longed-for

---

[28] https://answersingenesis.org/bible-timeline/how-long-did-it-take-for-noah-to-build-the-ark.

[29] *Ezekiel Daniel – a Self-Study Guide*. I.L Jensen, Moody Bible Institute of Chicago, 1968, p.74.

Messiah. It was as if God had forgotten about his people until, as Paul wrote, '*When the time had fully come, God sent forth his Son, born of woman...*' (Galatians 4:4) The timing, you see, had to be right. Why?

The first chapter in the New Testament gives us a clue. Here Matthew provides a complete genealogy from Abraham to Jesus Christ. He sums it up in verse 17 like this, '*So all the generations from Abraham to David were fourteen generations, and from David to the deportation to Babylon fourteen generations, and from the deportation to Babylon to the Christ fourteen generations.*' If you want evidence that God has a thing about timing, this is it![30]

The special day

So what has all this to do with God's creation of the world? According to Genesis chapter 1, he took six days to do this. God reiterated this in the famous Ten Commandments, which God gave to Moses just after the exodus of the Hebrew people from Egypt. The fourth of his commandments was this:

> "*Remember the sabbath day, to keep it holy. Six days you shall labour, and do all your work; but the seventh day is a sabbath to the Lord your God; in it you shall not do any work... for in six days the Lord made heaven and earth, the sea, and all that is in them, and rested the seventh day; therefore the Lord blessed the sabbath day and hallowed it.*"
>
> Exodus 20:8-11

---

[30] In Luke's version two names, Arni and Admin, come between Hezron and Amminadab, where Matthew has only one name, Ram. (Luke 3:33; Matthew 1:4) Two names would make 41 generations from Abraham to David, not 40. However, some ancient manuscripts of Luke's Gospel have Aram (similar to Ram) instead of Arni, and others omit Admin. If these versions are what Luke originally wrote then they would match Matthew's genealogy, and Matthew's genealogy would be correct as it stands. There are no known variations of Matthew's version.

'Sabbath' means simply 'rest'. Every seventh day was to be a rest day for God's people, and the reason God gave for this was that he himself had made everything in six days and had rested on the seventh. Some people argue that he really meant it took him six long periods of time, but I can't make sense of the instruction 'six days shall you work and one day you shall rest because that's what God did' if that wasn't what God did. Since he himself wrote the Ten Commandments on stone (Exodus 31:18) that would have made him a liar!

Actually, the only reason for interpreting the 'days' in Genesis chapter 1 to mean six long periods of time is that most scientists believe the universe took far longer than six days to evolve. But all scientific calculations of the age of the universe are based on the unprovable assumption that the universe was not created supernaturally. Therefore the only reason not to believe that the Genesis account is literally true is that many people believe the Genesis account is not literally true!

It seems to me that by carefully defining each day in turn as 'evening and morning, one day' the writer of Genesis was deliberately making it clear he meant seven *literal* days. I don't see any way to get away from that. It's obviously what was meant in the fourth commandment; it's obviously what the people who heard it would have understood it to mean; and it's equally obvious that God would have known they would understand it to mean that.

I believe God neither lies nor deliberately misleads us, so he would never have told the people of Israel he had made the world in six days if he had not really done so. As my old friend the evangelist Don Double used to say, *"God says what he means, and he means what he says."*

One reason God chose to complete his work of creation in six days and spend another day resting, was to set a pattern of life for us all, but particularly for his chosen people:

- It was to give physical rest to their bodies and to their beasts of burden once a week, and to release them from feeling that they must keep working continuously to stay alive.

- It gave them an opportunity to enjoy the fruits of their labour.
- It was to be 'to the Lord', i.e. it was to give them an opportunity to draw near to the Lord God in worship and thanksgiving and to rededicate themselves to his service.
- It was to be a sign, a perpetual sign, to remind the people of Israel that the Lord had made heaven and earth in six days and rested on the seventh one. *"The people of Israel shall keep the sabbath, observing the sabbath throughout their generations, as a perpetual covenant. It is a sign for ever between me and the people of Israel that in six days the Lord made heaven and earth, and on the seventh day he rested, and was refreshed."* (Exodus 31:16,17)

The commandment about keeping the sabbath is the only one of the Ten Commandments which God specifically singled out to be observed as a 'perpetual covenant'. It was to be observed for ever, never to be overridden by any later covenant, presumably not even by the New Covenant which Jesus instituted. Once a week throughout their life and as long as the people of God endured, the sabbath was to be observed as a reminder that God made everything in six days and rested on the seventh day.

I wonder how many Jews continue to observe that commandment in that way today?

The secret of the sabbath

Why did God single out this particular commandment for such special treatment? Why was he so insistent that people should keep remembering he made the world in six days and then rested for one day? After all, if a man erected a timber frame house in six days, he might justifiably be proud of his achievement, but his family would soon get fed up with him if he reminded them every week that he had done this! And isn't it rather strange that God had to rest on the seventh day, when the prophet Isaiah said he does not grow weary? It's difficult to make sense of it, unless God intended it to tell us something very, very important.

I showed earlier that all the most significant events in the Old Testament were models of events yet more important which were to come. By far the most important of all the events described in the Old Testament was the creation of the world. So I suggest that when God created the world, he chose to do it in the way he did, not only as an example of a weekly pattern of work for people to follow, but as a model of something far more important which he planned to do in the future. The week of creation was a model, set out at the beginning of time, to reveal God's plan for the whole of this present age!

The key to its meaning is given by Peter, to whom Jesus once said, *"I will give you the keys of the kingdom of heaven..."* (Matthew 16:19) In his second letter Peter explained to his readers why Christ hadn't yet returned as they had been expecting him to. He said it was because *'with the Lord one day is as a thousand years, and a thousand years as one day.'* (2 Peter 3:8)

Putting this key into the lock of Genesis chapter 1, the six days of God's work and his one day of rest turn into six thousand years of something represented by work followed by a thousand years of something represented by rest. Is this fanciful? The authors[31] of the New Testament letter to the

---

[31] My belief is that the authors of the letter to the Hebrews were a married couple known as Priscilla and Aquila. Saint Paul referred to them as his helpers, and they had a church in their house. Firstly, they mostly refer to themselves as 'we' (e.g. Hebrews 5.11), whereas the other New Testament writers do not do that except where it is evident that they are referring to themselves and other apostles. Secondly the letter is soaked in the teaching of the Old Testament, and Priscilla and Aquila knew the Old Testament very well, for they had taught Apollos from it (Acts 18:26). However, Saint

Hebrews didn't think so. They wrote, *'For he has somewhere spoken of the seventh day in this way, "And God rested on the seventh day from all his works." And again in this place he said, "They shall never enter my rest." So then, there remains a sabbath rest for the people of God... Let us therefore strive to enter that rest...'* (Hebrews 4:4-11)

Hebrews urges us to believe in a coming period of rest analogous to entry into the promised land, a period of rest that somehow corresponds to a seventh day of rest each week. The author or authors of the Hebrews letter might well have seen this promised future sabbath rest as lasting a thousand years, because they kept referring to Moses, and it was Moses who wrote, *'A thousand years in thy sight are but as yesterday when it is past...'* (Psalm 90:4)

The idea of a thousand-year period of 'rest' perfectly matches what the risen Jesus revealed to the author of the last book of the New Testament, the Revelation to John. Revelation chapter 20 describes a thousand-year period at the end of the present age under the rule of Christ, which will precede a day of judgement and the creation of a new earth.

Then I saw an angel coming down from heaven, holding in his hand the key of the bottomless pit and a great chain. And he seized the dragon, that ancient serpent, who is the Devil and Satan, and bound him for a thousand years, and threw him into the pit, and shut it and sealed it over him, that he should deceive the nations no more, till the thousand years were ended... Also I saw the souls of those who had been beheaded for their testimony to Jesus and for the word of God... They came to life, and reigned with Christ a thousand years.

Revelation 20:1-4

Paul once wrote that he did not permit women to teach men (1 Timothy 2:12), and that attitude was widespread in the culture of the time. So if they did write the letter to the Hebrews, particularly if Priscilla was the lead author, they might well have thought it best to write it anonymously.

This period of rest from Satan and all his temptations will take place on earth, not in heaven. Earlier, Revelation says believers in Christ from every tribe and nation 'shall reign on earth'.[32] (Revelation 5:10) If the present earth is no more than six thousand years old, a subsequent thousand years of rest would reflect exactly the predictive model that God set out when he created the world!

But could the earth really be so young?

Six thousand years young?

According to the Hebrew Bible, on which the King James version and most other English versions of the Old Testament are based, the world began only about four thousand years before Christ was born. The widely quoted date of 4004 BC for the creation of the world calculated by James Ussher, a former Archbishop of Ireland, is only one of many dates people have worked out, but those based on the Hebrew Bible are all fairly similar. The Wikipedia article 'Dating creation' lists 25 calculations made by people as famous as Isaac Newton, Martin Luther and the Danish astronomer Johannes Kepler. They range from 4194 BC to 3616 BC, with an average date of 3946 BC.

Here is one relatively simple way I worked out that the calculation can be done. The book of Genesis tells us how old Adam was when his son, Seth, was born, and then carefully records the age of the father when each successive eldest son was born, down to the year that the Israelites settled in Egypt. (Genesis 47:7-9)[33] Over 22 generations this gives a total of 2238 years from the creation of Adam to the settlement in Egypt.

---

[32] Saint Paul referred to this period of reigning with Christ on earth in his letter to the Christians who lived in the city of Corinth. *'Do you not know that the saints will judge the world?'* he asked in 1 Corinthians 6:2.

[33] It is possible that the named sons were not always the eldest ones, rather those in the ancestry of Abraham, the father of the Hebrew nation.

To this must be added another 11 years, because when the Bible says, for example, that Adam was 130 years old when Seth was born, he could have been any age from exactly 130 years to 130 years plus 364 days, in other words half a year older on average than the Bible says. This gives us 22 generations x 0.5 = 11 extra years, making 2249 years in total.

Exodus chapter 12 verse 40 then says the Hebrews were in Egypt for 430 years until the time of the Exodus, taking us to 2679 years from creation to the Exodus.

By far the most likely pharaoh at the time of the Exodus is Ramesses II. It is known that Ramesses engaged in vast building projects, for which he would have needed many slaves. His building work included the cities of Pi-Atum and his new capital Pi-Ramesses in the eastern Nile Delta. These correspond to the cities of Pithom and Raamses, which Exodus 1:11 tells us the Hebrews built. In fact Numbers 33 verses 3 and 5 tell us they lived at Rameses, which has to have been the same place in spite of the change of spelling.

Finally, Pharaoh Ramesses's eldest son, Amenhirwenemef, is believed to have died 25 years after his father began his long reign.[34] If you know the Bible story you will recall that the eldest son of every Egyptian family, including Pharaoh's, died on the night of the Exodus. (Exodus 12:29; Numbers 33:4) It was the death of his son that finally persuaded the pharaoh of the Bible to allow Moses and all his people to leave Egypt.

Egyptologists differ in their estimates of the year when Ramesses II began his reign, but the consensus of most scholars is 1279 BC.[35] Adding 25 years to this gives a possible date of 1254 BC for the Exodus on the night Pharaoh's firstborn son died.

---

[34] *The Complete Royal Families of Ancient Egypt.* A.Dodson & D.Hilton, Thames & Hudson Ltd, 2010, p.170. Amenhirwenemef was buried in tomb KV5 in the Valley of the Kings.

[35] *The Complete Royal Families of Ancient Egypt.* As above, p. 291.

Hence, 1254 + the 2679 years from creation to the Exodus takes us back to 3933 BC for the date when the world was created, provided that:

- the Biblical records are complete and correct
- the pharaoh of the Exodus was Ramesses II
- the Egyptologists have got the date of the death of Ramesses's son right.

A date of 3933 BC is close to the 3928 BC derived by the famous sixteenth century cartographer Gerardus Mercator. Ussher himself traced the Biblical dates beyond the Exodus to 584 BC, when the final deportation of the Jews to Babylon was known to have taken place under King Nebuchadnezzar, but he appears to have made several errors.[36]

It must be admitted there is a historical problem with all such chronologies. According to the Bible, the First Egyptian Dynasty must have been founded after the flood, for during the flood everyone except Noah and his family drowned. However, the most widely accepted date of 3150 BC for the start of the First Egyptian Dynasty was 873 years *before* the date of the flood based on the above calculations. There is a detailed discussion about this problem in Annex 1: 'Egyptian chronology and the date of the flood'.

In any case it is clear that according to the Bible the entire universe is only about six thousand years old. In contrast, most scientists believe it began 13.7 billion years ago. A number of scientific measurements and mathematical calculations can demonstrate this, and they generally agree with each other.

---

[36] http://www.answersingenesis.org/articles/am/v1/n1/world-born-4004-bc. In spite of Ussher's amazing knowledge of the Bible, biblical languages, ancient history, ancient calendars, astronomy and chronology, he did make three known errors. He was probably trying to reach a date for creation exactly 4000 years before the birth of Christ, which he took to have been in 5 BC.

There is probably nothing wrong with most of them except for one thing: as I stated earlier, they all depend on the assumption that the universe was not created supernaturally. My book *God, Science and the Bible* explains how this assumption produces such great apparent ages for the earth itself and for the universe as a whole.

The secret revealed

Thus the composite picture given in the Bible is that humanity will live for six thousand years, subject to deception by Satan and the ravages of sin and death. Then, just as Adam came to life at the end of the sixth day of creation, those who publicly acknowledge Jesus and believe in God's word will be brought to life again in resurrection bodies like that of Jesus at the end of those first six thousand years. They will then enjoy a thousand years of rest from struggle and persecution, sharing in Christ's reign on the earth.

And it's those seven thousand years of life on this earth, which God was modelling for us in the first chapter of Genesis!

Although I came to see all this for myself during my own studies of the Bible, I learned later that Jewish teachers, both before and after the time of Jesus, shared similar beliefs, and that nearly all the Christian teachers in the early centuries were of the same mind. Annex 2 records what some of them wrote.

Here's just one example. It is from the Epistle of Barnabas, which was written in about AD 100. This particular document almost made it into the New Testament. It includes the passage: '*As there have been two thousand years from Adam to Abraham, and two thousand from Abraham to Christ; so there will be two thousand years for the Christian era and then will come the millennium.*' By 'the millennium' Barnabas meant the one thousand year reign of Christ on earth. These were evidently intended only as round figures. According to the Bible there were 1948 years from Adam's creation to Abraham's birth, and no one knew exactly how many years there were from Abraham's birth to Christ's birth.

Once it became apparent that Jesus was not going to return immediately, pretty well all the early Christian teachers came to believe, along with the Jewish rabbis, that the present age would end six thousand years after creation. Even in AD 1552, Bishop Hugh Latimer, who was martyred in Oxford, wrote: *'The world was ordained to endure, as all learned men affirm, for six thousand years.'*

It is easy to dismiss the beliefs of all those 'learned men', both Jews and Christians, as primitive ideas based on a mistaken belief in the literal truth of the Bible. But suppose that instead it is the modern belief – that the world is 4 billion years old and that life as we know it will end when the sun swells up in 5 billion years' time – suppose it is this belief which is mistaken. Could the world really be only a few thousand years old after all? And if it is, just how near are we now to the return of Jesus Christ?

3. Can we know when Jesus will return?

"Of that day and hour no one knows"

In a manuscript now in the Jewish National and University Library in Jerusalem[37], the great physicist and mathematician Sir Isaac Newton explained why he believed from his study of the Bible and history that the world would end no earlier than AD 2060. In publishing this date, he wrote:

> *This I mention not to assert when the time of the end shall be, but to put a stop to the rash conjectures of fancifull* (sic) *men who are frequently predicting the time of the end, and by doing so bring the sacred prophecies into discredit as often as their predictions fail. Christ comes as a thief in the night, and it is not for us to know the times and seasons which God hath put into his own breast.*

Jesus certainly told his first disciples, *"It is not for you to know times or seasons which the Father has fixed by his own authority."* (Acts 1:7) *"Of that day and hour no one knows, not even the angels of heaven, nor the Son, but the Father only. ...the Son of man is coming at an hour you do not expect."* (Matthew 24:36,44) And Paul wrote, *'...the day of the Lord will come like a thief in the night.'* (1 Thessalonians 5:2)

So is it wrong to try to predict when Christ will return? Will Christ's return be so sudden and unexpected that no one will

---

[37] *Works of Sir Isaac Newton, Yahuda manuscript 7.3g, folio 13 verso.* Jewish National and University Library. Quoted by S.D.Snobelen in his British Journal for the History of Science paper 'Isaac Newton, heretic: the strategies of a Nicodemite', 1999, pages 391-2.

know about it until it happens? In that case should I end this book right here? I was tempted to leave the rest of this page blank as a joke, but the question is serious and it requires a serious answer. It definitely sounds as though no one can know the timing of Jesus's return, but let's look at a fuller account of his teaching.

What Jesus said about his return

Here is the main passage about Jesus's return, from Matthew's Gospel, chapter 24, verses 29 to 44. Jesus says much the same thing in the gospels of Mark and Luke.

"Immediately after the tribulation of those days (which he had just been describing) *the sun will be darkened, and the moon will not give its light, and the stars will fall from heaven, and the powers of the heavens will be shaken; then will appear the sign of the Son of man in heaven, and then all the tribes of the earth will mourn, and they will see the Son of man coming on the clouds of heaven with power and great glory; and he will send out his angels with a loud trumpet call, and they will gather his elect from the four winds, from one end of heaven to the other.*

"From the fig tree learn its lesson: as soon as its branch becomes tender and puts forth its leaves, you know that summer is near. So also, when you see all these things, you know that he is near, at the very gates. Truly, I say to you, this generation will not pass away till all these things take place. Heaven and earth will pass away, but my words will not pass away.

"But of that day and hour no one knows, not even the angels of heaven, nor the Son, but the Father only. As were the days of Noah, so will be the coming of the Son of man. For as in those days before the flood they were eating and drinking, marrying and giving in marriage, until the day when Noah entered the ark, and they did not know until the flood came and swept them all away, so will be the coming of the Son of man. Then two men will be in the field; one is taken and one is left. Two women will be grinding at the mill;

one is taken and one is left. Watch therefore, for you do not know on what day your Lord is coming. But know this, that if the householder had known in what part of the night the thief was coming, he would have watched and would not have let his house be broken into. Therefore you also must be ready; for the Son of man is coming at an hour you do not expect."

The passage is followed by two stories or parables. They are both about people who were not ready for the person they were waiting for: the steward of a household for the return of his master, and some bridesmaids for the arrival of the bridegroom. (In the Western world it's usually the bride who keeps people waiting!) Jesus concluded these two stories with the words, *"Watch therefore, for you know neither the day nor the hour."* (Matthew 25:13)

Notice Jesus did not merely say, *"You know neither the day nor the hour."* He said, *"Watch therefore, for you know neither the day nor the hour."* What is the point of watching? It is to avoid being taken by surprise. The steward who pleased himself, and the bridesmaids who ran out of oil, were foolish because they allowed themselves to be taken by surprise.

So while Jesus repeatedly taught in this long passage that his return would be at an unexpected hour, it is clear that his reason for doing this was to encourage us to remain vigilant, so that we shall be prepared for his coming. The unbelieving world around Noah was not prepared for the flood when it came, but Noah and his family were prepared because they had listened to God. The householder whose house was burgled would not have been taken by surprise, Jesus said, if he had been on the lookout for a break-in. The foolish bridesmaids would not have been caught out if they had prepared for a delay in the arrival of the groom as the wise bridesmaids did.

Finally, Jesus said that just as when the appearance of leaves on a fig tree told people summer was near, so when his disciples saw all the things he had been predicting in the preceding verses take place, then they too would know his coming was near.

In other words, if we heed Jesus's instructions we shall know when his return is imminent, and we shall be ready for it.

What Paul wrote about Christ's return

This is exactly the message Paul gave to the Thessalonians:

> *But as to the times and the seasons, brethren, you have no need to have anything written to you. For you yourselves know well that the day of the Lord will come like a thief in the night. When people say, "There is peace and security," then sudden destruction will come upon them as travail comes upon a woman with child, and there will be no escape. But you are not in darkness, brethren, for that day to surprise you like a thief... So then let us not sleep, as others do, but let us keep awake and be sober.*
>
> 1 Thessalonians 5:1-4,6

'*You are not in darkness, brethren,*' Paul wrote, '*for that day to surprise you like a thief... So then let us not sleep.*' People only stay awake at night if they have reason to believe that a thief is coming. My purpose in writing this book is to tell you that Jesus is indeed coming very shortly, so that you will not be taken by surprise when he does.

Actually, everyone who knows and believes God's Word will know without doubt when Jesus will return, seven years beforehand. For in the next chapter we shall see that, just as John the Baptist announced Jesus's arrival prior to his first coming, so two prophets will announce his imminent arrival prior to his second coming. They will begin their prophetic ministry seven years before Jesus returns in power and glory, and, more importantly, three and a half years before Resurrection Day. Resurrection Day is the day when all believers in Christ, past and present, will rise from the dead. Clearly if we are part of the generation who are alive at his coming, and if we remain spiritually awake, we cannot possibly be taken by surprise, for we shall have had at least three and a half years to prepare ourselves for it!

Then is not now - now the time of revelation has come

The only other passage I can think of that suggests the time of Christ's return isn't for us to know in advance, is the one referred to by Isaac Newton, which I quoted earlier.

Jesus's disciples were talking to him after his resurrection from the dead. *'So when they had come together, they asked him, "Lord, will you at this time restore the kingdom to Israel?" He said to them, "It is not for you to know times or seasons which the Father has fixed by his own authority."'* (Acts 1:6,7) Jesus then proceeded to tell them that their job was to be his witnesses to the (geographical) end of the earth.

Now, when Jesus said these things, he was addressing his first disciples, not you and me. *"It is not for you to know..."* he told them, and they never did know. Those first disciples all died long before he returned. That is all we should conclude from these particular verses.

Dr. David Stern, in his *Jewish New Testament and Commentary*, includes this interesting extract from the Zohar:

> *Rabbi Yose and Rabbi Y'hudah were in a cave where they found a supernatural book. They began studying it, but it disappeared in a flame and a gust of wind. When they came and told Rabbi Shim'on what had happened, he said to them, "Perhaps you were examining the letters that deal with the coming of the Messiah?... It is not the will of the Holy One, blessed be He, to reveal too much to the world. But when the days of the Messiah approach, even children will be able to discover secrets of wisdom, and through them be able to calculate the time of the end; then it will be revealed to all."*
>
> Zohar 1:117b-118a

There are times when God does reveal what he is about to do. Through Isaiah God declared, *"...I am God, and there is none like me, declaring the end from the beginning and from ancient times things not yet done, saying, 'My counsel shall stand, and I will accomplish all my purpose...'"* (Isaiah 46:9,10) As a result, Isaiah was able to prophecy that Cyrus would conquer Babylon and allow the exiled Jews to return to Jerusalem.

The prophet Daniel spent many hours in prayer asking God to reveal the future to him. When God did so in great detail, Daniel recorded it in writing for the benefit of others.

Finally, from his place of exile on the island of Patmos, John wrote the last book of the Bible, Revelation. It begins, *'The revelation of Jesus Christ, which God gave him to show to his servants what must soon take place; and he made it known by sending his angel to his servant John.'* (Revelation 1:1) Far from telling us we should not try to know the future, John wrote, *'Blessed is he who reads aloud the words of the prophecy, and blessed are those who hear, and who keep what is written therein; for the time is near.'* (Revelation 1:3) Clearly, John wanted his readers to know what was going to happen, and equally clearly Jesus revealed this to him so that he could share this knowledge with us all.

Moses told the Israelites, *"The secret things belong to the Lord our God; but the things that are revealed belong to us and to our children for ever, that we may do all the words of this law."* (Deuteronomy 29:29)

So what we have to do is to study, not the secret things which only God may know, but the things which God has revealed to us for our benefit. He has revealed them to help us to do his will, to trust him, and to remain faithful to Jesus Christ when life gets tough, so that we can prepare ourselves and others to be ready for his return.

So what exactly has God revealed to us about the times to come?

4. The first three and a half years

The book of Revelation

The first book in the Bible, Genesis, describes how everything began. The last book, Revelation, describes how it will all end, at least so far as this earth is concerned. Its full title is 'The Revelation to John'.[38]

Revelation is a series of visions John received from the risen Lord Jesus, mostly describing events leading up to Jesus's return and God's re-creation of the earth. John wrote the book while he was in exile on the island of Patmos, almost certainly in or around the year AD 68.[39] It was not long after a terrible persecution of Christians by the emperor Nero.

---

[38] Although Bible scholars disagree about who this John was who wrote Revelation, my feeling is that it was the original apostle John. The author calls himself simply 'John', so he must have been writing to people who knew him well. Revelation begins with letters to seven churches, the first to the church at Ephesus and the rest to churches in neighbouring towns, and the apostle John had settled in Ephesus. Furthermore, if the author was not the apostle John it is unlikely that he would have identified himself simply as 'John' without explaining that he was not the apostle whom they all knew. Finally, because the Greek of Revelation appears to be so bad, some Bible scholars believe that it was originally written in Aramaic (the local language of Palestine that John the apostle would have spoken) and was then translated by someone else very literally into Greek. John the apostle was uneducated (Acts 4:13), so writing in exile without the assistance of a scribe who could have translated into good Greek what he dictated, he would either have had to write it in Aramaic or else in his own bad Greek.

[39] Some scholars believe Revelation was written around AD 96 in the reign of the emperor Domitian, but others date it around AD 68 during the brief reign of the sixth Roman emperor, Galbus. Revelation 17:9,10 speaks about seven Roman emperors, and says that the first five had died

John's overwhelming motive in writing Revelation was to encourage Christians to remain faithful to Christ, even if it cost them their life. *'Be faithful unto death, and I will give you the crown of life'* is a constant refrain, in those or similar words. (e.g. Revelation 2:10)

Near the end of the book, Jesus shows John a vision of the life to come, when mourning, crying, and pain will no longer exist, and death will finally be abolished. Then God himself speaks, encouraging John's readers to hold on to their confession that Jesus is Lord, even when threatened with death unless they deny Him. He says: *"He who conquers shall have this heritage, and I will be his God and he shall be my son. But as for the cowardly, the faithless, the polluted, as for murderers, fornicators, sorcerers, idolaters, and all liars, their lot shall be in the lake that burns with fire and sulphur, which is the second death."* (Revelation 21.7,8). In other words: "Whatever you do, don't be among those people. Something much, much better awaits you."

Between 2000 AD and 2010 AD, a million Christians worldwide are known to have been murdered for their faith. The actual number was probably even higher.[40] Today some 200,000 people may lose their lives each year for their faith in Christ. More than ever before, the book of Revelation is needed to encourage followers of Jesus to maintain their hope of resurrection and an inheritance of life in all its fullness in the new world promised by God.

If you found what I wrote in Chapter 1 alarming, I'm afraid you'll find this chapter positively terrifying, unless you hold on to the repeated message of Revelation, that the Lord Jesus will keep those who trust in him safe in the tumultuous days to come. That is one reason why it's so important to know Jesus for yourself. A yet better reason is that if you remain faithful to

---

at the time of writing. The book's closing words, 'Surely I am coming soon!', also support the earlier date, for the other New Testament writers had abandoned hope in Christ's imminent return well before AD 96.

[40] *An Insider's Guide to Praying for the World.* B.C. Stiller, Bethany House, 2016, p.176.

him in spite of everything life throws at you, he promises you a reward exceeding anything you or I could ever imagine, a reward which is not for this short life only but until the end of eternity.

Revelation uses a literary style with which John's contemporary readers would have been familiar, but which sounds very strange to our ears. From chapter 4 onwards, nearly all his teachings and visions are drawn from the Old Testament or from other Jewish writings in circulation at the time.

For example, in Revelation 6:12-17 John sees an awesome preview of the coming Great Tribulation, including the words, '...*the stars of the sky fell to the earth as the fig tree sheds its winter fruit when shaken by a gale; the sky vanished like a scroll that is rolled up...*' This echoes Isaiah 34:4: '*All the host of heaven shall rot away, and the skies roll up like a scroll. All their host shall fall, as leaves fall from the vine, like leaves falling from the fig tree.*'

Similarly, Revelation 7:16,17 describes the happy state of believers who have come out of the Great Tribulation. *"They shall hunger no more, neither thirst any more; the sun shall not strike them, nor any scorching heat. For the Lamb in the midst of the throne will be their shepherd, and he will guide them to springs of living water; and God will wipe away every tear from their eyes."* Most of this is an exact repetition of Isaiah 49:10 and 40:11.

Again, Revelation 22:2 is almost identical to Ezekiel 47:12.

Some Bible scholars maintain that the visions in Revelation are not intended to describe in chronological order what is going to happen, but provide little evidence for such a claim. John's repeated use of phrases related to time, such as, 'When the Lamb opened one of the seven seals', 'After this I saw', 'Then came one of the seven angels', all seem to demonstrate that he was describing the various visions in the order he saw them. And in that order, they generally provide a logical chronological sequence of events, which is supported by other scriptures.

Perhaps the one exception is Revelation 7:9-17, in which John sees a multitude of Christians 'who have come out of the great tribulation'. As I'll shortly explain, I believe it's chapters 8 and 9 which describe John's vision of the Great Tribulation, so the passage in chapter 7 should come after chapters 8 and 9.

Table 4 lists the principal events described in the book in order.

Table 4: Principal end-time events from the book of Revelation

Symbol	Duration	Event
7 churches 2:1 - 3:22	Brief period in the first century	Letters to seven churches in Asia Minor
7 seals* 5:1 - 8:1	Not specified	Prophesied events – the world, Israel and the Church.
6 trumpets 8:2 - 9:21	Brief period	**The Great Tribulation**
10:1 - 11:14	Three and a half years	Two prophetic witnesses in Jerusalem speak about Christ's return.
The 7th trumpet 11:15 – 12:17	Brief period	**The resurrection of believers in Christ**
7 bowls 13:1 – 16:21	Three and a half years	A satanically inspired ruler commonly called Antichrist takes over the world, supported by a false prophet and of course the devil. Only people who give their allegiance to him can buy or sell anything. Most people continue to reject any belief in God, but many Jews and others believe in Jesus as the

		Messiah. Those who do turn to him are persecuted or murdered. **God's wrath** is poured out in the form of worldwide plagues.
19:11 – 20:3	Brief period	**The return of Jesus Christ** in power and glory, accompanied by angelic armies and resurrected believers. (1 Thess. 3:13) The destruction of Rome, or possibly the destruction of worldly political, economic and religious powers. The Antichrist, the false prophet and their supporters are destroyed. Satan is bound for a thousand years.
20:4 – 20:6	A thousand years	Christ's millennial rule on earth
20:7 – 21:8	Brief period	The final battle The destruction of Satan, death and Hades The resurrection of unbelievers The last judgement – everlasting life for the righteous, final death of body and soul for the unrighteous A new heaven and earth
21:9 – 21:17	Eternity	The kingdom of God is inaugurated fully on the earth under the everlasting rule of Jesus Christ, with a permanent

		end to sin, suffering, sorrow and death.
* Wax seals on a prophetic scroll, not seals as in sea creatures!		

So let's look at these events in more detail, as foretold in the Bible as a whole.

Prophesied events

In the world there will be stress, materialism, rebellion, godlessness; anarchy, terrorism and wars; famines and earthquakes. (Always present, but perhaps a little more so now.)

In the church there will be religiosity, loss of faith, false prophets; the persecution and murder of true Christians, an outpouring of the Holy Spirit, the gospel preached throughout the world. (Always present, but the last in particular now.)

In Israel there will be the destruction of Jerusalem and the temple; the return of exiled Jews to the land of Israel, the re-establishment of Jerusalem as the capital of Israel, a restoration of the Hebrew language to common use, planting of trees, conversion of deserts to fertile land, protection from enemies; possibly the rebuilding of the temple. (All accomplished, except for the last.)

The Great Tribulation

(i) Overview

Isaiah chapter 2 contains the famous words quoted on a wall near the entrance of the United Nations Building in New York, '*Nation shall not lift up sword against nation, neither shall they learn war any more.*' But then Isaiah went on to describe what will happen before the Lord comes back to rule the earth. Three times he describes in the same way the terrifying days that will precede the Lord's return. '*Men shall enter the caves of the rocks and the holes of the ground, from before the terror of the Lord, and from the glory of his majesty, when he rises to terrify the earth.'* (Isaiah 2:19)

In Matthew chapter 24 and in a similar passage in Mark's Gospel, Jesus prophesied a time of great tribulation:

> *"So when you see the desolating sacrilege spoken of by the prophet Daniel, standing in the holy place (let the reader understand), then let those who are in Judea flee to the mountains... For then there will be great tribulation, such as has not been from the beginning of the world until now, no, and never will be. And if those days had not been shortened, no human being would be saved..."*
>
> Matthew 24:15,16,21,22

Judea meant Jerusalem and the area of land around it. So in saying 'let those who are in Judea flee to the mountains' Jesus was undoubtedly prophesying the forthcoming destruction of Jerusalem. He had made a similar prophecy at the end of the previous chapter. As I mentioned previously, over a million people died of starvation during the siege of the city, so it's not surprising that Jesus foresaw it as an unequalled time of great tribulation. No doubt he was thinking of a prophecy in Daniel chapter 12. This speaks of *"...a time of trouble, such as never has been since there was a nation..."* (Daniel 12:1).

In that verse an angel was speaking to Daniel. The angel continued, *"...but at that time your people shall be delivered..."* 'Your people' meant Jews, the inhabitants of Judea. Not the whole world. If the Jews had taken Jesus's advice and fled to the mountains, they would have been delivered.

It's true that the words 'if those days had not been shortened, no human being would be saved' sound more like a reference to a worldwide cataclysm, but Jesus almost certainly meant only that 'no human being in Judea will be saved'. In Britain, we might say, "No one wants to see the death of the English pub," but we wouldn't mean no one in the whole world. In teetotal Muslim nations they probably couldn't care less.

So Jesus's prophecies of a time of great tribulation referred to a time of tribulation for the inhabitants of Judea surrounding the coming destruction of Jerusalem in AD 70.[41] When he said in Matthew 24:34, *"This generation shall not pass away until all these things take place,"* that was literally true, at least so far as the destruction of Jerusalem was concerned.

However, in Revelation 7:9 the story is different. Here John sees *'a great multitude which no man could number, from every nation, from all tribes and peoples and tongues, standing before the throne…'* John asks an elder who these people are. He is told, *"These are they who have come out of the great tribulation; they have washed their robes and made them white in the blood of the Lamb."* (Revelation 7:14)

The vision clearly referred to a time in history when there would be believers in Christ throughout the world – 'from every nation, from all tribes and peoples and tongues.' The elder says the reason they died is that they have come 'out of the great tribulation'. Since you can't come out of something

---

[41] The reason some people believe Jesus's prophecy of a great tribulation refers to the end times is that in Matthew 24:29 and similar passages he continued, *"Immediately after the tribulation of those days… they will see the Son of man coming on the clouds of heaven with power and great glory."* In reality Jesus was saying that he would return immediately after the fall of Jerusalem. For he went on to say in Matthew 24:34, *"Truly, I say to you, this generation will not pass away till all these things take place,"* 'All these things' included the fall of Jerusalem and the accompanying period of great tribulation, and his return in power and glory. Regarding the fall of Jerusalem he was exactly right. The city surrendered to the Roman armies in AD 70, which was 37 years later and within that same generation. (In Psalm 95:10 and other places a generation is considered to last 40 years.) Regarding his return, the New Testament epistles written shortly before AD 70, including the book of Revelation, state that his return was very near, presumably because the generation Jesus had addressed was approaching its end. But when he did not return immediately after the fall of Jerusalem, the New Testament writers no longer had any idea when he would come, so the epistles written after that date do not refer to his imminent return. In Chapter 8 I've dealt with the question as to whether Jesus was mistaken in teaching that he would return so soon.

60

you have never been in, they must have been in it. The reason they are in heaven is that they have died, so the great tribulation has killed them, whatever it is. There is no escaping the unpleasant truth that even believers will have to experience a time of terrible suffering to come, and this time it will be worldwide.

(ii) Nuclear war?

What is this coming time of great tribulation which the world is about to endure? I believe it is described in the next two chapters of Revelation. In chapters 8 and 9, which cover the period of the seven trumpet blasts, a third of the earth is destroyed and over a third of mankind dies. [42] There could hardly be a spell of greater tribulation than this, and nothing worse has been described in earlier chapters. So why does Revelation chapter 7, in which John sees a multitude who have 'come out of the great tribulation', precede the description of great tribulation in chapters 8 and 9? I think Jesus was simply encouraging John and his readers to remember that even if they had to die as a result of what he was about to reveal, their final destination would be secure. And that is true for everyone today who commits himself or herself by faith to live for Jesus Christ and his kingdom.

It is hard to know whether the vivid descriptions of blazing stars falling from heaven, poisoned drinking water, smoking pits releasing giant stinging locusts, and 100 million horses that breathe fire and smoke are descriptions of genuinely supernatural events, or symbols which require interpretation to be understood, or whether John was doing his best to describe, in the nearest terms he could think of, a genuine preview of future kinds of warfare far beyond his own experience.

---

[42] It is estimated that the Black Death killed almost a third of the population of Europe and Asia in the 14th century. It can happen!

Obviously if the Lord had shown John a squadron of helicopter gunships for example, John could only have described what he saw in terms of the nearest things he knew – giant locusts with '*scales like iron breastplates, and the noise of their wings was like the noise of many chariots with horses rushing into battle*'. Only 200 years ago, if an inhabitant of the British Isles could have seen a video of a helicopter from the future he would have described it in much the same terms, perhaps substituting 'giant dragonfly' for 'locust'. Certainly Bernhard Philberth, whose impressive achievements and honours in science and engineering are listed on Wikipedia, wrote, '*Revelation recounts, in a logical sequence, the events and consequences of nuclear war, in every particular material detail.*'[43]

Every year that passes by, a nuclear war seems more likely. Having produced nuclear missiles capable of reaching the USA, it's hard to believe the unpredictable Kim Jong-un will dispose of them as he once suggested he might. Israel is convinced Iran's goal is to produce nuclear weapons, and if Israel were attacked, even US president Joe Biden might be inclined to intervene on her behalf. As I prepare this book for printing, the Russian president Vladimir Putin has ordered his nuclear weapons to be made ready in case his invasion of Ukraine incites NATO to intervene.

Back in 2004, Bryan Lawton, a former reader at the Royal Military College of Science, Shrivenham, predicted in his award-winning book *Various and Ingenious Machines* that statistically we were due for a global war in 2020. No wonder every public building in Finland has to have a bombproof shelter.

---

[43] *Lo he comes!* M.Basilea Schlink, The Faith Press, 1965, p.57. Philberth wrote something similar in *Christliche Prophetie und Nuklear Energie*. B.Philberth, Christiana-Verlag, Stein am Rhein, 1982, p.168f. An English translation was published by the Christian Catholic Bookshop in 1994.

(iii) Supervolcanoes?

However, there is another possible source of coming great tribulation for the world. When Peter was writing in 2 Peter 3 about the end of this age, he referred to God's earlier destruction of the earth by water and said that the next time it would be by fire. The water in the flood was real water, not supernatural water, so the fire too might be real fire, not supernatural fire. It could be spewed out by a series of volcanoes erupting simultaneously all around the earth, just as water did long ago.

In a passage from the prophet Joel, which Peter quoted in his very first public speech, God said, *"I will give portents in the heavens and on the earth, blood and fire and columns of smoke. The sun shall be turned to darkness, and the moon to blood, before the great and terrible day of the Lord comes."* (Joel 2:30,31)

When the Indonesian volcano Krakatoa exploded in 1883 after three months of rumbling and spitting, the resulting column of smoke and ash rose 50 miles (80 km) above the earth. The sun was indeed darkened for three days, and the moon turned red.

What's interesting is that there aren't any volcanoes in or near Israel, so Joel had probably never seen a real volcanic eruption when he pronounced that prophecy. Consequently, if the Lord had shown him a vision of one, he might easily have described the glowing red lava flow as blood, accompanied as he said by fire and columns of smoke. Or if the Lord spoke to him in words and if there was then no word for 'lava' in Hebrew, he might have said 'blood' to Joel instead, lava being the lifeblood of a volcano.

Notice that 'portents' and 'columns' are in the plural, and they will appear in the heavens and the earth, not merely in the land of Israel. That suggests widespread volcanic eruptions, not one isolated one.

The Krakatoa eruption ejected 50 cubic miles of rock into the air with a force equivalent to 13,000 Hiroshima bombs. The ash continued to encircle the earth for three years and it took five years for normal weather patterns to be resumed. At least 36,000 people died.

In May 2021 the US Geological Survey reported 1722 earthquakes in and around the Yellowstone National Park in Wyoming during the previous year. Although this figure was not unusual, the website states that *'if another large, caldera-forming eruption were to occur at Yellowstone, its effects would be worldwide. Such a giant eruption would have regional effects such as falling ash, and changes to the global climate lasting from years to decades'.*[44]

The Daily Star put the matter rather more dramatically in 2017: *'Should the Yellowstone Caldera erupt, it would kill 87,000 people instantly and render large parts of the US uninhabitable. It would then plunge the world into a 'nuclear winter' as ash clouds blotted out the sun – potentially threatening all life on Earth.'*

However, after prophesying blood and fire and columns of smoke, Joel gave a more reassuring message from the Lord. *"It shall come to pass that all who call upon the name of the Lord shall be delivered; for in Mount Zion and in Jerusalem there shall be those who escape, as the Lord has said, and among the survivors shall be those whom the Lord calls."* (Joel 2:32) That sounds like a special promise of safety for those who dwell in Mount Zion, where there are no volcanoes.

It may be that if you are a Jew living elsewhere, particularly in the USA, the time has come for you contact the Jewish Agency and start making preparations for aliyah to Israel. Is the Lord calling you to come home?

(iv) Earthquakes?

There is yet another possibility. Jesus prophesied that there would be earthquakes before his return. *"For nation will rise*

---

[44] https://www.usgs.gov/faqs/what-would-happen-if-a-supervolcano-eruption-occurred-again-yellowstone?qt-news_science_products=0 qt-news_science_products. Accessed May 2021.

against nation, and kingdom against kingdom; there will be earthquakes in various places, there will be famines; this is but the beginning of the birth-pangs." (Mark 13:8) There have always been wars, earthquakes (1 Samuel 14:15; Amos 1:1) and famines (Genesis 26:1; 41:54), so presumably Jesus meant that these would markedly increase at the end of this age. His phrase 'birth-pangs' pictures the earth writhing in agony, just as it does in a major earthquake.

Whether the coming tribulation will be the result of conventional warfare, earthquakes, famines, volcanic eruptions, nuclear war or a combination of these, I don't believe its cause will be supernatural. 'Tribulation' simply means 'suffering'. 'Wrath' is more likely to come only from God, and it is only later, after Resurrection Day, that Revelation tells us God will pour out his supernatural wrath upon the remaining inhabitants of the earth.

(v) God's protection

Do not be afraid! Remember how the Lord protected my family from harm in our house fire in Chile!

A Japanese Christian family called Tsutada once had a similar but still more dramatic experience. In August 1945 Mrs. Tsutada said, "I have an insistent thought that we should leave and go to another city." Her neighbours told her she was foolish, but the feeling was so persistent that eventually she persuaded her family to act on it. One evening they all left the city where they had lived. That city was Hiroshima, and the very next day, August 6th, an atom bomb utterly destroyed it. In time the entire Tsutada family became Christian missionaries, one daughter in Africa, another in Europe, and the parents with their two sons in India.

Peter wrote, *'If God... preserved Noah, a herald of righteousness... when he brought a flood upon the world... and if he rescued righteous Lot* [from the fire and brimstone which fell on Sodom and Gomorrah]... *then the Lord knows how to rescue the godly from trial…'* (2 Peter 2:4-10)[45] If you are among the godly and if you keep in touch with the Lord you need not be afraid of anything that is going to happen. *'God is our refuge and strength, a very present help in trouble. Therefore we will not fear though the earth should change, though the mountains shake in the heart of the sea.'* (Psalm 46:1,2)

Two prophetic witnesses

Following the Great Tribulation, Jesus says in Revelation 11:3, *"I will grant my two witnesses power to prophesy for one thousand two hundred and sixty days, clothed in sackcloth."* That number of days is exactly equal to three and a half years of 360 days. The previous verse speaks of 42 months, again equal to three and a half years, as though to confirm that this period was meant literally.

According to Dr. David Stern, there is a popular belief in Judaism that Moses and Elijah will return to the earth. The last but one verse of the Old Testament (the Tanakh) says, *"Behold, I will send you Elijah the prophet before the great and terrible day of the Lord comes."* In his commentary[46] on Revelation chapter 11, Stern writes, *'Rabbi Yochanan ben Zakkai* [taught that God] *said, "Moses, I swear to you that in the time to come, when I bring Elijah the prophet to Israel, the two of you will come together."'* (Deuteronomy Rabbah 3:17)

Assuming the two witnesses will be real people and not merely symbolical representations of the Law and the Prophets or the Bible and the Church, the most likely candidates at first sight are Moses and Elijah. Firstly, these two appeared to Jesus on a mountainside shortly before his crucifixion, where they spoke to him about his coming death and resurrection. (Luke 9:28-36) Secondly, Revelation 11:6 goes on to say that the two

---

[45] Several YouTube videos report archaeological excavations that appear to confirm the destruction by incredible heat of ancient buildings in the likely vicinity of Sodom and Gomorrah.

[46] *Jewish New Testament Commentary*. D.H.Stern, Dayspring, December 1998.

witnesses will have power to stop rain falling – something Elijah famously did for three and a half years – and power to turn water into blood and produce every kind of plague – something Moses did to the kingdom of Egypt.

However, Revelation 11:9 says that after three and a half years they will be put to death, and *'for three days and a half men…* [will] *gaze at their dead bodies and refuse to let them be placed in a tomb.'* I think it is most unlikely that God will bring Moses and Elijah back to life once more in mortal bodies to die a second time. But the death of the two witnesses does imply they will be two actual people, not symbolical representations of the Law and the Prophets or anything else.

I believe the clue to their identity is given in Luke 1:17, where an angel tells the old priest Zechariah that his wife's coming baby will go before the Lord *'in the spirit and power of Elijah…'* When Jesus's disciples asked him why Elijah himself hadn't come as the prophet Malachi had foretold, Jesus said in effect that he had come, in the guise of Zechariah's son, John the Baptist. My sense therefore is that the two witnesses will come in the spirit and power of Moses and Elijah, but will not be those two men in person.

Whoever the two witnesses turn out to be, their ministry in Jerusalem will give the clearest possible notice to believers that Resurrection Day is near. As I wrote earlier, just as God sent one prophet – John the Baptist – to prepare people for Christ's first coming, so he will send two prophets to prepare us for Christ's second coming. And just as Revelation 11:10 implies, their words and actions will be seen and heard by people all over the world – by means of television and the Internet.

The first three and a half years

5. Resurrection Day

Replacement guarantee

Many churches still regularly recite the Apostles' Creed. It includes the words, *'I believe... in the resurrection of the body...'*

A central part of the Christian faith is that one day everyone will be brought back to bodily life, either to live for ever or to be condemned to final death. Jesus said, *"...the hour is coming when all who are in the tombs will hear [my] voice and come forth, those who have done good, to the resurrection of life, and those who have done evil, to the resurrection of judgement."* (John 5:28,29)

If we have 'done good', Jesus promises that our present body will be replaced by a new body like the one he had after his resurrection. It will be a body which will never wear out or die again. *"...because I live, you will live also,"* Jesus told his disciples on the evening of his resurrection. (John 14:19) 'Doing good' means what it says, but it includes living by faith in Jesus Christ.

> *For as by a man* (Adam) *came death, by a man* (Jesus) *has come also the resurrection of the dead. For as in Adam all die, so also in Christ shall all be made alive... For the trumpet will sound, and the dead will be raised imperishable, and we shall be changed. For this perishable nature must put on the imperishable, and this mortal nature must put on immortality.* [47]
>
> 1 Corinthians 15:21,22,52,53

---

[47] According to the theory of evolution, death existed long before the first man 'evolved'. Either Paul was wrong or the theory of evolution is wrong.

This promise of resurrection for those who have put their faith in Jesus Christ is a central part of the good news. It is good news that every church and every individual believer is called to share. *"With respect to the resurrection of the dead I am on trial before you this day,"* Paul told Marcus Antonius Felix, the Roman governor of Judea Province from AD 52 to AD 58. (Acts 24:21)

The last trumpet

The question is, when will this amazing transformation take place? When will this wonderful change to our bodies happen? It will happen to Christians – true believers in Christ – all on the same day and at the same moment, whether they have died or are still alive. It will happen, both Jesus and Paul tell us, when an angel in heaven sounds a trumpet, in particular when 'the last trumpet' is sounded. And that's why I believe it's when we get to the last of the seven trumpets in John's vision that Resurrection Day arrives.

This is what John wrote in Revelation chapter 10: *'And the angel that I saw standing on sea and land lifted up his right hand to heaven and swore by him who lives for ever and ever... that there should be no more delay, but that in the days of the trumpet call to be sounded by the seventh angel, the mystery of God, as he announced to his servants the prophets, should be fulfilled.'* What was that 'mystery'? Paul told us the answer in 1 Corinthians 15:51,52. *'Lo! I tell you a mystery. We shall not all sleep, but we shall all be changed, in a moment, in the twinkling of an eye, at the last trumpet.'*

If you look back to Table 4, you will see that the last trumpet will be blown when the two witnesses have completed their three and a half years of work. At that point Revelation 11 tells us that 'the beast that ascends from the bottomless pit' will succeed in killing off the two witnesses. ('The beast' is normally considered to be someone referred to as the Antichrist.) But a few days later they come back to life and are taken up to heaven in a cloud. It is then, finally, that the seventh angel blows his trumpet. *'Then the seventh angel blew his trumpet, and there were loud voices in heaven, saying, "The kingdom of the world has become the kingdom of our Lord and of his Christ... and the time* [has come] *for... rewarding thy servants, the prophets and saints, and those who fear thy name, both small and great, and for destroying the destroyers of the earth."* (Extracts from Revelation 11:15-18)

I was born in London three years before World War II ended. When I was two years old my mother took me and my baby sister on a very crowded train to North Wales, beyond the reach of the German bombs and V2 rockets. One rocket had come down in the street next to ours. Hundreds of families made similar journeys to places of safety. It was called the Evacuation.

Revelation tells us that Resurrection Day will take place just before the Antichrist takes over the world and God pours out his wrath in a last attempt to lead an unbelieving world to repent. Resurrection Day will be the divine evacuation day for those who believe in Jesus, to escape from the outpouring of God's wrath. But this time believers will be travelling in a train of angels!

Jesus was a real man. Jesus rose from the dead. Jesus was taken up into heaven. It happened to Jesus, so it can happen to us.

As if to confirm that the seventh trumpet will announce evacuation day, the next verses in Revelation chapter 12 describe a dramatic vision. The vision is of a woman producing a male child who is to rule the nations. A huge red dragon awaits the child's birth in order to devour him, but the child is saved by being 'caught up' to God in heaven. The Greek verb translated 'caught up' or 'snatched up', *harpazō*, is exactly the same verb Paul used in 1 Thessalonians 4:16,17: '*...the dead in Christ will rise first; then we who are alive, who are left, shall be caught up together with them in the clouds to meet the Lord in the air...*'

The woman in the vision is clothed with the sun. She has the moon under her feet, and a crown of twelve stars on her head. After her child is snatched up to heaven, she flees into the wilderness, where she is nourished for three and a half years.

The most obvious interpretation of the vision is that the woman is the nation of Israel. In Genesis 37:9,10 twelve stars represent Israel's twelve sons, and the sun and moon represent Israel and his wife Rachel. (God later changed Jacob's name to Israel.) In the vision, the child that the woman gives birth to and who will rule the nations is Jesus (Psalm 2:8,9); and the dragon is Satan who tried to destroy Jesus soon after his birth by the hand of King Herod. (Matthew 2:13)

The woman's flight to a place of safety means, I believe, that Israel as a nation will in some way be protected by God during the last three and a half years before Christ's return. God will provide for them, as he provided food and drink for Elijah when he was in the wilderness; but they must flee there, just as Jesus told the Jews in Jerusalem to flee to the mountains prior to the city's destruction by the Romans. (1 Kings 19:1-8; Matthew 24:15-20)

The child's ascension to heaven to rule the nations does not represent Jesus and his ascension, because Jesus ascended to heaven 40 years before Revelation was written, and the first verse of the book declares that the visions in it were for events soon to come. Instead, it represents the resurrection of all believers in Christ, dead and alive; for believers will join Jesus in ruling the earth. (1 Corinthians 6:2; Revelation 5:10)

If the vision does not symbolize the resurrection of believers, then either they will be raised before the last trumpet sounds, which is clearly unbiblical, or else they will remain on earth after the seventh trumpet sounds. In this case they would have to suffer what comes next, which is an outpouring of God's wrath on earth. (Revelation 15:1) And the wrath of God is something that believers will not have to suffer, because '*God has not destined us for wrath.*' (1 Thessalonians 5:9) This is the whole purpose of the evacuation.

But what does the last verse of chapter 12 mean? It says, '*Then the dragon was angry with the woman, and went off to make war on the rest of her offspring, on those who keep the commandments of God and bear testimony to Jesus.'* (Revelation 12:17) Who are these people who keep God's commandments and testify to their belief in Jesus? If the child's ascension into heaven symbolizes the resurrection of all believers in Christ, how can there be obedient believers on the earth after Resurrection Day when the seventh trumpet sounds? For what follows next in Revelation is the outpouring of God's wrath upon the earth (Revelation 15:1), and the wrath of God is something believers will not have to suffer. As I wrote just now, *'God has not destined us for wrath...'*

The answer lies in the phrase 'the rest of her offspring'. These are not the resurrected Christians, represented by her male child, but the rest of the offspring of Israel, i.e. Jews who had hitherto not believed in Jesus.

After such a stunning, earth-shattering, worldwide event as the Evacuation, many people who remain on earth will at last believe the truth about Jesus and will become his followers as well, particularly God-fearing Jews. Paul, writing in Romans 11, says that at the end of this age, Israel as a nation will turn to Christ. It's easy to imagine that even if Israel in general doesn't immediately believe the testimony of the two witnesses in Jerusalem, once these witnesses and millions of other believers in Christ disappear from the earth on Resurrection Day, Jews will finally realize the truth and turn to God in repentance for their unbelief. And there's no doubt that many non-Jews will do the same. Perhaps John's words about 'those who keep the commandments of God and the faith of Jesus' refer to believing Jews and Gentiles respectively: *'Here is a call for the endurance of the saints, those who keep the commandments of God and the faith of Jesus.'* (Revelation 14:12)

Journey into space

For this we declare to you by the word of the Lord, that we who are alive, who are left until the coming of the Lord, shall not precede

73

> *those who have fallen asleep. For the Lord himself will descend from heaven with a cry of command, with the archangel's call, and with the sound of the trumpet of God. And the dead in Christ will rise first; then we who are alive, who are left, shall be caught up together with them in the clouds to meet the Lord in the air; and so we shall always be with the Lord.*
>
> 1 Thessalonians 4:15-17

This is Paul's description of Resurrection Day for everyone who has believed in Jesus. He told the Christian believers in Thessalonica that he had received this teaching 'by the word of the Lord'. Either one of Jesus's original apostles had told him what Jesus had said, or he had had some direct conversations with the risen Jesus after he met him on the road to Damascus.

The idea of meeting Jesus in the air may sound implausible to us, but flying through the air non-stop from London to Australia would have sounded even more implausible to Paul and his readers. To Jesus's disciples, who had watched him disappear into the sky at the time of his ascension, it would have seemed an obvious way to follow him there if he wasn't intending to return to the earth immediately.

This coming journey into space is what popular writers call 'the rapture'. That word is not in the Bible: it means 'seizing or snatching away'. Paul's teaching probably explains what Jesus meant when he said, *"For as the lightning comes from the east and shines as far as the west, so will be the coming of the Son of man. Wherever the body is, there the eagles will be gathered together."* (Matthew 24:27,28) Jesus was apparently drawing a picture of a flock of eagles fluttering around a body – in this case not a dead body but the glorious resurrected body of Jesus Christ himself, with all his resurrected followers fluttering around him!

"...they will see the Son of man coming on the clouds of heaven with power and great glory," Jesus said. *"...he will send out his angels with a loud trumpet call, and they will gather his elect from the four winds, from one end of heaven to the other... Then two men will be in the field; one is*

74

taken and one is left. Two women will be grinding at the mill; one is taken and one is left." (Matthew 24:30,31,40,41)

This really is going to happen! It is the word of the Lord Jesus, who cannot lie. Jesus warned his listeners again and again to believe what he said and to be ready for evacuation day by committing their lives to him in repentance, trust and obedience before it comes. Either be ready, or be left behind! *"As were the days of Noah, so will be the coming of the Son of man. For as in those days before the flood they were eating and drinking, marrying and giving in marriage, until the day when Noah entered the ark, and they did not know until the flood came and swept them all away, so will be the coming of the Son of man."* (Matthew 24:37-39)[48]

In 2021 unprecedented floods in Germany, Belgium and the Netherlands killed at least 120 people. Whole villages were swept away. Hardly anyone was prepared for the torrents of water that seemed to come from nowhere and sweep over them. Yet staff at the European Flood Awareness System said that alerts had been sent out several days earlier. *"Forecasters issued alerts early in the week, and yet the warnings were not taken seriously enough and preparations were inadequate,"* said spokesperson Professor Hannah Cloke. *"There were alerts going out... saying there's some very serious rain and floods coming: be aware."* Yet by and large neither the local authorities nor the people believed the warnings. They said, "It's never happened in my lifetime." They didn't prepare for what was coming, and as a result many of them lost their lives.

Do not ignore Jesus's warnings about the coming day of resurrection! Do not say, "It's never happened before." It *will* happen. He is coming for his elect. Are you among them? Does your life truly belong to him? He gave his life for you. Are you willing to do the same for the sake of his name?

---

[48] It is true that in these verses Jesus used the term 'the coming of the Son of Man,' an event which will happen three and a half years after Resurrection Day. But the very next verse begins, "Then two men will be in the field; one is taken and another is left." Jesus was clearly speaking about evacuation day, not his later triumphant return to the earth as king.

> *"Take heed to yourselves lest your hearts be weighed down with dissipation and drunkenness and cares of this life, and that day come upon you suddenly like a snare; for it will come upon all who dwell upon the face of the whole earth. But watch at all times, praying that you may have strength to escape all these things that will take place, and to stand before the Son of man."*
>
> Luke 21:34-36

Resurrected bodies

(i) The promise of resurrection

Anastasis, the Greek word for resurrection, literally means 'standing again', i.e. 'raising back to life'. The New Testament tells us our present bodies will be raised back to life again, but in a form that will no longer be subject to death.

Four days after his friend Lazarus died, Jesus told Lazarus's sister, *"Your brother will rise again."* She replied, *"I know that he will rise again in the resurrection at the last day."* Jesus answered her with these famous words, *"I am the resurrection and the life; he who believes in me, though he die, yet shall he live, and whoever lives and believes in me shall never die."* (John 11:25,26)

Jesus wasn't promising Martha he would restore her brother to life again in his old body, even though he did exactly that. Lazarus's old body, like all our bodies, was never going to last for ever. No, what Jesus was talking about was a life to come in a new body which would be immortal. He was able to make this astonishing statement because he knew that he himself would rise from the dead, never to die again, having conquered death on behalf of us all for ever, if only we will believe fully in him.

(ii) Our new bodies

The best way to understand this idea of an immortal body is to read what happened when Jesus himself rose from the dead. He appeared to his disciples on the evening of what we now call Easter Sunday, when they were huddled together in a locked room, terrified that they would be arrested by Roman soldiers for their association with a 'rebel leader'. Suddenly, without knocking on the door, Jesus was in their midst. Apparently his resurrection body was not bound by the normal rules of three-dimensional space. An hour earlier he had been talking to two other disciples in a nearby village and had then vanished in front of their eyes. (Luke 24:31)

Yet he was not a ghost. He invited his incredulous disciples to feel his body, to prove to them it was real: ' *"See my hands and my feet, that it is I myself; handle me, and see; for a spirit has not flesh and bones as you see that I have." And while they still disbelieved for joy, and wondered, he said to them, "Have you anything here to eat?" They gave him a piece of broiled fish, and he took it and ate before them.'* (Luke 24:36-43) Clearly ghosts don't eat fish, even angelfish. Even before he died, Jesus promised that when God's kingdom finally came, he would return to eat the Passover meal and drink new wine with his friends in celebration of their final deliverance from death. (Luke 22:14-18) Jesus's body may now be immortal, but he will still be able to enjoy a good feast.

"Blessed are those who are invited to the marriage supper of the Lamb," cries an angel in Revelation 19:9. Why? For one thing, a body like Christ's resurrection body is promised to everyone who believes in him. He will '...*change our lowly body to be like his glorious body,*' Paul wrote. (Philippians 3:21)

So what was Jesus Christ's new glorious body like? It was recognizably the same as it was before he died; it even bore the scars of his crucifixion.[49] But I think we can safely conclude that in every other way it was perfect, without any physical or mental handicap whatsoever.

That is how our new bodies will be! '*Then the eyes of the blind shall be opened, and the ears of the deaf unstopped; then shall the lame man leap like a hart, and the tongue of the dumb sing for joy,*' the prophet Isaiah declared. (Isaiah 35:5,6) If we have grown past our prime, we shall find ourselves back in it once again. Ageing is caused by the degradation of DNA. It was part of the curse of death incurred by Adam in the beginning, a curse Christ took on himself in order to liberate us from it. (Romans 5:12; 1 Corinthians 15:21,22) So our new resurrection bodies will no longer be subject to ageing and death: they will be eternally beautiful and strong.

> *What you sow is not the body that is to be, but a bare kernel, perhaps of wheat or of some other grain, So it is with the resurrection of the dead. What is sown is perishable, what is raised is imperishable. It is sown in dishonour, it is raised in glory. It is sown in weakness, it is raised in power. It is sown a physical body, it is raised a spiritual body... Just as we have borne the image of the man of dust, we shall also bear the image of the man of heaven... When the perishable puts on the imperishable, and the mortal puts on immortality, then shall come to pass the saying that is written: "Death is swallowed up in victory."*
>
> 1 Corinthians 15:37,42-44,49,54

Paul did get carried away from time to time!

---

[49] The fact that the two disciples who walked with the risen Jesus to Emmaus did not immediately recognize him does not mean that he looked totally different in his resurrection body. Certainly he would have looked astonishingly fit and well in comparison with the last time they saw him, but the main reason was that '*their eyes were kept from recognizing him*'. (Luke 24:16)

(iii) What is a spiritual body?

If we shall still look the same and be able to eat and drink, why does Paul say that our new body will be a spiritual body instead of a physical one? Doesn't that sound like something totally different from a flesh and blood body? It does sound like that, but Paul's use of the words 'spiritual' and 'flesh' was different from ours.

When he visited the Christians at Corinth, Paul discovered some serious misbehaviour. Afterwards he wrote a letter to them. *'I could not address you as spiritual men, but as men of the flesh,'* he wrote. (1 Corinthians 3:1) Paul tended to think of the flesh as bad: *'I know that nothing good dwells within me, that is, in my flesh. …those who live according to the flesh set their minds on the things of the flesh, but those who live according to the Spirit set their minds on the things of the Spirit.'* (Romans 7:18; 8:5) In Paul's thinking, a man of the flesh is governed by the worst kind of animal instincts, while a spiritual man lives the way God wants him to live.

So when Paul said that our body will be sown a physical body and raised a spiritual one he meant that our new body will be *morally* different. One definition of the Greek word translated 'physical' in the RSV and 'natural' in the AV, *psuxikos*, is 'governed by the sensuous nature with its subjection to appetite and passion.'[50] In Paul's thinking, our present bodies are governed by our sensuous animal instincts rather than by the Spirit of God, but in our resurrection bodies there will be no fleshly desires contrary to the will of God: they will therefore be 'spiritual' bodies. Nevertheless, they will still be bodies, as fully human as the body of Jesus was after his resurrection!

Actually, the Greek word for 'physical' in the way we understand the word is not *psuxikos* but *phusikos*. That's where our word 'physical' comes from. If Paul really meant that we

---

[50] According to Grimm's and Wilke's Greek-English Lexicon, Paul might just as easily have written *sarkikos* i.e. fleshly.

were no longer going to have physical bodies, he would have used the word *phusikos*.

There is support in the last chapter of Revelation for the idea that our resurrection bodies will be similar to Adam's and Eve's. Here John sees a vision of a river flowing through the middle of the main street in the city of God, and *'on either side of the river, the tree of life with its twelve kinds of fruit, yielding its fruit each month; and the leaves of the tree were for the healing of the nations.'* (Revelation 22:1,2) Even in the resurrection, our bodies may sometimes need to be healed, perhaps when we cut our hand sawing up logs, or we break a leg in a skiing accident.

Pay attention! Jesus in his resurrection body ate and drank. He said that he looked forward to eating the Passover meal with his disciples when he returned to the earth, and to drinking 'the fruit of the vine' again. (Luke 22:15,16,18) Food and fluid are needed not only for energy, but for the constant replacement of cells, the continuing growth of hair and nails, and the production of hormones used in the management of internal messages. Our new bodies may be spiritual, as Paul wrote, but we shall not be spirits. A human being can break a leg: a ghost can't.

(iv) Guaranteed to last a lifetime!

The other difference between our present body and our new one is that our new body will no longer be 'perishable': in other words, it will last for ever. Paul says this four times in this passage from 1 Corinthians chapter 15. Once the ravages of age and other kinds of damage to our bodies and minds have been repaired by God, our new bodies will be much like the bodies Adam and Eve had when God first made them. So could their bodies have lasted for ever? Yes, they could! Death resulting from DNA degradation only entered Adam and Eve's bodies after they had disobeyed God and fallen into sin. *'...sin came into the world through one man and death through sin, and so death spread to all men because all men sinned,'* Paul wrote in Romans 5:12. As though to make this truth doubly clear, God planted a 'tree of life' in the Garden of Eden, and Genesis 3:22 specifically says that if Adam and Eve had eaten of that tree they would have lived for ever.[51]

(v) Teleporting and flying

But what about this business of vanishing from people's sight and appearing again in a locked room, like Harry Houdini in reverse? How could Jesus have done that if he still had a solid body? I don't know, but he had already been able to do that kind of thing before he died, when his body was exactly like ours are now. On several occasions his claim to be equal to God upset people so much that they seized him to kill him, either by pushing him over a cliff or by stoning him to death, and time and again he somehow wasn't among them any more. (Luke 4:29; John 8:59; 10:31,39) Once or twice he appeared to his disciples walking on the Sea of Galilee at night in the middle of a storm.

Moreover, Jesus wasn't the only human being who could teleport in a normal human body. In the early months of the church's life, the evangelist Philip preached the gospel to a royal official from Ethiopia and finished up baptizing him in a stream by the roadside. *'And when they came up out of the water,'* Luke tells us, *'the Spirit of the Lord caught up Philip; and... he was found at Azotus.'* (Acts 8:39,40) Even in our present bodies, all

---

[51] ' *The 'capping' at the end of each chromosome, called a telomere, is like the capped tip of a shoelace, necessary to prevent the ends fraying. The telomere shortens with each cell division, and once the limit is reached, the cells can no longer divide and reproduce themselves. This is one way in which our limited life spans are 'programmed' into us. There is no biological reason why people could not live much longer than they do at present, if they had the appropriate genetic makeup.'* From *Living for 900 years* by Carl Wieland. *Creation* 20(4):10–13, September 1998.

kinds of things are possible when we live close to the Lord, and we shall all do that in the resurrection. [52]

According to my son, we cannot dream of something unless we have experienced it in reality. If he's right, then somehow I must have experienced flying, because I have often dreamt I was flying, and I don't mean in an aeroplane. In fact there are three things I intend to do at the first opportunity following my resurrection. The first is to find a mirror to see what I look like in my renewed body. The second is to discover whether I can fly. And the third is to find my wife and go with her – if possible – to meet Jesus and thank him for bringing us together and saving us.

(vi) No more babies

When God 'made them male and female' (Matthew 19:4) he made Adam and Eve different in character as well as in body, and those differences must surely remain in the age to come. They are an essential part of our humanity as God designed it. Yet in spite of all I have just written, our bodies may not be exactly the same as they were.

In Luke 20:35 Jesus said, *"Those who are accounted worthy to attain to that age and to the resurrection from the dead neither marry nor are given in marriage."* The principal purpose of marriage is to produce and raise children. If there is to be no marriage in the resurrection, the implication is that no more children will be produced. That must be so, for Judgement Day will be over so

---

[52] If this three-dimensional universe were part of a four-dimensional one, it would be possible to travel via the four-dimensional part from point A to point B, without travelling through any intermediate points such as doors and walls in the three-dimensional part. Imagine a lot of ants scurrying around on a flat patio. If you were to pick one up from one spot and place it down on another, the ants around it would ask, in ant language, "Where did you come from?" The ant would reply (again in ant language), "From the other side of the patio. I don't really know how I got here. I certainly didn't crawl all that way." Ant language is obviously quite advanced.

the number of the elect will be complete. In any case, if children continued to be born on a finite earth while nobody died, eventually there would be standing-room only. In the new earth, nobody will die and nobody will be born.

It follows that our new bodies, even though they will be in the prime of life, will be incapable of producing babies. For women this will mean an end to menstruation, which I imagine will be great news. Whether it will also mean the end of sexual activities is another question. We shall still look like men or women, for I am sure that Jesus still looked like a man after he rose again, and that implies continuing physical differences between us, even if the associated functionality changes.

Perhaps men and women will relate to each other in a manner akin to a sexual relationship but somehow unimaginably better. This seems to have been the view of C.S.Lewis. *'We know the sexual life; we do not know, except in glimpses, the other thing which, in Heaven, will leave no room for it,'* he wrote.[53] *'The whole man is to drink from the fountain of joy…'*[54]

(vii) The mystery of Noah

One question about the resurrection of believers still has to be answered. If it is only people who have believed in Jesus who will take part in the resurrection, will the men and women of God who lived in the Old Testament days be left out? Noah would have believed in Jesus if he had known him. So would Abraham and Moses and the prophets and their wives. But they didn't know Jesus, so will they be left out?

The Old Testament taught that when people die, good and bad alike, they go to a realm for departed spirits called Sheol, awaiting a day of judgement at the end of the world. (Job 3:16-

---

[53] *Miracles*. C.S.Lewis, HarperOne, Revised Edition, 21 April 2015.
[54] *The Weight of Glory and Other Addresses*. C.S.Lewis, Zondervan, 2001.

19; 17:12-16; Psalm 30:3)[55] In the New Testament this place is called Hades. 1 Peter 3:18,19 tells us that when Jesus died on Good Friday he too went to this same place in spirit. And 1 Peter 4:6 explains why he went there. '...*the gospel was preached even to the dead, that though judged in the flesh like men, they might live in the spirit like God.*' In other words, Jesus told Noah and everybody else who had died before he came that he was their promised Messiah. He told them that if they would believe this and put their trust in him as Lord and Saviour, God would indeed welcome them into his kingdom.

Jesus didn't remain in Hades of course, for on Easter Sunday he returned to bodily life. John 20:17 tells us that after appearing to Mary Magdalene he then ascended to his Father. This must just have been a quick celebratory visit home on that same Easter Day, since he was back with his disciples in the evening. But what a joyful reunion with his Father that must have been!

When Jesus ascended on high, Paul tells us in Ephesians 4:8-10 that 'he led a host of captives'. This appears to refer to those who had been imprisoned in Hades but had responded in faith to Jesus as he preached the gospel to them. Whatever Paul meant, it seems clear that the Old Testament saints and other righteous people who died before the time of Jesus will be included in the resurrection as believers when that day comes, otherwise there would have been no point in Jesus's preaching the gospel to them.

So where do people who believe in Jesus go when they die now? Jesus said to one of the thieves who was being crucified with him, *"Truly, I say to you, today you will be with me in Paradise."* (Luke 23:43) That's how most versions of the Bible translate what he said. But there was no punctuation in the original Greek texts, so what Jesus actually said could equally well have

---

[55] Jesus's parable of the rich man and Lazarus contradicts this teaching about Sheol or Hades. I have explained the reason for this in Annex 3: The truth about eternal punishment.

been, *"Truly, I say to you today, you will be with me in Paradise."* In that case he would simply have been promising the thief a ticket to heaven on Resurrection Day.

And that must have been what he meant. He couldn't have promised the thief they would be in Paradise together that very day, for he didn't return to his Father until after Easter Sunday morning. (John 20:17) He spent the intermediate two days not in Paradise but in Hades, preaching the gospel! So while this verse proves that true repentance and faith alone are necessary to be with Jesus in the life to come, it does not prove that all believers in Christ consciously enter his presence as soon as they die.

It's true that in Revelation 7:9-14 John saw a vision of believers who had died in the Great Tribulation, and they were in heaven before Resurrection Day. It isn't clear whether they were in their final resurrection body in the vision or in some temporary heavenly kind of body such as those experienced by people who have a near-death experience. It may even be that the vision John saw was simply intended to reassure believers who will die in the Great Tribulation that they will live in the presence of Jesus in the age to come.

One thing is clear. The New Testament consistently describes the condition of death as 'sleep', and the principal characteristic of sleep is unconsciousness. Therefore it doesn't make much difference where we go when we first die. Whether we are believers or not, we shan't be aware of our surroundings. We shall be safe, and our surroundings will not matter.

Bearing in mind the Bible verses we've just looked at, my feeling is that when *unbelievers* in Jesus die they still go to Hades to await Judgement Day. Remember that Hades isn't hell: it's not particularly nasty but it's not particularly nice either. Believers on the other hand will sleep in some pleasant heavenly place akin to a garden. 'Paradise' means a garden, so we might describe it as a true garden of rest.

85

Wherever we first go to when we die, we shall know little or nothing more until we wake up in the presence of Jesus. And that will be either to greet him with joy on Resurrection Day as a believer and follower of Jesus, or else much later to stand in trepidation as an unbeliever before his throne of judgement on Judgement Day. Where will it be for you?

6. The second three and a half years

The evil triumvirate

Table 4 briefly summarizes the events of the second period of three and a half years. During this time the world, no longer protected by the prayers and godly influence of the Christian church (2 Thessalonians 2:7), will be dominated by three figures: the dragon, the beast, and a second beast described as a false prophet.

The dragon represents Satan, '...*that ancient serpent, who is called the Devil and Satan, the deceiver of the whole world.*' (Revelation 12:9)

The first beast is also referred to as the Antichrist. He will be an evil person motivated by Satan who, like the Roman emperors of John's time, will compel people to worship him or face death. (Revelation 13:1-10)

The second beast, the false prophet, will perform miraculous signs and will institute 'the mark of the beast', which will somehow be associated with the number of the beast, 666. People will be required to have this printed on their forehead or hand in order to buy and sell. (Revelation 13:11-18) Perhaps it will be a tattoo or even a holographic barcode. The three pairs of longer lines used to locate the beginning, middle and end of a barcode do appear to represent three 6s.

The law of the Lord (e.g. Deuteronomy 6:8) commands Jews to fasten the Ten Commandments to their wrists and forehead, and some devout Jews do this today when they pray. So being compelled to replace these by the number of the beast would appear to be a deliberate attack on any Jews who don't flee into the wilderness in time.

The false prophet will also set up an image of the beast, which people will have to worship. (Revelation 13:14,15) That would represent a further attack on Jews, for the second commandment forbids them to bow down to any kind of image. (Deuteronomy 5:8,9) Because the image will be able to speak, it may well be a robot equipped with massive artificial intelligence. This isn't so far-fetched as it might sound. In 2015 Oxford philosophy professor Nick Bostrom published a letter warning that artificial intelligence could go wrong and take over the world. Among those who agreed with him and who added their signatures to the letter were Bill Gates, the founder of Microsoft; Elon Musk, the founder of Tesla Cars and SpaceX; Lord Martin Rees, the UK's astronomer royal; and the late Stephen Hawking, who was one of the greatest brains of his generation.

Revelation 13:15 adds the chilling information that the image will be able to cause those who will not worship it to be slain. Does that sound unbelievable? Professor Stuart Russell in the BBC's 2021 Reith Lecture said, "Artificial intelligence algorithms that have the power to kill human beings and can decide to do so already exist."

Computers have already beaten the world's best chess and Go players, as well as America's two top champions in the general knowledge quiz show Jeopardy! The Megatron Transformer knows the whole of Wikipedia in English, 63 million English news articles from 2016-2019, 38 gigabytes' worth of Reddit discourse, and a huge number of creative commons sources.[56] It is frighteningly easy to envisage a time when all decisions of government and justice will be left to a supercomputer which has access to all human knowledge and exceeds all human beings in intelligence.

---

[56] *We invited an AI to debate its own ethics in the Oxford Union – what it said was startling.* A.Connock and A.Stephen, www.theconversation.com, 10 December 2021.

This evil triumvirate of Satan and the two beasts will be a parody of the Holy Trinity – God the Father, God the Son, and God the Holy Spirit. Some Bible commentators see the two beasts not as diabolically evil men, but merely as representing anti-Christian government and anti-Christian religion. However, the Bible is clear that the Antichrist at least will be a real person, and I have no doubt that the false prophet will be too.

Let no one deceive you in any way; for that day will not come, unless the rebellion comes first, and the man of lawlessness is revealed, the son of perdition, who opposes and exalts himself against every so-called god or object of worship, so that he takes his seat in the temple of God, proclaiming himself to be God. And then the lawless one will be revealed, and the Lord Jesus will slay him with the breath of his mouth and destroy him by his appearing and his coming.

2 Thessalonians 2:3,4,8

The temple

Paul's words about a man of lawlessness who would proclaim himself to be God in the temple at Jerusalem echoed prophecies in the Old Testament book of Daniel. (Daniel 7:25; 8:9-14; 11:31-37) Daniel chapter 11 verses 31 and 37 say: *"Forces from* ['a contemptible person to whom royal majesty has not been given'] *shall appear and profane the temple and fortress, and shall take away the continual burnt offering. And they shall set up the abomination that makes desolate. ...he shall not give heed to any other god, for he shall magnify himself above all."*

Paul wrote his letters to the Thessalonian Christians in about AD 50, twenty years before the Romans destroyed the temple in Jerusalem. At that time, Paul and the other apostles still believed Jesus would return within their lifetime. So he probably assumed that the coming 'man of lawlessness' would set himself up as God in the temple as it still then existed.

So will a real literal temple have to be built again in Jerusalem before the final seven years begin, or won't it? Let's look at both sides of the argument.

Religious Jews today believe the Jerusalem temple will be rebuilt before the Messiah comes. Malachi 3:1 says: *"Behold, I send my messenger to prepare the way before me, and the Lord whom you seek will suddenly come to his temple; the messenger of the covenant in whom you delight, behold, he is coming, says the Lord of hosts."* They believe the Messiah will enter the temple area via the Eastern Gate to the city, also known as the Golden Gate. This has been walled up for the last 500 years. The prophet Ezekiel had a vision: '[The angel] *brought me to the gate, the gate facing east. And behold, the glory of the God of Israel came from the east; and the sound of his coming was like the sound of many waters; and the earth shone with his glory. ...the glory of the Lord entered the temple by the gate facing east...'* (Ezekiel 43:1-4)

The Temple Institute is a Jewish organization located in Jerusalem's Old City. It has already prepared vestments and equipment for use in a new temple. In August 2016 the International Middle East Media Center reported active preparations by at least two organizations for building a temple on the site of the present Al-Aqsa Mosque. That is where they believe Herod's Jewish temple stood.[57] They claimed that the work could be completed in three years once it started. President Donald Trump's decision in December 2017 formally to recognize Jerusalem as the capital of Israel would have given further encouragement to these people.

---

[57] In 1927 the Al-Aqsa mosque was severely damaged by an earthquake. The British archaeologist Robert Hamilton was given permission to excavate its exposed foundations. He discovered numerous fragments from an earlier Byzantine church and even a Jewish mikveh. This was a ritual pool used for purification, and it dated back to the era of Herod's Jewish temple. The full story was reported on the website of Israel and stuff.com: www.israelandstuff.com/second-temple-era-mikveh-discovered-under-al-aqsa-mosque.

The existence of a temple halfway through the last seven years appears to be supported by Revelation 11:1,2: '*Then I was given a measuring rod like a staff, and I was told: "Rise and measure the temple of God and the altar and those who worship there, but do not measure the court outside the temple; leave that out, for it is given over to the nations, and they will trample over the holy city for forty-two months."*'

However, to demolish the Al-Aqsa mosque, the third holiest site in Islam, appears at the time of writing to be a political impossibility. In my view, the most likely scenario which could change the situation would be an Arab attack on Israel or possibly a pre-emptive strike by Israel on Iran. In either case, Israel might finally decide to ignore pro-Arab sympathies and retake the whole city of Jerusalem, which it has always believed was given to the nation by the Lord God. They could then build whatever they wanted to. According to the Temple Institute and Israel's Chief Ashkenazi Rabbi David Lau, there is sufficient space for a Jewish temple on Temple Mount, next to the Muslim Dome of the Rock. Building a temple there could be a compromise. Hopefully, none of this will happen before this book is published. I wouldn't like you to think I'd predicted something after the event!

Another possible scenario is that the Jews might be permitted to build a new temple as part of an international peace agreement to end the Great Tribulation, brokered by the emerging figure of the Antichrist. The prophet Daniel spoke of a 'prince who is to come': "*He shall make a strong covenant with many for one week; and for half of the week he shall cause sacrifice and offering to cease.*" (Daniel 9:27). This prophecy would match the Antichrist's requiring everyone to worship his statue during the second period of three and a half years ('half a week'), as Revelation chapter 13 prophesies.

What about the other side of the argument? Does a new temple have to be built before Christ returns? Since Jesus would have entered the city through the East Gate from Bethany on Palm Sunday, the prophecies in Malachi and Ezekiel were both fulfilled by Jesus Christ at his first coming.

They are therefore no proof that another temple has to be built before he comes again.

The instruction to John in Revelation chapter 11 to measure the temple 'and those who worship there' except for the outer court of the Gentiles, could mean symbolically that he was to count the total number of Israel's descendants alive at the midpoint of the last seven years, perhaps with a view to providing a degree of protection for them during the Antichrist's forthcoming reign. That would agree with Revelation 12:1-6, which says the nation of Israel will have a place of protection prepared for them by God during the last three and a half years.

In any case, why should God want a new temple to be built? There certainly won't be a temple in the new Jerusalem. (Revelation 21:22) The main purpose of the Jewish temple was to be a place where animal sacrifices could be offered, for in every other way God can be worshipped in a synagogue, a home or even in the open air. Chapters 9 and 10 of the Epistle to the Hebrews explain that God abolished animal sacrifices once and for ever by the sacrificial death of Jesus Christ. (Hebrews 10:5,6,9,19) Naturally, this doesn't mean the Jews won't build a new temple. But once Jesus returns to set up the millennial kingdom, there will be no more priests and no more sacrifices. Any temple will have to be used for other purposes, which could of course include the praise and worship of God.

The wrath of God

Once Christians depart on Resurrection Day halfway through the last seven years, most people will happily go along with the mark of the beast and with the prophet's demand for its image to be worshipped. However, God will demonstrate his displeasure by an outpouring of his wrath in the form of seven terrible plagues. (Revelation 15:5 to 16:21) The central theme of Revelation chapters 14 to 16 is the wrath of God:

14:9,10   *"If any one worships the beast and its image, and receives a*
          mark on his forehead or on his hand, he also shall drink the
          wine of God's wrath."

14:19   *'The angel swung his sickle on the earth and gathered the*
          vintage of the earth, and threw it into the great wine press of the
          wrath of God.'

15:1   *'Then I saw... seven angels with seven plagues, which are the*
          last, for with them the wrath of God is ended.'

15:7   *'And one of the four living creatures gave the seven angels seven*
          golden bowls full of the wrath of God who lives for ever and
          ever.'

16:1   *'Then I heard a loud voice from the* (heavenly) *temple telling*
          the seven angels, "Go and pour out on the earth the seven bowls
          of the wrath of God."'

These chapters on the wrath of God are exceptionally important. While everyone who lives through the coming days must endure *tribulation*, those who genuinely believe in Christ before Resurrection Day will not have to suffer God's *wrath*. Tribulations are man-made. Wrath has its source totally in God.

In his highly theological letter to Christians in Rome, Paul wrote, *'Since, therefore, we are now justified by* [Christ's] *blood, much more shall we be saved by him from the wrath of God.'* (Romans 5:9) When Paul spoke about God's wrath, he was usually thinking about the fate of the unrighteous on the day of judgement. (Romans 2:1-11) Sometimes he was thinking of more immediate examples of God's judgement on individuals or groups of people. (Romans 1:18-27; 1 Thessalonians 2:16)

However, here in Revelation we have an outpouring of God's wrath upon the world as a whole during the three and a half years preceding Christ's actual return. If those whose trust is in the death of Christ for salvation are to be saved from his wrath, they must leave the earth before these last three and a half years of wrath begin. So where Paul taught about the coming day of resurrection in 1 Thessalonians chapter 5 we can understand it like this: *'God has not destined us for wrath, but to*

93

obtain salvation through our Lord Jesus Christ, who died for us so that whether we wake (are still alive when Resurrection Day comes) *or sleep* (have already died) *we might live with him* (as a result of being raised to life again before the outpouring of God's wrath on the earth).'

That is why the last trumpet will be blown at the midpoint of the final seven years, and not at the end of them. Resurrection Day will come before the last three and a half years of God's wrath begin.

The harlot of Babylon

After God's wrath is completed a fourth figure appears in the story, pictured as a harlot seated upon seven mountains. She is identified as *'Babylon the great'* and *'the great city which has dominion over the kings of the earth'*. (Revelation 17:5,18)

Babylon was almost certainly a code name for Rome[58], for it would have been suicidal to prophesy the destruction of Rome if the ruling Roman emperor got to hear of it, whereas Babylon itself had long since ceased to be a city of great importance. Rome was built on seven hills (Revelation 17:9), it fed itself on the sweat and blood of millions of slaves (Revelation 18:13), and Nero had just crucified an immense multitude of Christians (Revelation 17:6; 18:24). So chapters 17 and 18 of Revelation are principally a vision of the forthcoming destruction of Rome. The Visigoths accomplished this in AD 410.

The German writer Basilea Schlink widened the interpretation. She saw the visionary fall of Babylon as the

---

[58] In the Jewish apocryphal book of 2 Esdras, also known as 4 Ezra, there are two references to the coming destruction of 'Babylon and Asia'. (In the Bible 'Asia' refers mainly to modern Turkey.) This book was written in the first century AD, when the New Testament was also written and Babylon itself had ceased to be a great city. Tom Wright in *What St Paul Really Said* commented, *'There was no problem in mentally deleting 'Babylon' and substituting 'Rome'.'*

coming destruction of every worldly political, religious and economic power.

In fact there are hints that Revelation chapter 17 refers, not only to the destruction of Rome or to worldly powers in general, but to what will happen when Christ returns. The beast on which the woman was seated *'was, and is not, and is to ascend from the bottomless pit and go to perdition'* (Revelation 17:8). Its ten horns represented ten kings who had not yet received royal power but would do so and would make war on the Lamb who would conquer them. (Revelation 17:12-14) These are all references to chapters 19 and 20 when Jesus returns.

Another resurrection?

In Revelation 19:11 to 20:3 Jesus returns to the earth in power and glory. He destroys the Antichrist, the false prophet, and all their armed supporters. He ties Satan up and casts him into a pit, where he will remain for a thousand years. But then in Revelation 20:4-6 we read these rather confusing words:

> *I saw the souls of those who had been beheaded for their testimony to Jesus and for the word of God, and who had not worshipped the beast or its image and had not received its mark on their foreheads or their hands. They came to life and reigned with Christ a thousand years. The rest of the dead did not come to life until the thousand years were ended. This is the first resurrection. Blessed and holy is he who shares in the first resurrection! Over such the second death has no power, but they shall be priests of God and of Christ, and they shall reign with him a thousand years.*
>
> Revelation 20:4-6

I have argued that Resurrection Day will take place at the midpoint of the final seven years, when the angel blows the last trumpet; but the verses above appear to say that Resurrection Day will be at the end of the seven years, after God's wrath has been poured out on the earth. Furthermore, John seems to be

95

telling us that only those who are beheaded by the Antichrist regime will be in the first resurrection and will reign with Christ. Hence, these verses appear to contradict directly Christ's teaching and Paul's teaching that every believer in Christ who dies will be raised from the dead in the first resurrection, and that believers are not destined for wrath. (1 Corinthians 15:51,52; 1 Thessalonians 5:9)

Here's the explanation as I see it. Those who are martyred during the reign of the Antichrist will be raised from the dead in the same way as believers who have earlier been raised from the dead on Resurrection Day. The phrase 'this is the first resurrection' does not mean 'this is the first time that resurrection will take place'. It means, 'this is the first *kind* of resurrection', the same kind as the resurrection of believers, the resurrection which frees us from judgement. It is not the second kind of resurrection that will take place at the end of the thousand years, when everybody else will be brought back to life to face judgement according to their works. (John 5:28,29; Revelation 20:12)

John was telling his readers the welcome news that believers martyred for Christ after Resurrection Day in the days of the Antichrist, particularly those many Jews who will repent of their unbelief in Jesus when he raises Christians from the dead, will also be raised from the dead and reign with Christ a thousand years. They will not miss out because they become believers only after the 'official' Resurrection Day takes place.

Summary of the last seven years

Summarizing the final seven years leading up to Christ's return we have, in order:

- The Great Tribulation
- three and a half years of relative calm with the two witnesses announcing Christ's imminent return

- Resurrection Day for believers in Christ, both dead and alive
- three and a half years of almost total ungodliness and God's wrath
- Christ's final triumphant return, accompanied by an army of angels and all the resurrected believers, and his defeat of all ungodly powers.

Christ's millennial rule

And then in Revelation chapter 20 we come to the beginning of Christ's millennial rule. In this final millennium of the present age, Jesus Christ will rule the earth assisted by the resurrected believers who will return to the earth with him. Paul speaks of '...*the coming of our Lord Jesus with all his saints* (holy ones)' (1 Thessalonians 3:13); Jesus tells his twelve disciples, "...*in the new world, when the Son of man shall sit on his glorious throne, you who have followed me will also sit on twelve thrones, judging the twelve tribes of Israel*" (Matthew 19:28); and John writes in Revelation 20:4, '*Then I saw thrones, and seated on them were those to whom judgement was committed. Also I saw the souls of those who had been beheaded for their testimony to Jesus and for the word of God... They came to life, and reigned with Christ a thousand years.*'

It will be '...*a sabbath rest for the people of God*' (Hebrews 4:9), corresponding to the seventh day of creation.

Picturing this requires a determined effort of imagination. As I understand it, Jesus will come back to live on the present earth for a second time, but this time in his resurrected body. (Revelation 19:11) Accompanying him will be an army of angels and all the resurrected believers to enjoy their thousand years of rest from struggle and persecution under the earthly rule of Jesus Christ. (Daniel 7:18,22; 1 Corinthians 6:2; Matthew 16:27; Revelation 19:14)

The earth will still be populated by the relatively few people who have survived the tribulation and the wrath of God in all its forms, and who were not taken off the earth as believers on

97

Resurrection Day.[59] In general, they will not have repented of unbelief, rebellion and idolatry, for in spite of God's wrath '...*they did not repent and give him glory*' (Revelation 16:9), and they '...*cursed the God of heaven for their pain and sores, and did not repent of their deeds.*' (Revelation 16:11)

However, there will be two major improvements. Currently Satan occupies himself by planting thoughts, desires and emotions in us, to ruin our health, relationships, peace, prosperity and fellowship with God. (John 8:44; 10:10) But at the start of the final thousand years, he will be trussed up out of harm's way. '*Then I saw an angel coming down from heaven, holding in his hand the key of the bottomless pit and a great chain. And he seized the dragon, that ancient serpent, who is the Devil and Satan, and bound him for a thousand years, and threw him into the pit, and shut it and sealed it over him, that he should deceive the nations no more, till the thousand years were ended...*' (Revelation 20:1-3) No doubt everybody will be far more sensible and governable as a result.

The second improvement will be that Jesus will rule with a rod of iron. (Revelation 19:15) This will deter even the most hardened souls from crime. When we lived in Chile under the military rule of General Pinochet, armed police were constantly in evidence. In consequence, we felt extremely safe – so long as we kept the law!

Being mortals, the surviving population will still marry and have children (or have children and not bother to marry), and they will continue to grow old and die. Meanwhile, living among them and assisting in Christ's administration of the world, will be the saints, resurrected believers with immortal bodies like the body of Jesus. (Revelation 20:4-6) When John says that judgement has been committed to them, he means they will help Jesus to rule the people like the Old Testament judges did. He doesn't mean they will decide the destiny of everybody at Judgement Day. Only Jesus will do that.

---

[59] Revelation 6:8 and 9:18 suggest that only a twelfth of the world's population will still be alive by Resurrection Day.

At the end of the thousand years Satan will be released from his imprisonment, and the underlying rebelliousness of the nations will explode in a massive attack on Jerusalem and the camp of the saints, the famous Battle of Armageddon. (Revelation 16:14-16; 19:19-21) It is said that Napoleon Bonaparte once stood at the head of the valley of Megiddo, which is a large area of land to the south of Galilee, and remarked, *"All the armies of the world could manoeuvre their forces on this vast plain."* The attack will fail. The world's armies will be consumed by fire from heaven, and Satan will finally be destroyed. (Revelation 20:7-10)

And then it will be time for the Last Judgement. But that needs a chapter to itself.

The second three and a half years

7. Judgement

The Basis of Divine Judgement

Then I saw a great white throne and him who sat upon it... And I saw the dead, great and small, standing before the throne, and books were opened. Also another book was opened, which is the book of life. And the dead were judged by what was written in the books, by what they had done. And the sea gave up the dead in it, Death and Hades gave up the dead in them, and all were judged by what they had done. Then Death and Hades were thrown into the lake of fire. This is the second death, the lake of fire; and if anyone's name was not found written in the book of life, he was thrown into the lake of fire.

Revelation 20:11-15

Judgement Day will be for everybody who has ever lived and who for one reason or another has not already been resurrected to eternal life as a believer in Jesus Christ. Those who believe in him before they die will not come up for judgement. (John 5:24) That's one extremely good reason for putting your trust in Jesus now. A very, very good reason!

Years ago, I read about someone who refused to believe that trusting in Jesus was the only way to heaven because, he said, of the Pygmies![60] His argument was that since people living in remote African jungles had no knowledge of Jesus, they had no opportunity to put their trust in him, so to exclude them from heaven on the grounds that they didn't believe in Jesus would be totally unjust. Well, it certainly would be unjust

---

[60] Maurice Smith in his autobiography *Five five fifty-five*, Christian Literature Crusade, 1969.

if that is what the Bible teaches. Instead, the verses above from Revelation chapter 20 explain that some people who have never heard of Christ will still be welcomed into the kingdom of God.

'The dead were judged by what was written in the books, by what they had done.' People who have never heard of Jesus will not be condemned because they have not believed in Jesus: that would be totally unjust, and God is not unjust. Instead, they will be judged by what they have done or not done. In Biblical language, they will be judged according to their works.

I'm sure this makes perfect sense to any readers of this book who are not Christians, but it will sound like heresy to many Christian readers. That's because Christians are taught that *'by grace you have been saved through faith; and this is not your own doing, it is the gift of God, not because of works...'* (Ephesians 2:8,9) Nevertheless, judgement on the basis of our works would not have sounded like heresy to the author of Revelation, nor to Jesus, nor even to Paul who wrote the words I have just quoted. So for the sake of both Christian and non-Christian readers, let me explain why. You ought to stick with me on this, because your eternal destiny could depend on understanding what I'm going tell you, and then acting on it!

First, those words in Ephesians 2 were written to Christians, to those who had believed in Jesus. They had indeed been saved, as are all true believers in Christ, through faith in him and not by their good deeds, which can never be perfect in the sight of God. So what Paul wrote in Ephesians is true *for Christians.*

But for those who have never heard of Jesus Christ as the saviour of the world, and who therefore do not believe in him, their final destiny will be decided at the last judgement, on the basis of how they have lived. Even so, if they are accepted into the everlasting kingdom of God it will still not be because their good deeds have earned them a place in it. Not one of us deserves salvation. It is only by God's grace that we can be granted forgiveness of our sins and a place in his eternal kingdom.

In order for that great day of judgement to take place at the end of the last thousand years of this earth, there must be a second resurrection, a resurrection of everyone who has not been part of the first resurrection as a believer in Jesus Christ three and a half years before he returns at the start of the thousand years. No unbelievers, however good or bad, will be left out. Here are Jesus's own words on the subject, from John 5:26-29.

"For as the Father has life in himself, so he has granted the Son also to have life in himself, and has given him authority to execute judgement, because he is the Son of man. Do not marvel at this; for the hour is coming when all who are in the tombs will hear his voice and come forth, those who have done good, to the resurrection of life, and those who have done evil, to the resurrection of judgement."

John 5:26-29

This doesn't mean there will be two different resurrections at the end of the thousand years. It means that this second resurrection will result either in everlasting life for 'those who have done good', or in condemnation for 'those who have done evil'. Those are Jesus's words! Once again, this second resurrection is not for believers, for immediately before those words of Jesus, he said, *"Truly, truly, I say to you, he who hears my word and believes him who sent me, has eternal life; he does not come into judgement, but has* [already] *passed from death to life."* (John 5:24)

John chapter 5 isn't the only place in the Gospels where Jesus teaches that people who are not believers will be judged according to whether they have done good or evil. In Matthew chapter 25 he says, *"When the Son of man comes in his glory, and all the angels with him, then he will sit on his glorious throne. Before him will be gathered all the nations, and he will separate them one from another, as a shepherd separates the sheep from the goats..."* He goes on to explain that whether people are classed as sheep or goats will depend on whether they have visited and cared for the hungry and thirsty, the stranger, the naked, the homeless, the sick and the prisoner. He says that on this basis the 'goats' will go away into eternal punishment, but the 'sheep' into eternal life.

That is how people who have not known about Jesus will be judged. Both groups of people, the righteous and the unrighteous, will ask him the same question, *"Lord, when did we see thee hungry and feed thee, or thirsty and give thee drink? And when did we see thee a stranger and welcome thee, or naked and clothe thee? And when did we see thee sick or in prison and visit thee?"* Evidently the people gathered before Jesus on his throne will be people who have had no real knowledge of him.

However, there will be another group of people present at the last judgement, people who *have* known about Christ, but who have deliberately rejected him as their Saviour and Lord. They too must stand before the throne of judgement, but they will already have been condemned. *'He who believes in him is not condemned; he who does not believe is condemned already, because he has not believed in the name of the only Son of God.'* (John 3:18)

Believing in Jesus means believing he is the promised Messiah and the Son of God who died to save us from sin and eternal death. But it means more than that: it means obeying him too. *'He who believes in the Son has eternal life; he who does not obey the Son shall not see life, but the wrath of God rests upon him.'* (John 3:36) Believing in Jesus means committing yourself to obey him as your Lord, as well as to trust him as your Saviour. Both! How many churches teach this nowadays?

I can easily imagine a Christian family having a nice framed text hanging on their living room wall, which says, 'He who believes in the Son has eternal life.' But can you imagine a family putting up a text which says, 'He who does not obey the Son shall not see life, but the wrath of God rests upon him'? Yet Jesus said both things. He made it very plain:

> *"Not every one who says to me, 'Lord, Lord,' shall enter the kingdom of heaven, but he who does the will of my Father who is in heaven. On that day many will say to me, 'Lord, Lord, did we not prophesy in your name, and cast out demons in your name, and do*

*many mighty works in your name?' And then I will declare to
them, 'I never knew you; depart from me, you evildoers.'"*

Matthew 7:21-23

So what is the will of our Father in heaven: what is it that
he wants us to do? For a start, if those who have not heard of
Jesus are expected to feed the hungry and thirsty, welcome
strangers, etc., how much more should those who believe in
him do the same! Yet when I offered temporary
accommodation to someone who had been rescued from
modern slavery, several Christians refused to support my
decision! Mahatma Gandhi once told some Christian
missionaries, *"If Christians would really live according to the teachings of
Christ, as found in the Bible, all of India would be Christian today."*

Actually, believing in Jesus means even more than trusting
in him as saviour and obeying him as lord, if that is only out of
a sense of duty. It means loving him. *"If you love me you will keep
my commandments,"* he said. (John 14:15) It means being filled
with his Spirit. *'Anyone who does not have the Spirit of Christ does not
belong to him.'* (Romans 8:9) It means being transformed into a
son or daughter of God by the power of that Spirit, for
"...unless one is born anew, he cannot see the Kingdom of God."
(Romans 8:14; 2 Corinthians 5:17; Galatians 3:26; John 3:3)
Jesus Christ himself will make all this and more happen once
you put your trust in him to be your Saviour and commit your
life to obey him as your Lord.

That explains why Paul was able to write to the Christians
in Ephesus: *'For by grace you have been saved through faith; and this is
not your own doing, it is the gift of God - not because of works...'*
(Ephesians 2:8) Paul was not writing to unbelievers or to
people who had never heard of Jesus and therefore could only
hope that the Lord would accept them at the Last Judgment on
the basis of how they had lived (Romans 2:6-8,14-16). He was
writing to people who had trusted Jesus to save them. So no
matter what kind of life they had previously led, their eternal
destiny was now secure. As the apostle John wrote in his old

105

age: *'I write this to you who believe in the name of the Son of God, that you may know that you have eternal life.'* (1 John 5:13)

And that is something you too can know. In the old black and white movie *The King of Kings*, the Roman governor Pontius Pilate asked the Jewish leaders' rent-a-mob, "Do you want this man to be your king?" What would you have answered? What is your answer now? Do you truly want Jesus to be your king?

The destiny of the damned

Often people look at all the evil in the world and ask, "If there is a God, why doesn't he do something about it?" Well, here in Revelation we are told that on the day of judgement God will at last do something about it. But why the long delay? Jesus explained this in a parable.

A farmer discovered that an enemy had sown weeds in his wheat field. He couldn't uproot them without damaging the wheat, so he left both to grow together until harvest time. At harvest time he gathered the wheat and the weeds, separated them from each other, and burned the weeds up. Jesus concluded his story, *"Just as the weeds are gathered and burned with fire, so will it be at the close of the age. The Son of man will send his angels, and they will gather out of his kingdom all causes of sin and all evildoers, and throw them into the furnace of fire; there men will weep and gnash their teeth. Then the righteous will shine like the sun in the kingdom of their Father."* (Matthew 13:36-43)

In Revelation, John pictures the awesome day of judgement as a great white throne, before which everyone who has ever lived will stand, except those already raised as believers. Jesus will be sitting on the throne as judge. As I quoted at the start of this chapter, *'...the dead were judged by what was written in the books, by what they had done... Then Death and Hades were thrown into the lake of fire. This is the second death, the lake of fire; and if any one's name was not found written in the book of life, he was thrown into the lake of fire.'* (Revelation 20:12-15)

A few verses earlier Satan had been thrown into the lake of fire, and now:

- Death is thrown into the lake of fire to be destroyed. Revelation 21:4 says, "*...death shall be no more...*".
- Hades is thrown into the lake of fire, also to be destroyed. There will be no further any need for it, because in the future no one will die.
- Those whose names are not written in the book of life are thrown into the lake of fire. The obvious implication is that they too are thrown into it to be destroyed. Revelation 21:4 says, "*...neither shall there be mourning nor crying nor pain any more, for the former things have passed away.*"

John describes the destiny of unrepentant sinners in the lake of fire as 'the second death'. Their first death is physical death, when their body dies. Their second death will occur at the last judgement, after their dead body has been resurrected and reunited with their spirit. They will then be consigned to final, permanent death, the death of both their body and spirit. Jesus said, "*...do not fear those* (i.e. men) *who kill the body but cannot kill the soul; rather fear him* (i.e. God) *who can destroy both soul and body in hell* (Gehenna).*"* (Matthew 10:28)

Again and again the Bible tells us that the fate of sinners is death and destruction, while the reward for those who believe in Jesus Christ is eternal life. As Jesus clearly said, the second death means the destruction of both soul and body. The choice is not between eternal life and eternal death. It is between eternal life and *death*. 'For God so loved the world that he gave his only Son, that whoever believes in him should not perish but have eternal life.' (John 3:16) 'But all the wicked He will destroy.' (Psalm 145:8-20) 'The soul that sins shall die.' (Ezekiel 18:20) 'For the wages (or penalty) of sin is death, but the free gift of God is eternal life in Christ Jesus our Lord.' (Romans 6:23)

Perish, destroy, die, death. Death means death, not continuing life. At least nine out of ten Bible verses on the subject make this absolutely clear. Most ideas of everlasting torment in hell originate from mediaeval teaching rather than the Word of God.[61]

I agree that some other verses in the New Testament appear to support the idea of everlasting punishment. Since an explanation of these verses is somewhat technical, I've put it into an annex, Annex 3, for readers who want to look at this subject in more detail.

But for now, let's simply note that a belief in never-ending punishment has no place in the ancient creeds of the Christian church. These creeds were formal statements of the essential Christian beliefs, agreed after widespread and prolonged consultations among the church leaders. If a Christian believed what was in the creeds then he or she believed all that was necessary. Two of the earliest creeds, the Apostles' Creed and the Nicene Creed, still define the essential components of the Christian faith in all the major branches of the church. *And they do not even mention the fate of the damned.*[62]

Similarly, in Great Britain the *39 Articles of Religion* have formed the basis of the Church of England's teaching since 1563. They reaffirm the authority of the two creeds mentioned above, and like them make no mention of the fate of unbelievers.

---

[61] Manuals by Muslim teachers such as the ninth century theologian al-Ghazali and the twelfth century scholar Qadi Ayyad *'dramatise life in the fire'*, and present *'new punishments, different types of sinners, and the appearance of a multitude of devils'* to exhort the faithful to piety. *The Garden and the Fire: Heaven and Hell in Islamic Culture.* N.Rustomji, Columbia University Press, 2009, Pages 118–9.

[62] The Nicene Creed dates from AD 325 and the Apostles' Creed from AD 390. A third creed, commonly called the Athanasian Creed, dates from the fifth or early sixth century. It says that the destiny of unbelievers is to 'perish everlastingly' in 'everlasting fire', but its authorship by the respected teacher Athanasius is strongly contested, and it has never been accepted by the Eastern Church.

Therefore if the idea of everlasting hellfire has put you off believing in God or the Christian faith, let me assure you of this: the mainstream Christian church in its fundamental declarations of faith does not require you to believe in any such thing.[63]

It is true that on Judgement Day severe punishment awaits the wicked and everyone who refuses to believe in the God who created them, especially for people who deliberately reject Jesus as their Saviour and Lord. This is clearly taught in the Bible. *"Vengeance is mine, I will repay, says the Lord."* (Romans 12:19) *'He who does not obey the Son shall not see life, but the wrath of God rests upon him.'* (John 3:36) *'God deems it just to repay with affliction those who afflict you... when the Lord Jesus is revealed from heaven with his mighty angels in flaming fire, inflicting vengeance upon those who do not know God and upon those who do not obey the gospel of our Lord Jesus.'* (2 Thessalonians 1:6-8)

It would be totally unjust for someone like Joseph Stalin, Adolph Hitler or Pol Pot to come to the same peaceful end as a little old lady whose only real crime had been selfishness. And because God is just, totally just, the punishment he metes out will be perfectly proportionate to the extent of everyone's guilt. *'...life for life, eye for eye, tooth for tooth, hand for hand, foot for foot, burn for burn, wound for wound, stripe for stripe.'* (Exodus 21:23-25) *"And that servant who knew his master's will, but did not make ready or act according to his will, shall receive a severe beating. But he who did not know, and did what deserved a beating, shall receive a light beating."* (Jesus's words in Luke 12:47,48)

So my point is not that wrongdoers and deliberate unbelievers will escape justice. It is that the punishment they will receive will not continue for ever. *'The Lord is _merciful_ and gracious... He will _not_ always chide, nor will he keep his anger for ever.'* (Psalm 103:8,9) *'He does _not_ retain his anger for ever.'* (Micah 7:18)

---

[63] The Roman Catholic Church and the Orthodox Churches have a lot of additional doctrines, which do include a belief in the everlasting torment in hell of those who have not been baptized.

How could it be merciful to consign someone to everlasting torture? To do that would mean the Lord *will* always chide: he *will* retain his anger for ever! A belief in everlasting punishment is in plain contradiction to the words of Holy Scripture.

The Bible says that eventually all things will be united in Christ. (Ephesians 1:10) That cannot happen if multitudes of evildoers and unbelievers, the vast majority of humanity, remains disunited from Christ in a place of eternal torment.

After the British people voted to leave the European Union, the new prime minister, Theresa May, endlessly repeated, "Brexit means Brexit." All that anyone could understand from this was that 'Brexit' didn't mean something else! In the same way, when the Bible says that the alternative to eternal life is to perish (John 3:16), 'perish' means 'perish': it doesn't mean something else. It does not mean to go on living in any way whatsoever. Even Theresa May couldn't have been clearer than that.

Whatever the fate of people who reject the salvation God offers us through faith in his Son, why not ensure here and now that your own destiny is everlasting life? All you have to do – and you do have to do it – is to invite Jesus to take his rightful place in your life as your Saviour and Lord, and then follow his instructions.

The day of judgement

At the beginning of this chapter, I said that even Paul would have agreed that men and women will be judged according to their works on that final day of judgement, if they have not known Jesus and received him as Saviour and Lord.

In chapter 2 of his letter to the Romans, there is a passage which I have never heard read in church: '*For* [God] *will render to every man according to his works: to those who by patience in well-doing seek for glory and honour and immortality, he will give eternal life; but for those who are factious and do not obey the truth, but obey wickedness, there will be wrath and fury.'* (Romans 2:6-8)

Paul went on to write, *'When Gentiles* (non-Jews) *who have not the law* (of Moses) *do by nature what the law requires... They show that what the law requires is written on their hearts, while their conscience also bears witness and their conflicting thoughts accuse or perhaps excuse them on that day when, according to my gospel, God judges the secrets of men by Christ Jesus.'* (Romans 2:14-16)

These words of Paul tell us three important facts about Judgement Day.

- God will judge the secrets of men by Christ Jesus. It is Jesus who will be the judge. The Father has given authority to the Son to judge the world, because having been a man himself Jesus understands human weaknesses and temptations. He will judge fairly and justly. (John 5:25-27; Hebrews 4:15,16)
- What the law requires is written on men's hearts. While Jesus will judge every man according to his work (and of course 'every man' means every woman too), it is what is in their hearts, their hidden secret thoughts and desires and character, which will really determine his decision. Jesus said that a tree is known by its fruits, for it is the fruit a tree bears which shows what kind of tree it is. That's why judgement will be based on works. But essentially Jesus will be looking for people who have demonstrated that they genuinely want to live in accordance with the laws of God's kingdom and will be happy to obey him as their king.
- He will *give* eternal life. However good one might have been, eternal life remains a gift. It is not something which anyone can earn or deserve through his own deeds or efforts. We could do nothing at all if God had not freely given us our life in the first place. As John Wesley declared, *'All the blessings which God hath bestowed upon man are of His free, undeserved favour... There is nothing*

we are, or have, or do, which can deserve the least thing at God's hand.'[64] Jesus said, *"...when you have done all that is commanded you, say, 'We are unworthy servants; we have only done what was our duty.'"* (Luke 17:10) Who can ever say he has done everything God has commanded him to do? As Paul wrote later in Romans, *'None is righteous, no not one.'* (Romans 3:10) So whoever we are, believer in Christ or someone who has tried to live a godly life while never having heard of him, we receive eternal life only as a gift from God, freely granted to us out of his undeserved grace and love and mercy.

SIN: Salvation Is Necessary

Life on earth is not how God meant it to be! When I was writing this part, 67 of the 194 countries in the world were involved in ongoing warfare [65]; 65 million people were refugees [66]; and 795 million people or 11% of the world's population were chronically undernourished.[67]

While millions starve to death, millions more eat too much for their own good! A third of the inhabitants of many Western countries are overweight and suffer or die from health problems caused by eating and drinking too much or by an unnatural diet created by a profit-motivated food industry. Many more die of excessive stress caused by the worship of money and the abandonment of God's plan for family life and a weekly day of complete rest from work.

In the USA 34,000 people are murdered by firearms every year, another 34,000 by motor vehicles, and 52,000 by

---

[64] *Sermon 1: Salvation by Faith.* J. Wesley, *Forty-Four Sermons,* The Epworth Press, London, 1944.

[65] www.warsintheworld.com.

[66] UN Refugee Agency, *Figures at a glance,* 2015. www.unhcr.org.

[67] UN Food and Agriculture Organization report for 2014-2016, uploaded on www.worldhunger.org, Jan 2017.

poisoning, mainly from alcohol.[68] In Russia over 600 women die at home *every month* as a result of domestic violence.[69] In the world as a whole between 40 and 50 million unborn children are killed every year – in the USA one in every five pregnancies is terminated. Generally, the more immediate neighbours someone has, the more likely he or she is to be lonely. In the UK 4000 people take their lives each year, in Russia 28,000, and in the USA nearly 40,000![70] Do you realize how bad human society has become?

What other intelligent race would spend a fortune erecting hospitals, schools, business premises and homes, and then wantonly destroy them all again with shells and bombs? Someone once wrote that if a Martian were to visit our planet he would conclude that the earth was an asylum for the criminally insane!

In many less dramatic ways also life has gone wrong. We have to lock the doors of our cars to prevent someone stealing them, we have to be constantly vigilant for ever more sophisticated scams, we fall out with colleagues and neighbours and even with family members or members of our church or mosque or synagogue. A large proportion of our nation's wealth is sucked up by armaments and defence; by police, prisons, the judiciary and the legal profession; by vastly overpaid executives in public office and private business; and by monitoring the performance of schools, hospitals, railway services, local authorities and other bodies because the people running them are not trusted to run them competently.

It is not good enough to say that such activities keep people in employment. All such expenditure could otherwise be spent on education, healthcare, house building, recreational facilities,

---

[68] Centers for Disease Control and Prevention: National Center for Health Statistics, 2014.

[69] http://www.bbc.co.uk/news/world-europe-38804687 viewed January 2017.

[70] *Suicide rates: Data by country.* World Health Organization, 2012. *World Population Prospects 2015,* United Nations.

public transport, infrastructure, the support of organic and environmentally sensitive food production, and other worthwhile causes.

Now, you may not personally be responsible for all the trouble in the world, but neither is anyone else. No one individual causes all the world's problems, yet we are all involved in causing them. Like a single stone in the Great Wall of China, our individual contribution to what is wrong with the world may appear to be totally insignificant, but it is from many such insignificant contributions that the whole edifice is built.

Who can say honestly he loves his neighbour as himself, or that he could not reasonably give more time and money to help the homeless, the lonely, the oppressed, the sick or the starving? Who can claim that she has never lied, or envied, or acted selfishly? How many have really forgiven from their hearts everyone who has wronged them? Above all, which of us loves our Creator with all our heart and mind and soul and strength, daily acknowledges with gratitude his gift of life and every other blessing we enjoy, and daily asks for his help to live the way he wants us to?

The Bible has a simple explanation for why we behave as we do. It's called SIN. Sin is much more than simply missing the mark or falling short of the life God meant us to live, which is clearly expressed in the Ten Commandments. It is more than missing a GCSE grade 9 in God's Certificate of Satisfactory Endeavour.[71] It's not just a failure to keep the whole law of Moses and all its rabbinic ramifications, nor a failure to observe faithfully the five pillars of Islam and the teachings of the Hadith. Sin is something far deeper, embedded within the human spirit. It is a disease of the human spirit which affects every single one of us. Even Paul, who probably tried harder than anyone to live a perfect life before he came to know Jesus,

---

[71] For non-British readers, GCSE or the General Certificate of Secondary Education is a school examination taken at the age of 15 or 16 in a range of subjects, with a pupil's attainment in each one assessed by a number from 1 to 9, with 9 being the highest attainment level.

complained, '*I can will what is right, but I cannot do it. For I do not do the good I want, but the evil I do not want is what I do. Now if I do what I do not want, it is no longer I that do it, but sin which dwells within me.*' (Romans 7:18-20)

Sin is not something bad that we do; it is what makes us do what is bad. It is what stops us being as good as we should be. It is a spiritual disease that we inherit from our parents. (Psalm 51:5; Romans 5:12)

Only one person can cure us of sin: Jesus Christ. Jesus, who was born of God, is the only human being who has ever lived his entire life without sin, and he is the only one who can deliver us from it. "*...every one who commits sin is a slave to sin,*" he said. "*So if the Son makes you free, you will be free indeed.*" (John 8:34,36)

When an angel told Joseph in a dream that Mary's new baby would save God's people from their sins (Matthew 1:21) he meant much more than saving them from sin's *consequences*. Jesus came to set us free from *sin itself*, to heal the spiritual disease from which we all suffer, to put us right so that we can finally live how God intended us to.

The reason it's so important to accept Jesus's help in this matter is that in the new world, when God's kingdom will at last be established, there will be no sin. Revelation 21:27 says, '*But nothing unclean shall enter it, nor anyone who practises abomination or falsehood, but only those who are written in the Lamb's book of life.*' Only a society totally and permanently free from sin can be a society in which no one suffers, no one is unhappy, no one is treated unjustly, no one is afraid. In the world to come there can be no sinful actions, no sinful thoughts, no sinful desires, no sin of any kind at all, ever! And therefore – have you worked it out? – there can be no sinners there.

That is why you and I need the help of Jesus to be saved. It doesn't matter whether you are an atheist, agnostic, Christian, Jew, Muslim, Hindu, Buddhist or a devotee of 'Thee Temple ov Psychick Youth' (sic): only Jesus Christ can set you free from sin. And I'll explain in the Epilogue how he can do that for you personally.

A new heaven and earth

Revelation chapter 21 begins, *'Then I saw a new heaven and a new earth; for the first heaven and the first earth had passed away, and the sea was no more. And he who sat upon the throne said, "Behold, I make all things new."'* (Revelation 21:1,5)

The prophet Isaiah brought a similar word from the Lord 750 years earlier: *"...I create new heavens and a new earth; and the former things shall not be remembered or come into mind."* (Isaiah 65:17) Peter wrote in his second letter, *'But the day of the Lord will come like a thief, and then the heavens will pass away with a loud noise, and the elements will be dissolved with fire, and the earth and the works that are upon it will be burned up. ... But according to his promise we wait for new heavens and a new earth in which righteousness dwells.'* (2 Peter 3:10-13)

God is going to start again! The almighty God who designed and created the present earth six thousand years ago is going to create a brand new one, as soon as Jesus Christ as Judge has pronounced his final sentence, justice has been carried out, and the heavenly court has been dissolved for ever.

'Then I saw a new heaven and a new earth...' The word 'heaven' is in the singular, and in some Bible passages when it's in the singular it clearly refers only to the earth's atmosphere. So this verse in Revelation 21:1 implies that it is only the earth and its atmosphere that God is going to remake. But Revelation 21:5 says, *'And he who sat upon the throne said, "Behold, I make all things new."'* This implies that the entire universe is going to be remade. Whichever it is may not be of much immediate importance to us, but if you are interested you can read what I think about it Annex 4: 'A new heaven or heavens?' What is certain is that God is going to make a new planet earth, and everything on earth will be new.

In many ways, the new earth won't be radically different from our current planet. [72] Jesus's resurrection body was apparently very similar to his pre-resurrection body: he still breathed air and ate and drank and walked around. So the promise that our resurrection bodies will be similar to that of Jesus's, means that air and water and food, the temperature and even the force of gravity will have to be much the same as they are now. [73] In Annex 5: 'Where will believers spend eternity?' I've shown that God is going to recreate the world just as it was in the beginning, and that this new earth, not heaven, will be the final and permanent home of believers.

Human life will continue in a familiar fashion. *"They shall build houses and inhabit them; they shall plant vineyards and eat their fruit."* (Isaiah 65:21) The prophets foresaw a somewhat rural and organic lifestyle in the coming kingdom, even though they were well acquainted with large cities. '...*they shall sit every man under his vine and under his fig tree...*' (Micah 4:4) '*Happy are you who sow beside all waters, who let the feet of the ox and the ass range free.*' (Isaiah 32:20) Many people will regard that as good news, judging from the popularity of the BBC's programme *Escape to the Country*. Only this morning, as I write, a psychologist on Radio 5 was analysing the additional stresses that people living

---

[72] Revelation 21:1 says, '...*and the sea was no more.*' Most people take this to mean that in the new earth there will be no sea. However, John was merely saying that the first heaven and earth had passed away, including the sea. He did not say whether there would be any seas in the new earth. When God made the first earth it included seas and lots of sea creatures, all of which he pronounced to be good. So there is no reason why he should not recreate them, just as he is going to recreate everything else. The Authorized Version correctly translates Acts 3:20,21, '...*he shall send Jesus Christ, which before was preached unto you: whom the heaven must receive until the times of restitution of all things...*'

[73] Certainly if I were the Lord God making a planet which I intended to replace one day with a more permanent one, I would make the first one as similar as possible to my final intended design to check that it would work!

in towns suffer, where access to green spaces and the natural environment is limited.

The new Jerusalem

It's true that in Revelation chapter 21 John sees a vision of '*the holy city, new Jerusalem, coming down out of heaven,*' but I don't believe we are intended to understand this vision as the description of a literal city. Logically I can't see how each of a literal city's gates can be made of a single pearl, nor what the point is of having such gates if they are never to be closed night or day, unless this is just a way of saying that there are no longer any enemies to fear. Above all, I can't see how a real city in a real earth can be 1500 miles square and have only one street in it, still less be 1500 miles high. Above 5 miles there isn't enough air to breathe!

But if this picture is not to be interpreted literally, what is the reality it symbolizes? There are two clues in this chapter. Verses 18 and 19 tell us that the wall of the heavenly city will be built of jasper, and its foundations will be made of twelve different kinds of precious stones. In Isaiah chapter 54, verses 11 & 12, God comforts the nation of Israel with the words, "*O afflicted one, storm-tossed, and not comforted, behold, I will set your stones in antimony, and lay your foundations with sapphires. I will make your pinnacles of agate, your gates of carbuncles, and all your wall of precious stones.*" In Isaiah a picture of a bejewelled city stands for Israel, the Old Testament people of God.

Verses 2 and 9 of Revelation 21 provide the second clue. In these verses the city itself is called 'the Bride of the Lamb'. It's hard to imagine Jesus coming to live on the earth in order to marry a city, however beautiful; but he might come to 'marry' a city which represents the church – his redeemed people who have committed their lives to him. For it's as the bride of Jesus that Paul describes the church in his letter to the Ephesians. In chapter 5 verses 25 to 27, he wrote, '*Husbands, love your wives, as Christ loved the church and gave himself up for her, that he might sanctify her, having cleansed her by the washing of water with the word, that he might present the church to himself in splendour, without spot or wrinkle or any such thing, that she might be holy and without blemish.'*

Just as a bejewelled city symbolized in the Old Testament a restored nation of Israel, so in the New Testament the beautiful holy city which John saw symbolizes the entire body of Jewish and Gentile believers, coming down out of heaven for their marriage to the Lamb of God, Jesus Christ. (Revelation 21:2)

Why will they come down out of heaven if they have already been living as resurrected believers on the earth for a thousand years? Because at the end of the thousand years God is going to destroy this old earth and create a new one. (Revelation 21:1) While the builders are knocking down their old home the occupants will be moved into temporary accommodation in heaven, where they will be *'prepared as a bride adorned for her husband'*. (Revelation 21:2)

Creation restored

In many respects the new earth will be similar to the old one, but in other ways it will be very different. The curses which came upon the present earth as a result of Adam's sin and the subsequent flood (Genesis 3:17-19; 7:11; 9:12-15) – thorns and thistles, pests and diseases, droughts and floods, earthquakes and tidal waves, hurricanes and volcanic eruptions – all these deviations from God's original perfect creation will belong to the past. Paul wrote, *'We know that the whole creation has been groaning in travail together until now.'* (Romans 8:22)

Just as people who have put their hope in Jesus are looking forward to being free from disability, disease and decay in their resurrection bodies, so the natural world is looking forward to its own redemption. *'For the creation waits with eager longing for the revealing of the sons of God; because the creation itself will be set free from its bondage to decay and obtain the glorious liberty of the children of God.'* (Romans 8:19,21)

119

In Revelation 21 a voice from God's throne declares, *"Behold, the dwelling of God is with men. …he will wipe away every tear from their eyes, and death shall be no more, neither shall there be mourning nor crying nor pain any more, for the former things have passed away."* (Revelation 21:3,4)

When I wrote this passage, Italian rescue teams were desperately trying to find survivors in a hotel buried under an avalanche. It was in the same region that had suffered three major earthquakes in the preceding year, and an entire village, Arquata del Tronto, was destroyed. Mourning, crying and pain inevitably follow avalanches, earthquakes, volcanic eruptions, hurricanes, floods, tidal waves, droughts, forest fires, and plagues like covid-19. So much has gone wrong with the natural world since the day the Lord God first contemplated his new creation and saw that it was 'very good'. (Genesis 1:31)

But these things will not continue for ever. The earth is going to be very good once more!

…the burning sand shall become a pool, and the thirsty ground springs of water…

Isaiah 35:7

Instead of the thorn shall come up the cypress; instead of the brier shall come up the myrtle…

Isaiah 55:13

…I will give you your rains in their season… and the trees of the field shall yield their fruit. And your threshing shall last to the time of vintage, and the vintage shall last to the time for sowing; and you shall eat your bread to the full, and dwell in your land securely.

Leviticus 26:4,5

The wolf and the lamb shall feed together, the lion shall eat straw like the ox… They shall not hurt or destroy in all my holy mountain, says the Lord.

Isaiah 65:25

A world free from sin

Yet all these improvements are as nothing when we think about the difference the end of sin will produce. For one of the 'former things' that will have passed away is sin. Try to imagine life in a world where everyone lives in perfect accordance with God's will. A world in which everyone loves his neighbour as himself, in which everyone is kind and helpful and generous and cheerful and truthful and responsible and trustworthy. A world in which nobody is selfish or greedy or dishonest.

In such a world no one will starve, no one will be homeless, no one will be lonely, no one will be afraid. There will be no war, no terrorism, no robbery, no violence. There will be no need for armies, policemen, judges or prisons, all of which consume labour and material resources and leave society poorer. People will never have to lock their doors or windows or cars or bicycles.

In the business world there will no longer be vast and morally unjustifiable differences in the pay of owners and employees; disputes will be resolved amicably and fairly, without any need for strikes, and no one will have to work excessive hours in a stressful environment. With no disease and no physical or mental handicaps there will be no need for hugely expensive health care. Everyone will have everything they need.

That is how it's going to be in the world to come!

...nation shall not lift up sword against nation, neither shall they learn war any more; but they shall sit every man under his vine and under his fig tree, and none shall make them afraid; for the mouth of the Lord of hosts has spoken.

Micah 4:3-4

Then justice will dwell in the wilderness, and righteousness abide in the fruitful field. And the effect of righteousness will be peace, and the result of righteousness, quietness and trust for ever.

Isaiah 32:16,17

And all these blessings shall come upon you and overtake you, if you obey the voice of the Lord your God. Blessed shall you be in the city, and blessed shall you be in the field. Blessed shall be the fruit of your body, and the fruit of your ground, and the fruit of your beasts, the increase of your cattle, and the young of your flock. Blessed shall be your basket and your kneading-trough.

Deuteronomy 28:2-5

And the ransomed of the Lord shall return, and come to Zion with singing; everlasting joy shall be upon their heads; they shall obtain joy and gladness, and sorrow and sighing shall flee away.

Isaiah 51:11

Practical considerations

I have been asked, "How could everybody who has ever lived possibly fit into one planet the size of this present earth?" That's a really good question. As I've said, our new immortal bodies are going to be like the resurrected body of Jesus. Apparently his new body was the same size as normal, and normal-sized bodies haven't been designed to live in a larger world with a greater force of gravity. Of course, gravity itself could change, but I think it's more likely that the Lord designed the present earth as a full-size prototype, don't you? Therefore I think it's certain that the new earth will be no bigger than this one.

So how many people might there be in it? Obviously, no one knows but God, nevertheless some reasonable predictions are possible.

The world's population is expected to reach 8.5 billion by 2030, so it's reasonable to assume that there will be enough room on earth for 8.5 billion people. However, Revelation 8:11 says that many will die in the Great Tribulation, and Revelation 9:18 says a further third of the world will die, so by Resurrection Day in Revelation chapter 12 the population will have been reduced by at least half to 4.25 billion people.

As we have seen, not everyone who has ever been born will inherit eternal life. *"For the gate is narrow and the way is hard, that leads to life, and those who find it are few,"* Jesus said. (Matthew 7:14) Currently about 30% of the world's population claims to be Christian, but many of these, perhaps most, are likely to be merely nominal adherents. So if 'the elect' represent 5% of the remaining 4.25 billion population in 2030, 0.21 billion believers will disappear on Resurrection Day. That will leave 4.04 billion people alive during the final three and a half years.

At the end of this period many of these unrepentant surivors will be slain at the battle of Armageddon. (Revelation 16:12-16; 19:17-21) So let's say there will be no more than 4 billion survivors on earth when Jesus returns with all the resurrected elect. (1 Thessalonians 3:13)

How many will the elect number in total? The Population Reference Bureau estimates that the total number of people who have ever lived will be about 117 billion by the year 2030.[74] So if the elect represent 5% of all humanity they will number $117 \times 5/100 = 5.85$ billion. Hence, when Jesus returns there will be 5.85 billion resurrected elect and 4.25 billion unresurrected survivors in the world, a total population of 10.1 billion.

10.1 billion is rather more than the current estimated population of 8.5 billion. But the prophets tell us that when the Lord comes, the trees of the field will clap their hands, deserts will be turned into pools of water, etc. So if 5% is a correct but sober estimate of the proportion of the saved, there will be room for everyone on the present earth, and the numbers of believers and surviving unbelievers will be somewhat similar.

---

[74] *How many people have ever lived on earth?* https://www.prb.org/articles/how-many-people-have-ever-lived-on-earth Viewed March 2022.

But what about life in the new earth? At the day of judgement most of the unsaved population will be consigned to the lake of fire (Revelation 20:15), but on that same day additional numbers of godly people who never had the opportunity to believe in Jesus while they were alive will be added to the community of the saved. (Matthew 25:31-46; Romans 2:6,7; Revelation 20:12) But no problem! If the new earth is going to be like the earth was before the flood, its habitable land area could be twice its current area. The oceans now cover some 70% of the world's surface, but according to the Bible there was far less water before the Flood. Geological evidence indicates that before the Flood the polar regions of the earth were temperate and habitable, and Isaiah prophesied that even the deserts will blossom, so the new earth, with an increased area of land which is nearly all habitable, will accommodate a population of many more people than it can now.

There are a hundred-and-one other questions one might ask about this amazing life to come. "Shall we all speak the same language? Shall we all be vegetarians? Will animals still give birth, grow old and die? Will great creative works like Shakespeare's plays and Beethoven's symphonies and Rembrandt's paintings be resurrected? Shall we be able to read each other's minds?" The Bible only hints at the answers to such questions.[75]

Upwards and onwards

One question about the new earth has exercised my mind in particular, and it's this. If we are truly going to live for ever, won't there come a time when we shall have explored everywhere, done everything and heard everyone's life story so

---

[75] The answers to many questions about life on the new earth are given in a book entitled *Heaven* by R.Alcorn, Tyndale House Publishers Inc, 2004.

many times that we know them all by heart? Eventually, won't we simply become bored? I know it will still be possible for creative people to compose music, paint pictures, write more books, do craft work, design buildings, redesign gardens, perhaps even continue to make scientific discoveries. But even so...

I think my favourite prophet Isaiah has an answer to my question. '*Lift up your eyes on high and see: who created these? He who brings out their host by number, calling them all by name; by the greatness of his might, and because he is strong in power not one is missing.*' (Isaiah 40:26)

Isaiah was telling us that the Lord God not only made 100 billion stars in each of an estimated 10 trillion galaxies[76], but that he is fully acquainted with each one of them individually! Knowing the Lord, every one of them will be different. And since hardly any of these innumerable stars can be seen with our naked eye, he can't have made most of them to make the sky look pretty, or even to help sailors and explorers navigate at night. Of course, he might have made them simply for his own amusement, but don't you think he might have made them for our benefit somehow?

From the earliest days of history men have had an urge to explore. When Christopher Columbus set sail across the Atlantic Ocean he had no idea whether he would discover another land, or whether he and his crew would keep sailing west until they ran out of food and water and died, or even fall off the edge. But something impelled Columbus to find out what was there.

In the nineteenth and early twentieth centuries, British missionaries, sailors and scientists explored Africa, the southern Pacific and even Antarctica. Now mankind is starting to explore other planets in the solar system. NASA aims to send astronauts to Mars by 2030.

---

[76] http://www.space.com/26078-how-many-stars-are-there.html

What made films and books such as Star Wars, Star Trek, 2001: A Space Odyssey, and Journey into Space so popular? Their amazing popularity sprang from a conviction in the human mind that there must be more out there waiting to be explored, and from an urge embedded deeply in the human spirit to explore it.

The Gospel accounts suggest that Jesus in his resurrection body could travel through space, at least for short distances, and perhaps that will be possible for us. But even if it isn't, history warns us not to limit the possibilities of travel by more natural means:

"How, sir, would you make a ship sail against the wind and currents by lighting a bonfire under her deck?" demanded Napoleon Bonaparte, when told of Robert Fulton's steamboat in the 1800s. *"I pray you, excuse me; I have not the time to listen to such nonsense."*

"Rail travel at high speed is not possible because passengers, unable to breathe, would die of asphyxia," affirmed Dr. Dionysius Lardner in 1830.

In 1933, when the twin-engined Boeing 247 airliner first left the ground, a Boeing engineer proudly announced, *"There will never be a bigger plane built."* It seated ten passengers.

And three years later, in 1936, the New York Times confidently informed its readers, *'A rocket will never be able to leave the Earth's atmosphere.'*

Yet in 2018 Materials World magazine [77] reported an experiment, partly funded by the European Space Agency, to develop graphene 'sails' which would accelerate a spaceship up to 20% of the speed of light and be capable of reaching the Alpha Centauri star system within twenty years!

Personally, I believe God has made an enormous and possibly an infinite number of habitable planets, every one of them waiting to be explored between now and eternity. One

---

[77] *Sailing space with graphene.* K.T.Lee, Materials World, Institute of Materials, Mining and Metallurgy, 1 February 2018.

day the resurrected children of God will begin to travel to them; they will discover and delight in the unimaginable flora and fauna they will find there; they will build holiday homes and botanical gardens and theme parks and adventure trails.

Not every planet will be a paradise to begin with, for human beings thrive on challenge, and great achievements are not served up on warm plates. But when a group of such pioneers fulfil their vision – and on each new planet they will have all the time in the world to achieve it – then they will invite their friends from New Earth to visit them. They'll show off the new paradise they have created and have all the fun in the world together!

I'm not suggesting they will live permanently on these other planets. I believe that Earth, where Jesus will reign, will remain the planet of everyone's permanent residence. For if a finite number of people were to spread out among an infinite number of stars it is hard to imagine how society could remain, in any meaningful way, under the kingship of Jesus.

And why stop at space travel? Jesus told his disciples, *"...with God all things are possible."* (Matthew 19:26) If we can travel through space, why not also through time? Might we visit scenes from Earth's history, either supernaturally or in a time machine like the Tardis, or at least holographically in something like a Star Trek holodeck?

Perhaps, like Doctor Dolittle, we'll be able to communicate with animals and birds, or even experience their lives in avatar bodies as Jake Scully did in the film Avatar.

"...whatever you ask in prayer, believe that you have received it, and it will be yours," Jesus said. (Mark 11:24) A wonderful promise, but not one for sinners! For imagine what would happen if God granted someone who asked for it the ability to burn up anyone they didn't like, as Jesus's disciples James and John once wanted to do. Think what would happen to business if God allowed everyone who asked to draw out unlimited money from a cash machine whenever they wanted to. Imagine what

127

might happen if we could all do anything we wanted to while we were still sinners!

But one day, when Jesus the Saviour has finally eradicated sin from our minds and hearts, when in the resurrection we have at last become like him and want only what is in accordance with his Father's will, then at long last it should be possible for Christ's promise to be fulfilled without any restrictions: *"Ask, and it will be given you."* (Matthew 7:7)

Does that sound too good to be true? *"You are wrong, because you know neither the scriptures nor the power of God."* (Matthew 22:29) The people Jesus was addressing when he said this were Sadducees who didn't believe in any resurrection, but he might well have said the same thing to us. It's not that we expect too much of God: rather that we expect too little from him. *'We are half-hearted creatures, fooling around with drink and sex and ambition, when infinite joy is offered us, like an ignorant child who wants to go on making mud pies in a slum because he cannot imagine what is meant by the offer of a holiday by the sea. We are far too easily pleased.'* So wrote C.S.Lewis in one of his most famous passages.[78] Paul would have agreed with him. In his first letter to the Corinthians he wrote, *'...no mere man has ever seen, heard, or even imagined what wonderful things God has ready for those who love the Lord.'* (1 Corinthians 2:9 TLB)

No wonder Jesus said, *"The kingdom of heaven is like treasure hidden in a field, which a man found and covered up; then in his joy he goes and sells all that he has and buys that field."* (Matthew 13:44) His point was that a place in God's everlasting kingdom is worth more than anything we can possibly find, earn, achieve or possess in this life. Believe it! Eternal life can be yours, but only as a gift from Jesus, a gift he is longing to give you, if you are willing to give yourself to him!

Some Christian preachers warn their hearers, "Don't delay. Christ could return at any moment." That isn't true, as we have seen. But it is true that you could die at any moment. Death

---

[78] *The Weight of Glory and Other Addresses.* C.S.Lewis, Zondervan, 2001.

comes unexpectedly for all kinds of reasons. So if you want to receive eternal life, do it now! You really don't want to be left behind to endure the years of God's wrath and then have to hope for the best when it comes to Judgement Day. In fact – and this is genuinely serious - if you reject Christ's offer of salvation now that you know about it, you can have no hope of salvation on that awesome day. *'He who believes in the Son has eternal life; he who does not obey the Son shall not see life, but the wrath of God rests upon him.'* (John 3:36)

So then, if Jesus Christ is not going to return at any moment, when exactly is he going to come? Before we can finally answer that, there's one more question we have to face up to: could Jesus have made a mistake? Didn't he tell his disciples he would return in their lifetime? For if he made a mistake about that, could he not have been mistaken in believing that he would ever come back?

Judgement

8. Did Jesus make a mistake?

The first disciples expected Jesus to return in their lifetime

There is no question that the first followers of Jesus Christ believed he would return within their lifetime, or at least within the lifetime of most of them.

Saint Paul wrote, '*We shall __not__ all sleep* (die)*, but we shall all be changed, in a moment, in the twinkling of an eye, at the last trumpet. For the trumpet will sound, and the dead will be raised imperishable, and we* (i.e. those of us who are still alive, to whom he was writing) *shall be changed.*' (1 Corinthians 15:51,52) With the possible exception of Jude, whose letter is very short, all the other writers of letters in the New Testament agreed that Jesus would return while most of them at least were still alive. (Hebrews 10:37; 1 Peter 4:7; James 5:7; 1 John 2:28; Revelation 22:20) Paul even attributed this teaching to Jesus. '*For this we declare to you by the word of the Lord, that we who are alive, who are left until the coming of the Lord, shall not precede those who have fallen asleep.* (1 Thessalonians 4:15)

So either Paul, Peter, John, James and the authors of Hebrews and Revelation, as well as the authors of the four Gospels, all misunderstood what Jesus had said about the time of his return, or else Jesus did indeed teach them that he would return within their lifetime. This is unquestionably what the writers of the Gospels understood him to have taught. Here are some of the teachings of Jesus about this, as they recorded them.

131

The teachings of Jesus

> *These twelve* [apostles] *Jesus sent out, charging them, "Go nowhere among the Gentiles, and enter no town of the Samaritans, but go rather to the lost sheep of the house of Israel. And preach as you go, saying, 'The kingdom of heaven is at hand.'...Truly, I say to you, you will not have gone through all the towns of Israel, before the Son of man comes."*

Matthew 10:5-7,23

> *"...the Son of man is to come with his angels in the glory of his Father, and then he will repay every man for what he has done. Truly, I say to you, there are some standing here who will not taste death before they see the Son of man coming in his kingdom."*

Matthew 16:27,28

> *"Immediately after the tribulation of those days* (the fall of Jerusalem) *...they will see the Son of man coming on the clouds of heaven with power and great glory... this generation will not pass away till all these things take place."*

Matthew 24:29,30,34

> *"...whoever is ashamed of me and of my words in this adulterous and sinful generation, of him will the Son of man also be ashamed, when he comes in the glory of his Father with the holy angels." And he said to them, "Truly, I say to you, there are some standing here who will not taste death before they see that the kingdom of God has come with power."*

Mark 8:38-9.1

> *"Truly, I say to you, this generation will not pass away before all these things take place."*

Mark 13:30

> *"And there will be signs in sun and moon and stars, and upon the earth distress of nations in perplexity at the roaring of the sea and*

132

the waves, men fainting with fear and with foreboding of what is coming on the world; for the powers of the heavens will be shaken. And then they will see the Son of man coming in a cloud with power and great glory. Now when these things begin to take place, look up and raise your heads, because your redemption is drawing near... Truly I say to you, this generation will not pass away till all has taken place."

Luke 21:25-32

"Let not your hearts be troubled... I will come again and will take you to myself."

John 14:1,3

Think about Jesus's opening words in Mark's Gospel: *'Jesus came into Galilee, preaching the gospel of God, and saying, "The time is fulfilled, and the kingdom of God is at hand; repent, and believe in the gospel."* (Mark 1:14,15)

The gospel or good news which Jesus announced was not that God was going to set up his promised kingdom. That wouldn't have been news at all, for his Jewish audience knew he was going to do that one day. The good news he proclaimed was that God was going to do it imminently, that the inauguration of his kingdom was at hand. That was the good news he brought. The promised new age, when men would beat their swords into ploughshares and the wolf would lie down with the lamb and unrighteousness and injustice would cease for ever under the everlasting worldwide reign of the promised Messiah was just round the corner. They were the generation which was going to see it happen! That was the good news Jesus told them to believe. Why would he have said it was good news if God's kingdom wasn't going to come for another 2000 years? If they were going to have to wait another 2000 years it would have been bad news, not good news!

Jesus clearly taught that he would return to inaugurate the promised kingdom of God within the lifetime of his hearers. The writers of the Gospels and Epistles did not misunderstand what he said. How could they have done? For almost six weeks after his resurrection he appeared to most of them, 'speaking of the kingdom of God'. (Acts 1:3) As a result they unanimously understood that he would come back from heaven to establish the kingdom before they all died.

Nevertheless Jesus did not return as they expected, and to most people today his return seems as far off as ever. How then can we reconcile what appears to have been a major mistake on his part with his claim that he said only what his heavenly Father told him?

Attempted explanations

Bible commentators come up with various explanations. The Jewish scholar David Stern says that the word 'generation' can mean 'people' or 'race'. He suggests that when Jesus said, *"This generation will not pass away before all these things take place,"* he was merely promising that the Jewish people as a race would survive until the end of the age.

If that is what he meant then he was simply echoing God's promise in Jeremiah 31:35,36 that Israel would continue as a nation for ever. It isn't the natural reading of Christ's words, and it doesn't explain some other passages in which he said he would return in power during the lifetime of his hearers, such as Mark 9:1: *'And he said to them, "Truly, I say to you, there are some standing here who will not taste death before they see that the kingdom of God has come with power."'*

William Barclay and other Bible commentators say that Jesus was referring only to his prophecies of the forthcoming destruction of Jerusalem when he said that his hearers would live to see it happen. In that respect Jesus was exactly right. Jerusalem fell in AD 70, 37 years after his prophecy and just within one generation of 40 years. (See Psalm 95:10) However in every passage above about Jerusalem's coming destruction Jesus also spoke about his own coming on the clouds of heaven in power and glory. And each time he said, *"Truly, I say to you,*

this generation will not pass away till all these things take place."
Matthew 24:34 is only one example.

Others suggest that when Jesus said, *"...there are some standing here who will not taste death before they see that the kingdom of God has come with power,"* he meant that some of his hearers would live to see powerful miracles performed, or perhaps the powerful growth of the church as it conquered a pagan world. But his hearers had already seen Jesus cast out demons and even raise the dead, and in the previous sentence he had not been talking about the growth of the church, but about the Son of man coming in the glory of his Father. Furthermore, in Mark 13:26 the phrase 'with great power' clearly referred not to miracles nor the growth of the church, but to Jesus's return. *"And then they will see the Son of man coming in clouds with great power and glory."*

Many Christian teachers try to solve the problem by reinterpreting the meaning of the kingdom of God to mean living with Jesus as king. This is a very popular teaching today. It is true that when we live with Jesus as our king, the kingdom of God has already come among us in a limited sense. But a minority of the population imperfectly obeying Jesus Christ on this present earth falls far short of the amazing promises about God's kingdom made by the Old Testament prophets. (e.g. Isaiah 65:17-25; Micah 4:1-4 and Zechariah 14:1-9)

Those promises, that God's kingdom of righteousness will one day be established throughout the earth, have still not yet been fulfilled, in spite of the fact that Jesus said their fulfilment was imminent. In fact many Jews would regard this as evidence that Jesus was *not* the Messiah. In Jewish eyes the kingdom of God has not come even now, let alone during the lifetime of the apostles.

In any case, Jesus didn't only say his hearers would see the kingdom of God come: he also said they would live to see him return!

The dispensational explanation

A more credible explanation of Christ's failure to return when he said he would is that God did indeed intend the world to be evangelized within a generation, but only the *Jewish* world. For example, in Matthew 15:24 Jesus declared, *"I was sent only to the lost sheep of the house of Israel,"* and in John 20:21 he told his remaining eleven disciples, *"As the Father has sent me, even so I send you."* According to this explanation, if the Jews as a whole had received Jesus Christ as their Messiah, then he would have returned within a generation, just as he had promised. However, when they rejected the message, God inaugurated a new plan, which was the evangelization of the Gentiles, something which would obviously have to take much longer. This is the explanation given by Michael Penny and others.[79]

Just as God was unable to keep the promise he made to the Exodus generation to bring them into Canaan because of their unbelief, so he was unable to keep the promise he made to the Jewish generation of Jesus's time about his Son's return as king, because of their unbelief. For, like all God's promises, this promise of Christ's imminent return had a condition attached to it, a condition which they did not fulfil.

In Acts chapter 3 Peter told the Jewish crowds who had collaborated in crucifying their Messiah, *"Repent therefore, and turn again, that your sins may be blotted out... and that* [the Lord] *may send the Christ appointed for you..."* (Acts 3:19,20) Plainly the promises of forgiveness and Christ's return were dependent on the Jews' repentance. And while many Jews did repent of their unbelief in Jesus, the Jews as a nation did not do so. The consequence was that their sins were not blotted out, the promised Christ did not return to them, and instead of living to see the coming of the Son of Man, they saw the destruction of their temple and much of the holy city by the Romans, just 40 years later.

---

[79] *A Key to Unfulfilled Prophecy.* M.Penny, The Open Bible Trust, Reading, Great Britain, 2011.

As a result God turned the apostles' attention to the Gentile world:

When [the local leaders of the Jews in Rome] *had appointed a day for* [Paul], *they came to him at his lodging in great numbers. And he expounded* [the gospel] *to them from morning till evening, testifying to the kingdom of God and trying to convince them about Jesus both from the law of Moses and from the prophets. And some were convinced by what he said, while others disbelieved. So, as they disagreed among themselves, they departed, after Paul had made one statement: "The Holy Spirit was right in saying to your fathers through Isaiah the prophet: 'Go to this people, and say, You shall indeed hear but never understand, and you shall indeed see but never perceive...' Let it be known to you then that this salvation of God has been sent to the Gentiles; they will listen."*

Acts 28:23-29

It is not strictly true to talk about a change of plan on God's part. There was only one plan, but it had several stages. In Acts 2:23 Peter told the listening crowd that Jesus was '*delivered up according to the definite plan and foreknowledge of God.*' In other words, God knew beforehand that the Jewish leaders in Jerusalem would reject Jesus as their Messiah, yet he went ahead and sent his Son into the world for their salvation. In just the same way, he knew that most of them would continue to reject Jesus after he had ascended to heaven. Yet he went ahead and told his apostles to preach Christ to the Jewish race throughout the known world, to give them a further opportunity to receive him as their saviour and king. It was only after they refused this opportunity too, that he inaugurated the next stage of his plan, which was to have the gospel preached to Gentiles, and to invite them to join his kingdom on equal terms with his chosen race.

The interesting thing is that Jesus predicted all this would happen:

The kingdom of heaven may be compared to a king who gave a marriage feast for his son, and sent his servants to call those who were invited to the marriage feast; but they would not come. …they made light of it and went off, one to his farm, another to his business, while the rest seized his servants, treated them shamefully, and killed them. The king was angry, and he sent his troops and destroyed those murderers and burned their city. Then he said to his servants, "The wedding is ready, but those invited were not worthy. Go therefore to the thoroughfares, and invite to the marriage feast as many as you find."

Matthew 22:1-10

Notice that the parable even included a prediction of the martyrdom of some early church leaders and the forthcoming destruction of the city of Jerusalem. It is hard to conclude that Jesus really didn't know exactly how things were going to work out!

The true explanation

While the dispensational explanation for Jesus's failure to return in the lifetime of his hearers is plausible, I have a fascinating alternative explanation, which I believe is the true one. It is supported by scripture, and it presents an incredible challenge to those of us who are his followers today.

In the first place, Jesus did indeed command his apostles to preach the gospel to all nations: not only to the Jewish people. In Matthew 28:18,19 he gave his remaining eleven apostles this great commission: *"All authority in heaven and on earth has been given to me. Go therefore and make disciples of all nations…"* The Greek actually says, 'disciple all the nations', and definitely not 'make disciples from *among* all the nations'.

Furthermore, the Greek word *ethna*, translated here as 'nations', is often used in the New Testament to mean the Gentile nations *as distinct from* the Jewish nation! For example, in Matthew 4:15 and 6:2, where the Authorized Version and the

Revised Standard Version speak of 'Gentiles', the Greek word is this same word *ethna!* So Christ's commission at the end of Matthew's Gospel was clearly to preach the gospel and make disciples of all nations, and *especially* the non-Jewish nations.

Jesus's intention was just as explicit in the Gospels of Luke and Mark. In Luke 24:46,47 we read, '*...and* [Jesus] *said to them, "Thus it is written, that the Christ should suffer and on the third day rise from the dead, and that repentance and forgiveness of sins should be preached in his name to all nations, beginning from Jerusalem."* The Greek unambiguously states, 'to all the nations'; not 'among all nations' or 'in all the world'.

Mark's account of Christ's instructions to his disciples is still more inclusive. '*And he said to them, "Go into all the world and preach the gospel to the whole creation"*'! (Mark 16:15) How could 'the whole creation' possibly have meant only Jews?

As if that isn't enough, there are around 60 verses in the Old Testament, from Genesis to Malachi, which say God's concern is for 'all nations', 'all peoples', 'all mankind', 'all creation', 'every creature', 'every knee', 'every tongue', 'men of every language' and 'the world' to know and worship him.[80] It is inconceivable that Jesus did not know these passages, and he did say that he had come to fulfil them. (Matthew 5:17) In the New Testament there are another 29 similar verses that speak of God's desire for people from every ethnic group to know and worship him.

It is true that Jesus said he was sent only to the lost sheep of the tribe of Israel during his first visit to the earth. In a ministry lasting little more than two years there was no time to preach to Gentiles as well as Jews. But when some Greek-speaking Gentiles wanted to meet Jesus during his final week among us, he said that after his death and resurrection things would be different. *"I, when I am lifted up from the earth, will draw all men to myself,"* he said. (John 12:32)

---

[80] At the time of writing, the verses mentioned are listed at ywam.org/get-involved-now/all-nations-verse-list.

The idea that Jesus meant the gospel to be preached only to Jews is not only unsupported by the Bible as a whole: it is comprehensibly rejected.

Once again, at the end of Matthew's Gospel, Jesus told his eleven remaining apostles, *"Go therefore and make disciples of all nations... and lo, I am with you always, to the close of the age."* The implication of those words is clear. When the apostles had made disciples of all nations, the end of the age would come. The apostles might have thought that to preach to all nations within their lifetime was an impossible task, but the fact is that they could have done it, and they could have done it long before they died! They could have completed the task quite easily by the power of *multiplication.*

The power of multiplication

Back in the garden of Eden the Lord told Adam and Eve to *'be fruitful and multiply, and fill the earth...'* If they thought that to be an impossible task it was because they too had not reckoned on the power of multiplication. Because they were fruitful and made a good number of children (Genesis 5:3,4), and because each of their children did the same (Genesis 5:6,7) and so on, two people eventually filled the earth with people![81]

In a similar way, Jesus told his remaining eleven apostles to *"...make disciples of all nations... teaching them to observe all that I have commanded you."* (Matthew 28:19,20) The task of making disciples of all nations *was* possible, because Jesus told them to

---

[81] It is estimated that the world's population at the time of Jesus's birth was around 300 million. If human life began with just two people in about 4000 BC, as the Bible implies it did, the population must have grown at an average annual growth rate of 0.48% to reach 300 million by start of AD 1. That is significantly *less* than the average growth rate in the world's population of 0.80% between AD 1750 and AD 2000, so it is perfectly feasible. On the other hand, if all human life restarted with Noah's family of eight after the Flood, an annual growth rate of 0.76% - almost exactly the growth rate in recent centuries - would still have produced the estimated population in AD 1.

teach their disciples to do the same thing that he had commanded them to do, to create spiritual children, grandchildren, great grandchildren and so on, in ever increasing numbers. It's exactly what Paul told his disciple Timothy to do. '...*what you have heard from me before many witnesses entrust to faithful men who will be able to teach others also.*' (2 Timothy 2:2) Once again it's the principle of multiplication at work.

If each wave of converts had taught the next wave to do the same, and if they had taught their converts in turn to do the same, then the whole world could have been reached *in one generation.* And that's what began to happen in the very beginning. When only Peter and the other apostles were preaching in Jerusalem '...*the Lord added to their number day by day those who were being saved.*' (Acts 2:47) But when the church spread throughout Judea and Galilee and Samaria and everybody began to share the good news with their neighbours the number of believers *multiplied.* (Acts 9:31)

Some six months after the day of Pentecost, Stephen was stoned to death. The new believers in Jerusalem fled to other parts of the country where they preached the word. (Acts 8:1-4) But suppose that they and every subsequent believer had been willing to keep moving on, in order to continue to share the good news of Jesus where it had never been heard before. And suppose that each believer led just *one* other person to believe in Jesus each year and that every new believer did the same. That's feasible, wouldn't you say? The astonishing fact is that if that had happened then within just sixteen years the first group of 3000 Christians who were baptized on the day of Pentecost would have multiplied to almost 200 million, the estimated population of the entire world at that time! *Just sixteen years!*

Let's say that at Pentecost in the year AD 30 there were 3000 Christians in total. In the year AD 31 the number would have doubled to 6000, in AD 32 it would have doubled again to 12,000, and so on. If you keep doubling the number you'll find that by AD 46 it would have reached 196.6 million! (Enter '3000 x 2^16' in a calculator if you don't believe me.) And that's not all. Not everyone who heard the gospel would have accepted it: perhaps only one in ten would have done so. In that case the task of converting 20 million people to Christ rather than 200 million could have been accomplished *in less than thirteen years!*

To be fair, the calculations assume no one would have died during that period. And in order for the multiplication process to continue as calculated, believers would have had to move to new places and even new countries as the evangelization of their current locations was completed. But isn't that exactly what Jesus expected many Christians to do? In Luke 18:29,30 he said, "*...there is no man who has left house or wife or brothers or parents or children, for the sake of the kingdom of God, who will not receive manifold more in this time, and in the age to come eternal life.*" Brian Stiller[82], writing about missionaries in the communist country Laos where only 1.5% of the population are Christians, said, '*We hear story after story of men, women, young people, and young and middle-aged couples with so much to gain by staying home who respond to the Lord's call to leave their homes for distant lands.*'

In practice some Christians with family responsibilities, health problems or a lack of zeal would have stayed put or fizzled out as evangelists. Nevertheless others on fire with the Holy Spirit could easily have made up for that by leading far more than one person to Christ every year. Multitudes of Samaritans responded to Philip's preaching, for example, and he wasn't even an apostle. (Acts 8:5,6)

The task of preaching the gospel to everyone on earth could have been accomplished well within one generation if the majority of believers and their converts had obeyed Christ's instructions to multiply! One reason he kept telling his disciples he might return at any time was surely to instil a sense of urgency into their evangelism.

---

[82] *An Insider's Guide to Praying for the World.* B.C.Stiller, Bethany House Publishers, 2016.

This principle of multiplication was evidently in the mind of Jesus in his parable of the yeast or leaven. *"To what shall I compare the kingdom of God? It is like leaven which a woman took and hid in three measures of flour, till it was all leavened."* (Luke 13:20,21) Yeast cells divide, reproduce and multiply. And while my calculations are based on everyone leading just one person a year to Christ for a maximum of sixteen years, I believe that Jesus expected his followers to lead significantly more than sixteen other people to faith during their lifetime. In his parable of the sower he said that the good soil represented people *"...who hear the word and accept it and bear fruit, thirtyfold and sixtyfold and a hundredfold."* (Mark 4:20) So it really isn't surprising that Jesus expected the task of world evangelization to be completed within a generation. *It could have been!*

The world's total population in 1 AD was only 250 or 300 million, compared with nearly 8 *billion* now. Moreover, more than 90% of the population lived in Europe and in the south and east of mainland Asia, all accessible from Israel by land. The southern hemisphere was virtually uninhabited.[83]

I know that before the age of translation apps and transatlantic aircraft there would have been problems concerning language and travel to any distant places, but with God all things are possible. He demonstrated on the day of Pentecost that the gift of tongues could cross language barriers, and perhaps that was intended to be its chief purpose. And even if God didn't enable people to walk across the sea as he enabled Jesus to do, or to move someone supernaturally from one place to another as he appears to have done with Philip in Acts 8:40, they did have ships in those days, and the Bering Strait between Russia and Alaska in North America is only 55 miles (88 km) wide at its narrowest point.

---

[83] *Long-term dynamic modeling of global population and built-up area in a spatially explicit way.* K.K.Goldewijk & P.Janssen. HYDE 3.1, The Holocene, June 2010, vol. 20, no. 4, pp.565-573.

So it seems to me that in the mind of Jesus, his disciples and their converts would spread the gospel throughout the earth by the process of multiplication within a generation, and that in consequence he would be able to return before they all died of old age. He intended his first apostles to blaze a trail into every inhabited land on the earth, and the resulting believers to commit their lives fully to spreading the message of Jesus Christ and his kingdom in the power of the Holy Spirit during the few years before his return. They were to forsake everything else and take up their cross to follow him. (Luke 14:25-27,33)

Even before the Holy Spirit was given at Pentecost Jesus sent out 72 men on a training run to tell people the kingdom of God was near and to heal the sick. (Luke 10:1-9,17) And Jesus reinforced his plan to involve *all* believers in evangelism on the day of his ascension. He told his eleven apostles, *"Go into all the world and preach the gospel to the whole creation. ...these signs will accompany <u>those who believe</u>: in my name they will cast out demons; they will speak in new tongues; they will pick up serpents, and if they drink any deadly thing, it will not hurt them; they will lay their hands on the sick, and they will recover."* (Mark 16:15-18) Clearly *all* the new believers were to be equipped to proclaim Christ in the power of the Holy Spirit, not merely the apostles.

That was the plan Jesus announced, and if it had been fulfilled then centuries of warfare would have been avoided and countless millions of people would not have been killed in the succeeding centuries by warfare, drought, flood, famine and plague.

So what went wrong?

When the vision fades

Although the early Christian church was in many ways amazing and it did change the world, it was far from perfect. There were quarrels and disputes in it (James 4:1; Acts 15:39; Galatians 2:11); jealousy and strife (1 Corinthians 3:3); instances of serious sexual immorality (1 Corinthians 5:1); and early departures from faith in Christ (Galatians 3:1-3). It appears to me that neither the apostles nor most of the early Christians fully grasped the vision that they were to preach the gospel to the whole world and to dedicate their lives to that one overriding purpose. For consider these facts:

- Jesus had commanded his eleven apostles to be his witnesses *'in Jerusalem and in all Judea and Samaria and to the end of the earth'* (Acts 1:8), but it was at least five and possibly ten years before any of them preached to a Gentile household (Acts 10), and some of them at least remained in Jerusalem for at least another seventeen years (Galatians 1:18 and 2:1,9).
- Peter, John and other 'pillars' of the church decided that their ministry was to be confined to Jews (Galatians 2:9), when Jesus had clearly commanded *all* the apostles to preach the gospel to *all* nations (Matthew 28:19; Mark 16:15; Luke 24:47,48; Acts 1:8).
- They decided (Galatians 2:9) that only Paul and Barnabas should preach to Gentiles, when in the Roman Empire Gentiles outnumbered Jews by 50 to 1!
- Instead of 'declaring the wonderful deeds of him who called you out of darkness into his marvellous light' (1 Peter 2:9) many ordinary believers became lukewarm (Revelation 3:15,16). They abandoned their first love for Jesus (Revelation 2:4) and became spiritually dead (Revelation 3:1), just as Jesus had predicted they would (Matthew 24:12).

Of course, it's easy for us to be critical: most of us haven't experienced the opposition, threats, arrests or the risk of martyrdom, which many of those early Christians faced daily. Nevertheless it seems to me that although things began well, within a few years both the original apostles and the first generation of Christians largely abandoned the worldwide mission Jesus had given to them. In consequence, although the church still grew rapidly in the confines of the Roman Empire, that first generation of believers never lived to see Christ's return. The promise Jesus had repeatedly made that he would return within their lifetime to set up the kingdom of God was never fulfilled, just as God never fulfilled his promise to the slaves in Egypt to bring them into the land of Canaan. Nearly all God's promises, perhaps all of them, come with conditions!

What about us?

I cannot possibly finish this chapter without applying its lessons to ourselves. As you will learn in the next chapter, we may not have many years left to encourage those we know or love to put their trust in Christ! If we have committed our lives to Jesus Christ and his mission, what are *we* doing about sharing the good news of eternal life with the world?

There are many ways to do this, but in my opinion there are at least five things every believer needs to do. Like the recommended 'five-a-day' fruit and vegetables in our physical diet, these are the essential spiritual vitamins we need to share the good news effectively:

(i) Join a church!

If possible, join a lively church which is committed to the teaching of the Bible and leading people to Christ. This will give you necessary encouragement, provide you with sound teaching and resources, and give you opportunities to invite people to social and evangelistic events. If joining a lively

146

church in your neighbourhood isn't possible, then at least ask the Lord to help you find one or two other Christians that you can share with and pray with regularly so that you can support and encourage each other in your outreach for Christ. Someone once advised John Wesley, *"The Bible knows nothing of solitary religion."*

(ii) Know the gospel!

Soon after I began my ministry, two members of my congregation asked me how they could know God personally. I didn't know how to answer them! If we are unclear ourselves what the good news is and how Jesus can change our lives for ever, how can we hope to explain it to anyone else? If no one in your church can explain the gospel to you in a way that you can understand, find two or three other Christians and try to sort out together with the help of the Bible what you believe. Practise sharing this with each other, if you think it would help. That's how sales staff are trained, and we have something far more important to offer than vacuum cleaners, sports cars, life insurance or beauty products. Practise what you'll preach! No one but Mozart and Superman ever became good at something without practice.

(iii) Work out and learn your own three-sentence testimony.

Peter wrote, *"If anybody asks why you believe as you do, be ready to tell him."* (1 Peter 3:15 TLB) Here's my three-sentence testimony:

When I was eighteen I decided that if there was a God who had a purpose in making me, the best thing I could do was to find out what it was.

After a long struggle I prayed, "O God, I'm still not sure whether you are real, but from this moment I'm going to believe you are and I will do whatever you tell me."

As I've learned to know God as Father, Son and Holy Spirit he has proved again and again that he is real, and he has given my life an exciting purpose which I am still happily fulfilling in old age.

Can you summarize in three sentences how your life used to be, how you came to know Jesus as your Saviour and Lord, and what difference it has made to you now? It doesn't have to sound spectacular: it just has to be the truth.

(iv) Love your neighbours!

Make an effort to get to know your neighbours, colleagues, fellow students, etc. Do some social stuff with them; help them practically when you can; help with homework, baby-sitting, car lifts or translation; be hospitable, visit them when they are in need, offer to pray with them when they are sick, go the extra mile. Putting love into practice can soften hearts. Then, when the Spirit gives you an opportunity to share the word of God, it can take root and perhaps produce the fruit of eternal life.

(v) Be open to the Holy Spirit's guidance.

When Jesus told the greedy chief tax collector Zaccheus to come down out of the tree he was hiding in, I don't suppose he had planned beforehand to seek Zaccheus out. He just kept his eyes open. He probably asked his disciples, "Who's that funny little man hiding in a tree up there?" Matthew, the former tax collector who might even have worked for Zaccheus, would have told him. So be open to the Holy Spirit as you travel around and meet people. You might just see someone God wants you to speak to. Be brave, open your mouth and trust the Spirit to tell you what to say.

(vi) Pray for people to be saved!

We are engaged in a spiritual battle for human souls, and this requires spiritual weapons. Above all it requires Spirit-empowered prayer. A principal result of praying for unsaved members of your family, school, college, workplace or neighbourhood is that it will keep you alert and willing to share God's love in word or deed with them, whenever he provides you with an opportunity to do so. Pray for yourself too. Every morning, offer yourself to Jesus for his service, asking him to make you bold in speaking and acting as his representative.

Ah yes, six ways, not five. Well, I did say 'at least five', so I'm not going to change that now!

Today there are believers in Christ throughout the world. There are believers in countries like Cuba, Iran, North Korea and even in our own country! If they currently number only 1% of a nation's population, the fact remains that if each one were to introduce one person to Christ every year and teach them to do the same then a third of that nation's population would be in God's kingdom within five years.[84] And since Jesus said that relatively few people will find the way to life, that would surely be more than enough to prepare the world for his imminent return! Come on people! Let's do it! Let's use with all our might whatever gifts and opportunities God has given us to fulfil Christ's great commission. That's how we can at last be the generation which sees his return in power and glory!

Rise up, O men of God! Have done with lesser things;
Give heart and soul and mind and strength to serve the King of
kings.

William Pearson Merrill

---

[84] At the end of the first year believers would constitute 2 % of the population; after two years, 4%; after three years 8%; after four years 16%; and after five years 32%, or very nearly a third of the population.

Did Jesus make a mistake?

9. The date of Christ's return

Is everyone agreed?

When all four reviewers of a bottle of Hardy's Stamp Cabernet Merlot South Eastern Australia wine give it a 5-star rating, the chances are that it's pretty good, provided of course that the four of them are independent of each other and are not employees of the firm which produces it.

In this chapter we shall see that a number of independent methods to determine the date of Christ's return agree with each other, giving us good reason to believe they are right. I accept that these methods are all based on the assumption that Bible's teaching is true, so in that sense they are not independent. But I have demonstrated in another book, *God, Science and the Bible*, that the Bible is true, so I hope you will feel able to come along with me.

So let's see, at long last, what the Bible has to tell us about the date of Christ's return!

Six thousand years

In Chapter 2 we saw how there will be six thousand years from creation to the return of Christ and the beginning of his thousand-year reign over this present earth. So if the world was created in 4004 BC, as Archbishop Ussher calculated, the millennial kingdom should have started six thousand years after that, in AD 1997. Clearly that didn't happen. However, we have also seen that most people who have attempted to calculate the date of creation based on the Hebrew text of the Old Testament have come up with rather more recent dates, most of which leave us still waiting for the millennial kingdom to

151

begin. With an average estimate of 3946 BC for creation, all one can conclude from this line of biblical prophecy is that Christ's return will be somewhere around the middle of this century. But that's only the first method of fixing the date.

Two thousand years

Fortunately there is a second way to hit the target. We've seen how the historical events recorded in the Old Testament were often models of much more important events which were to occur later in the life of Jesus. It's also true that in the Old Testament there are many words related to events of that time which prophetically foretold more important events in Jesus's life. One example is in Isaiah chapter 7.

King Ahaz, who then reigned in Jerusalem, was terrified to learn that the Syrian army had joined forces with the army of the northern tribes of Israel to attack his tiny two-tribe kingdom of Judah and Benjamin. The prophet Isaiah told him not to worry. *"Behold, a young woman shall conceive and bear a son, and shall call his name Immanu-el,"* he told the king. *"For before the child knows how to refuse the evil and choose the good, the land before whose two kings you are in dread will be deserted."* (Isaiah 7:14,16) Isaiah went on to tell him that Assyria would conquer both of them, which is exactly what happened.

Now what Isaiah said about the young woman was most peculiar. In the first place, to call her son 'Immanuel' amounted to blasphemy, because 'Immanuel' means 'God with us'. It was like calling her son 'God'. Imagine how the little chap would have felt when he went to school and told his teacher what his name was. It's unthinkable! Furthermore, Isaiah said that the young woman would name her child. In Hebrew culture naming one's child was always the father's responsibility.[85] In

---

[85] "His name is John," declared John the Baptist's father at his son's birth. "You shall call his name Jesus," said the angel to Joseph, when informing him that Mary was about to give birth to the Son of God.

fact, the way Isaiah put it, without any mention of a father, suggests to me that he did mean 'a virgin shall conceive', as the Authorized Version translates it, rather than 'a young woman shall conceive', as the Revised Standard Version does. In that case the birth of this child really would have been a miraculous sign to convince King Ahaz that Isaiah was telling him the truth about the invading kings.

As you may have realized, although Isaiah was speaking about something which was going to happen almost immediately, his words were an uncanny prediction of the birth of the Lord Jesus, who was indeed conceived by a virgin and was truly 'God with us'. Thus, a prophecy about something which happened at the time was fulfilled in another and deeper way many years later in the birth of Jesus Christ.

So why have I been telling you all this? In the book of the prophet Hosea, God says,

> *I will return to my place, until they acknowledge their guilt and seek my face, and in their distress they seek me, saying, "Come, let us return to the Lord; for he has torn, that he may heal us; he has stricken, and he will bind us up. After two days he will revive us; on the third day he will raise us up, that we may live before him. Let us know, let us press on to know the Lord..."*
>
> Hosea 5:15 to 6:1-3

God was saying that he would leave the rebellious northern kingdom of Israel to suffer the consequences of their wickedness until they truly repented and returned to him, knowing that just as he had brought trouble upon them so he would then rescue them from it.

That part makes sense, but what about, *"After two days he will revive us; on the third day he will raise us up, that we may live before him'*? Why should the Lord have promised to rescue them on condition that they said these strangely specific words? He must have wanted Hosea to write them, because 2 Peter 1:21 says, *'No prophecy ever came by the impulse of man, but men moved by the Holy Spirit spoke from God.'* So why did Hosea write these words?

We need 1 Peter 1:10,11 for an explanation. *'The prophets… inquired what person or time was indicated by the Spirit of Christ within them when predicting the sufferings of Christ and the subsequent glory.'* When Hosea's words are interpreted as referring to the suffering and resurrection of Jesus Christ, they become extraordinarily specific. They say that Jesus's crucifixion was in the will and purpose of God; that he would be dead for two days; and that he would then be resurrected and restored to life, enabling those who had repented and returned to God to live in his presence.

If fact this prophecy is almost certainly the one that Jesus was thinking of when he told his disciples, *"Thus it is written, that the Christ should suffer and on the third day rise from the dead."* (Luke 24:46)[86]

That seems to explain things, but the tangled knot of this prophecy isn't completely untied. For it says that on the third day the Lord will raise *us* up, and *we* shall live before him. Once again, Peter comes to the rescue. If we insert his 'key', that a day is equal to a thousand years, it all becomes plain. *"After two thousand years he will revive us; on the third thousand years he will raise us up, that we may live before him."* Ah! Now Hosea was prophesying that if we repent and turn to the Lord then after two thousand years we shall be raised from the dead and shall spend the next thousand years living with him on the earth, just as Revelation 20:4 says.

Just like Isaiah's prophecy about a virgin birth, Hosea's words might originally have applied to his own time, but they had a deeper fulfilment in the life of Jesus at his first coming, and they will have an even deeper fulfilment at his return.

---

[86] The other possibility is that Jesus was thinking of the story of Jonah, who was in the belly of a fish for three days, but that doesn't speak of Jesus's suffering in the same way that this verse in Hosea does.

What a fantastic revelation this is! Resurrection Day, when the Lord will raise us up, will be 'after two thousand years'! Here at last is an unambiguous timetable for the resurrection of believers. The only question is: two thousand years after what?

If Peter had thought about Hosea's prophecy like this, he would almost certainly have taken it to mean two thousand years after the good news of Christ's victory over sin and death was first announced. (1 Peter 1:12) In other words, two thousand years after Jesus Christ's resurrection!

In reality, Peter and the first Christians were so convinced Jesus would return in their lifetime that there is no evidence they ever thought of interpreting Hosea's prophecy in this way. If Peter had known that Jesus's return would be delayed by another two thousand years, I have no doubt that he would not only have reminded his readers that a day with the Lord is as a thousand years, but he would also have applied this to the prophecy of Hosea.

So we appear to have a clear message that Resurrection Day will be two thousand years after the year that Jesus Christ was resurrected. And that makes perfect sense, for while the date of creation is not certain, the range of possible dates calculated by various people shows that two thousand years after Christ's resurrection could well be six thousand years after creation. Thus the two methods of determining the end time – years since creation and years since Christ's resurrection – support each other. Which leads us to the next question: when was the year of Christ's death and resurrection?

The date of Christ's death and resurrection

The accounts of Jesus Christ's life in the four Gospels include many references to other known historical figures and events, such as Caesar Augustus (63 BC to AD 14); a first census conducted when Quirinius (or Cyrenius) was the governor of Syria; King Herod the Great (74/73 BC to 4 BC); Archelaus the ruler of Idumaea, Judea and Samaria from 4 BC to AD 6; and the Roman procurator Pontius Pilate who governed Judea from AD 26 to AD 36 or 37. The most complete example of such references can be found in Luke chapter 3, verses 1 to 3:

> *In the fifteenth year of the reign of Tiberi-us Caesar, Pontius Pilate being governor of Judea, and Herod* (a son of Herod the Great) *being tetrarch of Galilee, and his brother Philip tetrarch of the region of Ituraea and Trachonitis, and Lysani-as tetrarch of Abilene, in the high-priesthood of Annas and Caiaphas, the word of God came to John the son of Zechariah in the wilderness; and he went into all the region about the Jordan, preaching a baptism of repentance for the forgiveness of sins.*

External information about such people and events is provided by secular historians of the time such as the Roman historians Dio Cassius and Tacitus, and the Jewish historian Flavius Josephus. Other sources include contemporary calendars (there were more than one), astronomy, and even Roman coinage.

With all this information, modern historians can work out when the significant events in the life and ministry of Jesus Christ took place. To do this properly is far from easy, and I am certainly not going to attempt it here. What must be the most complete and definitive study is the book *New Testament Chronology*, written by Kenneth Frank Doig and published by the Edwin Mellen Press in 1990. Here is how Doig, supported by 216 references to other writers, summarized 68,000 words of investigation into the chronology of Christ's life:

- Jesus was born on about December 25 in 5 BCE.
- He was baptized by John the Baptist on about January 6 in 28 CE, when he was 31.
- After a ministry of two years and three months he was crucified on Friday, April 7, 30 CE, when he was 33.
- He was resurrected to eternal life on Sunday, April 9, 30 CE.

- This is the only dating that fully satisfies the Scriptures and the reconstruction of ancient history and calendars.

So there we are. Two thousand years after AD 30 gives AD 2030 for Resurrection Day!

It is possible, I suppose, that Resurrection Day might not be exactly two thousand years after Jesus's resurrection. It might happen a year or two later, because Hosea did say 'after two days he will revive us'. However, Hosea also said, 'on the third day he will raise us up,' which to my mind sounds as though he meant resurrection to take place at the start of the following millennium, or at least very soon after it starts.

Incidentally, a Google search for 'Jesus 2030' that I did produced over 13 million hits! It's evident that the Holy Spirit is telling Christians all over the world that 2030 will be a significant year in relation to Christ's return, even though many have different views about the order of events in the last seven years and what exactly will happen in 2030.

Is it possible to get any closer to the date of Resurrection Day than the year? Yes, it is! The Jewish feasts will tell us.

The Jewish feasts

This is a true story. A man was once babysitting for his small granddaughter. She had a toy tea set and brought him a little cup she had filled with water.

"Would you like a cup of tea, Grandad?" she asked.

"That would be nice, dear. Thank you," he said.

When he had finished, she asked, "Did you like your tea, Grandad? Would you like another cup?"

It was only a small cup, so he readily agreed. "Thank you very much."

When her mother returned home, he told her how hospitable her little daughter had been. She stared at him in horror. "But she can't reach the taps!" she exclaimed. "Where do you think she got the water from?"

In their playtime, children are practising skills for real use in adult life. When my younger sister was about six, she used to make me and my other sister sit on the floor as her pupils while she 'taught us', using the piano stool as her desk. She grew up to become not only a teacher but a much sought-after consultant to failing schools. One of my own children used to play endless games of Monopoly with seemingly unlimited supplies of money. He became a financial manager in one of Britain's major companies.

Something similar was going on when God established the annual Jewish feasts and temple rituals in the days of Moses. Their purpose was – and still is in the case of the feasts – to remind God's people of his historical dealings with them, and to teach them about gratitude, holiness, sin and forgiveness. What the people would not have realized is that, like children's tea parties, these feasts and rituals were also a preparation in heart and mind for the real thing, the coming of their Messiah. (Hebrews 9:23,24; 10:1)

Take the Passover feast for example. In the weeks preceding the exodus from Egypt, the Lord sent a series of increasingly horrible plagues on the Egyptians in an effort to persuade Pharaoh to free his army of Hebrew slaves. (At this time in history the descendants of Abraham, Isaac and Jacob were called Hebrews in the Bible.) When these efforts all failed, the Lord told Moses that he was going to do something even worse, and this time it would succeed: he was going to kill the firstborn child of every Egyptian family. This sounds heartless, but Hebrew slaves were probably dying every day under the lashings of their Egyptian taskmasters, and Pharoah had already ordered every Hebrew male child to be killed at birth.

In order that the angel of death should not make a mistake and kill some of the Hebrew children, Moses was to tell every Hebrew family to kill a lamb and smear its blood on the lintel and doorposts of their house. The killing angel would then pass over the houses with blood on them, and the children would be saved from death. God also told them to roast and eat the lamb that same night to give them strength for their flight from Egypt, for it was that very night that he was going to deliver them.

Thus it was that through the death of a lamb the people were themselves saved from death, freed from slavery, and given the physical strength to begin a new life under the rule of God on their way to the promised land of Canaan. Afterwards the Lord commanded them to remember this great deliverance at the same time every year by eating a special Passover meal of roast lamb and other symbolic ingredients in their homes.

The whole Exodus event, and the annual Passover meal which still recalls it in many Jewish homes every year, was an amazing trailer for the death of Jesus Christ and the salvation which his death has made available to us. Jesus's cousin John the Baptist called him *"...the Lamb of God, who takes away the sin of the world!"* (John 1:29) Even the blood-spattered upright and crosspiece of his crucifixion cross recalled the doorpost and lintel over the entrance to each Hebrew home on that dramatic night in ancient Egypt. Jesus died like a Passover lamb to save us, not from physical death but eternal death. Through him we can be rescued, not from slavery to an Egyptian pharaoh and his taskmasters, but to Satan and sin in all its forms. But what is more important for our investigation is the timing: Jesus died on the very same day that the Passover lambs were slaughtered.

Immediately after Passover week, on the first day of the following week, the feast of First Fruits is celebrated – the first signs of new life in the world of nature with the appearance of green barley grains. The return to life of the buried seeds of barley symbolized the resurrection of Jesus from the tomb two days later.

Thus two of the Jewish feasts prefigured the death and resurrection of the promised Messiah Jesus, but how do they tell us the month of his return? I will explain. Moses instituted three principal feasts which were to be celebrated each year by attendance at the tabernacle or later at the temple in Jerusalem. As stated in Deuteronomy 16:16 these three feasts were:

(i)   the Feast of Unleavened Bread, which began with the Passover meal in March or April on the anniversary of the Exodus and ended with the festival of First Fruits or Beginning of Harvest, the beginning of the barley harvest

(ii) the Feast of Weeks or Pentecost, in May, which celebrated the wheat harvest

(iii) the Feast of Tabernacles, also called the Feast of Booths, the Feast of Ingathering, or simply The Feast. This took place in September or October, and basically celebrated the fruit harvest, the final harvest of the year. It begins with the Feast of Trumpets, continues ten days later with the Day of Atonement, and finishes with the actual Feast of Booths - eight days of camping out on rooftops in memory of Israel's 40 years of sojourning in tents in the wilderness on their way to the promised land of Canaan.

The central meaning of each feast listed above clearly corresponds to three major events in the life of Jesus and his followers:

(i)   his death and resurrection

(ii) his gift of the Holy Spirit resulting in three thousand new believers

(iii) the resurrection of believers in Christ, the repentance of Israel, their reconciliation with their Messiah and their ingathering to his kingdom; and as a reminder that we are on a joyful journey to the promised land of a new heaven and earth.

As I wrote just now, Jesus's death actually took place in the Passover week, on the same day that thousands of lambs were slaughtered in Jerusalem in memory of the night the Hebrews marked their doorways with the blood of a lamb to save them from the angel of death.

His resurrection took place on the first day of the following week, the same day that First Fruits or the Beginning of Harvest was celebrated. Paul wrote, '...*Christ has been raised from the dead, the first fruits of those who have fallen asleep.*' (1 Corinthians 15:20)

The Holy Spirit was given on the day of Pentecost, which celebrated the wheat harvest. The three thousand new believers who were baptized that day represented a harvest of souls. "...*unless a grain of wheat falls into the earth and dies, it remains alone; but if it dies, it bears much fruit.*" (John 12:24)

It is clear that, in an amazing way, God arranged for these major events in the life and ministry of Jesus to occur on the very dates of the corresponding Jewish festivals. It would therefore be incredible if he did not time Resurrection Day to coincide with the third of the three principal annual festivals, the Feast of Tabernacles. This takes place in September or October, as I said.

In Annex 6 I have shown in more detail how Jesus fulfilled the symbolism of these feasts and how they all clearly point to him. For now, I just want to look at the Feast of Tabernacles, because it not only tells us in which month Resurrection Day will occur but also, I believe, the actual day!

The Feast of Tabernacles

The Feast of Tabernacles, or the Feast of Booths, involves making temporary shelters of branches and palm fronds – often on the flat roofs of houses – to remind the Jews of the time when their ancestors lived in tents in the wilderness. I say 'involves' rather than 'involved', because religious Jewish families do still celebrate it. God instituted the feast to be a happy time of celebration at the end of the summer's labour. For that reason, it is also called the Feast of Ingathering.

161

"You shall keep the feast of booths seven days, when you make your ingathering from your threshing floor and your wine press; you shall rejoice in your feast, you and your son and your daughter, your manservant and your maidservant, the Levite, the sojourner, the fatherless, and the widow who are within your towns. For seven days you shall keep the feast to the Lord your God at the place which the Lord will choose; because the Lord your God will bless you in all your produce and in all the work of your hands, so that you will be altogether joyful."

Deuteronomy 16:13-15

In essence, it is Israel's harvest thanksgiving.

When Jesus described the end of this age, he used a harvest metaphor: *"Let* [the wheat and weeds] *grow together until the harvest; and at harvest time I will tell the reapers, Gather the weeds first and bind them in bundles to be burned, but gather the wheat into my barn."* (Matthew 13:30)

Paul also linked resurrection with harvest: *'But someone will ask, "How are the dead raised?" ...what you sow is not the body which is to be, but a bare kernel, perhaps of wheat or of some other grain. ... So is it with the resurrection of the dead. What is sown is perishable, what is raised is imperishable. ... For the trumpet will sound, and the dead will be raised imperishable, and we shall be changed.'* (Extracts from 1 Corinthians 15:35-52)

There is even a hint of the harvest metaphor in a related prophecy of Zechariah in the Old Testament: *'Then the Lord will appear over them... the Lord God will sound the trumpet... On that day the Lord their God will save them... Grain shall make the young men flourish, and new wine the maidens.'* (Zechariah 9:14-17)

It is clear that in the Bible, Resurrection Day is likened to harvest time, and therefore it is linked in thought to the Feast of Tabernacles or Ingathering.

However, the Feast of Tabernacles comprises more than a week of living in temporary shelters or booths to celebrate the final harvest of the year. It begins on the Jewish New Year's day, the first day of the month of Tishri, with the Feast of

162

Trumpets. (Leviticus 23:23-25) Ten days later comes the solemn Day of Atonement (Leviticus 23:26-32), and only then is harvest time celebrated with the Feast of Booths. (Leviticus 23:33-36)

So if Resurrection Day is to coincide with the Feast of Tabernacles or Ingathering, at what point will it occur?

The exact moment of resurrection will be announced by a loud trumpet-call, which Paul described as 'the last trumpet'. *'Lo! I tell you a mystery. We shall not all sleep, but we shall all be changed, in a moment, in the twinkling of an eye, at the last trumpet.'* (1 Corinthians 15:51,52)

Have a think about this for a moment. If you asked me which road I lived in, and I replied, "It's at the last turning," you'd still be none the wiser. It would only make sense if you knew where all the preceding turnings were. So when Paul told his readers that they would be raised 'at the last trumpet', it would only have made sense if they knew what all the preceding trumpets were, or else what the last trumpet itself was. So what was this 'last trumpet' – or all the preceding trumpets – that Paul could confidently assume his readers were acquainted with?

By the time of Jesus and Paul, the service held on the Feast of Trumpets in the temple and synagogues involved a total of 100 trumpet blasts.[87] Nowadays, Jewish people see this as a summons to spend the next ten days that lead up to the Day of Atonement in self-examination and repentance.

The first 99 blasts were made up of repeated sets of three different kinds:

- Tekiah A pure unbroken sound. It calls a man to search his heart, forsake his wrong ways, and seek forgiveness through repentance. The tekiah calls people to attention and to consider again the teaching of Moses. In general, it

---

[87] The information on trumpet blasts is taken from Wikibooks, *Hebrew Roots/Holy Days/Trumpets/The Blowing of the Shofar.*

is a summons to listen to God and to receive from him the orders for the day.

- Teru'ah A broken, staccato, trembling sound. It typifies the sorrow that comes to man when he realizes his misconduct and desires to change his ways. It must comprise at least eight notes, so most trumpeters blow nine to be sure.

- Shevarim A wave-like sound of alarm, calling upon man to stand by the banner of God. Shevarim in Hebrew means not only a certain unique sound, it also denotes breaking something or causing damage or both. It is the note for bustling, speedy activity, the signal for striking tents and breaking camp. (I think it might also refer to breaking sinful habits and relationships.)

The resulting 99 blasts were followed by a single long trumpet blast, the Tekiah ha-Gadol. This is a prolonged, unbroken sound, held for as long as the tokea or trumpeter can manage. Where there are several trumpeters, they compete to see who can keep it up for the longest! This special blast is seen as a final appeal for sincere repentance and atonement. It is 'the last trumpet'!

The Jewish name for the Feast of Trumpets is Yom Teruah, 'Teruah day'. According to Christie Eisner[88], *'Judaism has three main shofar blasts. The one blown at Shavuot* (Pentecost) *is called "the first trump." The one blown at the first fall feast of Yom Teruah or Rosh Hashanah is called "the last trump". The one blown at Yom Kippur* (the Day of Atonement) *is called "the great trump". They are all recorded in Scripture and are still sounded to this day.'*

So when Saint Paul wrote 'we shall all be changed... at the last trumpet,' his meaning was as plain, to his readers at least, as though he had written, 'we shall all be changed one New Year's Eve'.

---

[88] *Finding the Afikoman.* C.Eisner, p.191. Ruth's Road, 2015.

The Feast of Trumpets is unique among the feasts prescribed in the Old Testament, in that the Lord didn't explain what its purpose was. Leviticus 23:23-25 simply says the people were to observe the first day of Tishri as a day of memorial and a sabbath rest, and they were to meet together for a blast of trumpets. Not a hundred trumpet blasts, but one loud blast by several trumpets simultaneously, to make as much noise as possible. The complicated series of different kinds of blasts practised in later years and their associated meanings were subsequent inventions of the rabbis. So why did the Lord want a special day to be observed by a loud trumpet blast, without attaching any clear meaning to it?

The most usual purpose of a trumpet blast in Biblical days was to warn people of impending danger and to call them to act accordingly. In Ezekiel chapter 33:2-5 the Lord said,

> *"If I bring the sword upon a land, and the people of the land take a man from among them and make him their watchman; and if he sees the sword coming upon the land and blows the trumpet and warns the people; then if any one who hears the sound of the trumpet does not take warning, and the sword comes and takes him away, his blood shall be upon his own head. He heard the sound of the trumpet, and did not take warning; his blood shall be upon himself."*

Jesus echoed those words about watching and heeding the warning of a trumpet when he was talking to his disciples about Resurrection Day in Matthew chapter 24. *"Then two men will be in the field; one is taken and one is left. Two women will be grinding at the mill; one is taken and one is left. Watch therefore, for you do not know on what day your Lord is coming."*

What are we to watch for? Jesus gave the answer a few verses earlier. *"Immediately after the tribulation of those days the sun will be darkened, and the moon will not give its light, and the stars will fall from heaven, and the powers of the heavens will be shaken; then will appear the sign of the Son of man in heaven, and then all the tribes of the*

165

earth will mourn, and they will see the Son of man coming on the clouds of heaven with power and great glory; and he will send out his angels <u>with a loud trumpet call</u>, and they will gather his elect from the four winds, from one end of heaven to the other." (Matthew 24:29-31)

We are to watch for a sign in heaven, for the appearance of Jesus in the sky, and to wait for the sound of a very loud trumpet. When we hear that we must drop everything and, not run, but fly!

Therefore it seems to me that God established the Feast of Trumpets as a prophetic sign pointing forward to the day of resurrection. It didn't celebrate something that had already taken place and it didn't require worshippers to take any immediate action, so no reason for it was given. Its symbolic meaning would be fulfilled only on the day when everyone who has accepted Jesus Christ as Saviour and Lord is raised to eternal life. The last thing we shall hear before we meet him in the sky will be a long and very loud trumpet blast. Only this time, it will be blown not by men but by a single angel, with no competitors.

One other thought. In Revelation chapter 11 it is the seventh trumpet blast which announces resurrection day. In Israel the first day of every new month was announced by a trumpet blast. (Psalm 81:1-3) Tishri is the seventh month in the Jewish religious calendar. So the trumpet blast which announced the beginning of the Feast of Trumpets was also the seventh trumpet-call of the year.

Shall I tell you something that excites me? The Feast of Trumpets has to be observed as a sabbath, and Tishri 1 when the Feast will take place in the year 2030 will already be a sabbath. When I discovered this, I felt the Lord was encouraging me to believe that 2030 will indeed be the year when that amazing last trumpet-call will finally be sounded.

Some Christian and messianic Jewish writers who, like me, connect the Feast of Trumpets with Resurrection Day, also connect the Day of Atonement to the events on earth that will follow the resurrection, when the Jews as a nation will realize

166

their error in rejecting Jesus as their Messiah and will turn to him as a body in repentance and faith. Since the Day of Atonement takes place nine days after the Feast of Trumpets, the Jewish nation will have nine days, after the stunning disappearance of all Christ's followers, to organize an ultimate national Day of Atonement for their rejection of Jesus as their Messiah. It will be rather like one of the national days of prayer which King George VI announced for the British nation during World War II.

The week-long Feast of Booths which follows the Day of Atonement will then be a celebration of their own ingathering into God's kingdom and a time of joyful looking forward to their promised everlasting life in the new earth. Thus the Feast of Ingathering prefigures the final harvest of the Jews who will at long last come out of the wilderness into the kingdom of Jesus Christ and will join resurrected Christians when he returns to rule the world. For, as I explained in Chapter 6, they too will be resurrected at the beginning of the final millennium, and will not have to wait until the day of judgement to come back to life.

The Jubilee Hypothesis

There were two other major calendar events instituted by the Lord through Moses. The people of Israel were commanded to observe every seven years as a day of rest for the land, a 'sabbatical year', when no crops were to be planted. This was another link in what we might call 'the chain of rest': a seventh day of rest, a seventh year of rest, and a seventh millennium of rest. And then every 50 years they had to provide a further year of rest for the land, release all slaves, and return all land taken in surety to its original owners. This fiftieth year was called a 'year of jubilee', and it was a very serious occasion.

*"And you shall count seven weeks of years, seven times seven years,
so that the time of the seven weeks of years shall be to you forty-nine*

years. Then you shall send abroad the loud trumpet on the tenth day
of the seventh month; on the day of atonement you shall send abroad
the trumpet throughout all your land. And you shall hallow the
fiftieth year, and proclaim liberty throughout the land to all its
inhabitants; it shall be a jubilee for you, when each of you shall
return to his property and each of you shall return to his family. A
jubilee shall that fiftieth year be to you; in it you shall neither sow,
nor reap what grows of itself, nor gather the grapes from the
undressed vines. For it is a jubilee; it shall be holy to you; you shall
eat what it yields out of the field."

Leviticus 25:8-12

Just as past events in the life of Christ have coincided with corresponding Jewish feasts, some people believe that either the resurrection or the return of Christ three and a half years later will take place at the beginning of a year of jubilee. The return of Christ at the start of the millennial kingdom would make the more obvious connection, for that is when the entire land of Israel will be returned to the nation of Israel.

Since a jubilee year was to be announced by a loud trumpet-call on the Day of Atonement, some people believe that this will be 'the last trumpet' to which Paul was referring when he wrote that believers would be resurrected 'at the last trumpet'. (1 Corinthians 15:52) In this case, Resurrection Day will take place, not on the Feast of Trumpets, but on the Day of Atonement ten days later. However, there is no reference to jubilee years in the New Testament, and jubilee years had not been observed since 122 BC or earlier. So it is most unlikely that Paul was referring to a jubilee year trumpet on the assumption that his readers would know what he was talking about. And even if he was, the only difference would be that Resurrection Day will take place ten days later than I have concluded it will.

The Jubilee Hypothesis itself is the idea that this present age of six thousand years has been divided into 120 jubilees of 50 years. There is at least one published book which asserts that

Abraham was born exactly on the fortieth jubilee after creation, the exodus from Egypt took place on the fiftieth jubilee, and Solomon's temple was completed on the sixtieth jubilee, etc. Sadly, such an ordered history of the world is nothing but wishful thinking. In Chapter 2 in the section headed 'Six thousand years young?' I explained how to calculate how many years after creation the Exodus and other early events occurred, using the chronologies of Adam's descendants recorded in the Hebrew text of Genesis as far as the Exodus. Adding information from 1 Kings chapter 6 these dates can be extended to work out when the temple of Solomon was completed. Table 5 shows the results.

Table 5: Comparison of key dates and jubilee years

Event	Calculated years from creation	Claimed years from creation
Birth of Abraham	1948	2000 = 40 jubilees
Date of the Exodus	2679	2500 = 50 jubilees
Completion of the first temple	3165	3000 = 60 jubilees
Decree of Cyrus allowing the Jews to return to Jerusalem*	3432	3500 = 70 jubilees
Birth of Jesus Christ*	3966	4000 = 80 jubilees
Start of the Millennium		6000 = 120 jubilees

*Based on a generally accepted date of 539 BC for the decree of Cyrus and 5 BC for the birth of Jesus Christ and a date of 3971 BC for creation. An alternative creation date of 4004 BC (Archbishop Ussher's date) would put Jesus's birth at exactly 80 jubilees, but all the other dates would still not match multiples of 10 jubilees.

Table 5 shows that none of the events mentioned occurred at an exact multiple of ten jubilees from creation. Some occurred earlier and some occurred later, so no kind of adjustment could make them all fit.

Actually, I think Resurrection Day may well be followed by a jubilee year. But to predict the year of resurrection or the return of Christ from the date of the next jubilee year seems to be impossible, for jubilee years are no longer celebrated, and no one knows for certain when the next one will be. Until about 2016 some writers were predicting Christ's return in 2016 or 2017 in the belief that one of those years would be a jubilee year.

The messianic Jew who coined the phrase 'the Jubilee Hypothesis' believes the next jubilee year will be 2027. This appears to be based on an incorrect belief that the historian Josephus said 24/23 BC was a jubilee year. At the time of writing, the Jubilee Hypothesis man is still predicting that Jesus will return in 2027, as are many other people. But Revelation clearly tells us that God's two prophetic witnesses will begin their ministry seven years before Christ's return, so we should have been hearing from them since 2020 if the Jubilee Hypothesis and the 2027 date are true!

A long and detailed historical examination of all the evidence about jubilee years was available at the time of writing on the website design-of-time.com/chronoj.htm. The 7000-word article 'Chronology of Jubilees' was based, not on years from creation, but on evidence from the Bible and several other historical sources as to when the Jews actually celebrated jubilee years. Its author concluded,

> *If a jubilee year were celebrated in this modern era – as a projection of jubilees celebrated in the Temple Era – it is probable that the next jubilee year would correspond to about the year 2029 CE plus or minus 1 year. Due to some uncertainty inherent in the assumptions currently made and due to the antiquity of the cited source material, the current analysis should be considered to be very speculative.*

Nevertheless, if the writer is correct, AD 2030 could mark the start of the final 120th year of jubilee, and according to my conclusions, that will be the year of resurrection! This then is the third method of dating resurrection year. For even if the date of the 120th year is only approximately right, it supports the conclusions of the first two methods, that the close of this age is at hand.

A bunch of dates

I've been keeping the box of dates well wrapped up until now, but finally we can open it and take some juicy dates out!

The Feast of Unleavened Bread takes place in either March or April and the Feast of Ingathering takes place in either September or October. They are actually on fixed dates in the Jewish calendar, but because the Jewish calendar differs from the Gregorian calendar which most of the world uses, they appear to vary. Nevertheless, for any particular year the exact dates of the Jewish feasts according to the more widely used Gregorian calendar can be obtained.

Assuming that Kenneth Doig is correct in dating Jesus Christ's resurrection to AD 30, and that Resurrection Day for believers will take place two thousand years later in line with Hosea's prophecy, then Resurrection Day will be in AD 2030 at the Feast of Trumpets. In that year the first day of Tishri, when the last trumpet will be sounded at the Feast of Trumpets, will be Saturday, September 28th, 2030. It is true that this date will be 2000 years plus six months after Christ's resurrection, so it might equally be 2000 years minus six months, in Tishri 2029. But since Hosea wrote '*after* two days the Lord will raise us up' I believe it will be in 2030 as I have said.

Jesus will then return three and a half years later, which will be in 2034 on or about March 28th. The two witnesses will have begun their ministry of announcing Christ's return seven years earlier, which means at the end of March 2027. That is when we shall know for certain whether the dates the Bible has led us to are indeed correct. If they are, the Great Tribulation will happen some time before this. So be prepared!

At the last supper with his disciples Jesus told them, *'I have earnestly desired to eat this Passover with you before I suffer; for I tell you I shall not eat it until it is fulfilled in the Kingdom of God.'* (Luke 22:15,16) In 2034 the Passover meal will be eaten on the evening of Monday 3rd April, a week after March 28th when Jesus will return. That would give Jesus a week to win the battle of Armageddon and prepare for the greatest Passover celebration in history. What a celebration that will be! *'And the angel said to me, "Write this: Blessed are those who are invited to the marriage supper of the Lamb."'* (Revelation 19:9)

Somehow – and only God knows how – Jesus will eat that amazing Passover meal not only with his original disciples as he promised, but with all the resurrected believers who have returned to the earth with him. For them at least, death will be no more. What a fantastic party that is going to be! Will you be there among the invited guests?

The previous day, Sunday April 2nd 2034, would have been celebrated by Christians as Palm Sunday if they had still been on the earth. That was the day in AD 30 that Jesus entered Jerusalem on a donkey, thereby announcing his claim to be Israel's saviour, but in humility and peace. This time however he will enter Jerusalem mounted on a white warhorse, and no one will be able to dispute his authority to be the king of Israel and of all the nations on earth.

> *...though he was in the form of God...* (he took) *the form of a servant, being born in the likeness of men. And being found in human form he humbled himself and became obedient unto death, even death on a cross. Therefore God has highly exalted him and bestowed on him the name which is above every name, that at the name of Jesus every knee should bow, in heaven and on earth and under the earth, and every tongue confess that Jesus Christ is Lord, to the glory of God the Father.*
>
> Philippians 2:6-11

Then I saw heaven opened, and behold, a white horse! He who sat upon it is called Faithful and True, and in righteousness he judges and makes war. On his robe and on his thigh he has a name inscribed, King of kings and Lord of lords.

Revelation 19:11,16

The date of creation

There is one final date to be deduced, namely the date of creation. If Resurrection Day is to take place in September 2030 and if God created the world exactly six thousand years before that, then creation took place in September 3971 BC. (There was no year zero.) Martin Luther worked out the year as 3961 BC, but the closest previous estimate seems to be 3967 by Heinrich Bünting.

Summary of forthcoming events

In summary, the Bible leads us to the dates shown in Table 6.

Table 6: Suggested biblically predicted dates for the events to come

Event	Date
The Great Tribulation – nuclear war, unprecedented volcanic eruptions, or something else unparalleled in history.	Some time before 2027
The two witnesses begin their three and a half-year ministry in Jerusalem.	Sunday March 28th or thereabouts in 2027
Resurrection Day.	Saturday September 28th, 2030 *The Feast of Trumpets, Tishri 1*

173

Three and a half-year rule of the Antichrist. Conversion of many Jews and others.	2030 – 2034
The return of Christ Jesus with all resurrected believers and the inauguration of the millennial kingdom.	Tuesday March 28th, *Nisan 8*, or thereabouts in 2034
Celebratory Passover meal, which might also be 'the bridal supper of the Lamb'.	Monday April 3rd, 2034, *the evening of Nisan 1*

One final reason

There is one final reason why God may have to intervene and bring this age to an end very soon. The British doctor Aubrey de Grey, a co-founder of the Methuselah Foundation, believes that through developments in tissue engineering and regenerative medicines, people will eventually be able to live as long as a thousand years.

Ray Kurzweil has gone even further. Kurzweil is a celebrated inventor who has made many correct predictions about the future in the last twenty years or so. *"I believe we will reach a point around 2029 when medical technologies will add one additional year every year to your life expectancy,"* he told Playboy magazine in May 2016. *"By that I don't mean life expectancy based on your birth date, but rather your remaining life expectancy."* Which means that anyone still alive by then will live for ever!

As I've previously mentioned, immortality would create insurmountable population problems if children continued to be born. It was to stop Adam and Eve eating of the tree of life and so living for ever that God expelled them from the Garden of Eden. Therefore if humanity does find its way back to the tree of life by 2029 or thereabouts, it is difficult to see how God could allow life as we know it to continue any longer.

Now boarding

In some airports you don't know whether your aircraft has even returned from its previous destination until a sign lights up at the departure gate saying, 'Now boarding'. Jesus promised that when his disciples eventually saw a fulfilment of all the things he had foretold, then they would know that his return was near. Once again, here's what he said:

> *"From the fig tree learn its lesson: as soon as its branch becomes tender and puts forth its leaves, you know that summer is near. So also, when you see all these things, you* [will] *know that he is near, at the very gates. Truly, I say to you, this generation will not pass away till all these things take place."*
>
> Matthew 24:32-34

In other words, the generation which sees a fulfilment of all the signs that Jesus foretold will be the generation which sees his return.

So what were those signs Jesus spoke of that would unambiguously announce his arrival at the departure gate? Some of them, like wars and persecution and signs in the heavens, have continued throughout the centuries, so they have not been much help. But there were two signs which Jesus did unambiguously relate only to the time of his return.

In Luke 21:24 Jesus said that Jerusalem would be trodden down by the Gentiles until the times of the Gentiles were fulfilled. Forty years after he said this, Jerusalem was destroyed, just as he had foretold. But in 1948 Palestine was re-established by international agreement as a homeland for the Jews, and Jerusalem was no longer trodden down by Gentiles. This was an unambiguous statement from God that the times of the Gentiles had been fulfilled. I don't want to make too much of this, but the average lifespan in the UK is currently 82 years. This means that the generation born in 1948 will come to an end in 2030, the very year that I believe will be Resurrection

175

Year. "...this generation will not pass away till all these things take place." What a privilege to be born into the generation who will finally see the return of Christ! It's so exciting!

But there's more. In Revelation chapter 7, John saw people in heaven from every nation, from all tribes and peoples and tongues. These were people who had died during the Great Tribulation, the period preceding the last seven years. It means that people from every language group must have had the opportunity to hear and respond to the gospel before the Great Tribulation comes and goes. Is that a possibility at this present time? It certainly is, at least from every significant language group.

In 1999, Wycliffe Bible Translators (WBT) set themselves a goal entitled 'Vision 2025'. In conjunction with other similar organizations it was *'to see a Bible translation programme begun in all the remaining languages that need one by 2025'*. This goal had become a possibility because computerization has enormously speeded up the process of Bible translation. If their goal is realized, by 2025 Bible translators from WBT and other groups will be working on the Gospels with native speakers in every remaining significant language group.

While this work is going on another organization, Global Recordings Network (GRN), is making recordings of the Bible available for even the tiniest language groups, using native-speaking recordists. People who cannot read or who have never seen a book can now listen to these recordings on their smartphones. GRN's phone App, downloadable from www.5fish.mobi, has the recorded story of Jesus and part or all of the Bible in 6,700 different languages! Even where there is no Internet access or electricity, people can still listen using hand-wound MP3 players provided by GRN. Chile for Christ, the charity I founded, supplied two of these machines to a Pehuenche community living high up in the Andes mountains.

Only in our generation has it become possible for the Gospel to reach people in every corner of the planet. Even in countries where evangelism is totally forbidden and people cannot buy a Bible or attend a church meeting, they can still read and hear the Gospel in secret, thanks to the World Wide Web. The Gospel is indeed being preached throughout the whole world, and it is happening in our generation.

When Jesus's disciples asked him, *"...what will be the sign of your coming and of the close of the age?"* (Matthew 24:3) his most significant reply was this: *"...this gospel of the kingdom will be preached throughout the whole world, as a testimony to all nations; and then the end will come."* (Matthew 24:14) This was the second unambiguous sign of his imminent return that Jesus told his followers to look out for, the sign that would declare beyond any further doubt that the end of this age has come at last. *"Then the end will come,"* he said.

That 'then' is now!

177

Epilogue

Jesus – the way, the truth and the life

Your place in eternity depends totally on your relationship with the living Lord Jesus Christ. As Peter told the Jewish rulers back in AD 33, *"There is salvation in no one else, for there is no other name under heaven given among men by which we must be saved."* (Acts 4:12)

The one thing which bars us from living for ever in the wonderful world to come is our sin, just as in the olden days leprosy barred people from human society. Trying to buy a place in God's kingdom by good behaviour would be like a leper offering money to his fellow villagers to let him live among them while he was still a leper. Jesus Christ is the only person who has ever lived without sin, and he is the only one who can deal with our sin and restore us to a right relationship with God the Father. *"Behold, the Lamb of God, who takes away the sin of the world!"* (John 1:29)

Jesus died for the whole world. He died for Christians, Jews, Muslims, Hindus, Buddhists, agnostics, atheists and you! Whether you think you are deserving or undeserving, loveable or unlovable; whatever you have done or not done in the past; however badly people may have treated you and whatever they may have said about you, none of this makes any difference. God wants everyone to be saved and to live in a loving fellowship with himself. (1 Timothy 2:4; 1 John 1:1-3)

With Jesus's help you can begin eternal life here and now, not because you've earned it, nor because you deserve it, but as a gift from the God who loves you more than you can possibly imagine. *'For the wages of sin is death, but the free gift of God is eternal life in Christ Jesus our Lord.'* (Romans 6:23)

To receive eternal life you must put your trust in Jesus to be your Saviour and Lord. That means being deeply sorry for your sins, for all the ways in which you have broken God's commandments by what you have done and by what you have not done; by what you have said and by what you have thought; by not loving God with all your heart and soul and mind and strength, and by not loving your neighbour as yourself. It means asking God to forgive you for the sake of Jesus, who gave his life for you on the cross. And it means asking Jesus to be the Lord of your life from this moment onwards, allowing him to help you to live a new and changed life that brings honour to his Father. That is the only way you can meet Jesus as your saviour on Resurrection Day, rather than meeting him as your judge at the end of this age. The way to Paradise is a one-way street, and that one way is Jesus.

Saying "I will" to Jesus

Find somewhere quiet where you can talk aloud to the Lord Jesus. He has been longing for this moment since before you were born. Use your own words, or say the following prayer if it expresses what's in your heart.

> *Lord Jesus,*
> *I believe you are the Son of God. You know who I am. I realize that because of my sin I am under a death sentence. I am truly sorry for all the wrong things I have done and said and thought.* (If there's anything in particular on your conscience mention it.) *Please forgive me. With your help I now want to live the way you want me to and to fulfil the purpose you made me for.*
> *Lord Jesus,*
> *I thank you very, very much that you died on the cross so that I can be forgiven and set free from sin to live for ever in your kingdom.*
> *I now open the door of my life to you. Please come in as my Saviour and Lord, and help me to live for you from this moment onwards.*
> *Thank you, Lord Jesus.*

Jesus said, *"All that the Father gives me will come to me; and him who comes to me I will not cast out."* (John 6:37) If you prayed like that and meant it, you can be confident that Jesus has accepted you and restored you to a right relationship with the Father, that all your sins have been forgiven, and that you have the promise of everlasting life.

'*If we confess our sins, he is faithful and just, and will forgive our sins and cleanse us from all unrighteousness.*' (1 John 1:9)

'*For God so loved the world that he gave his only Son, that whoever believes in him should not perish but have eternal life.*' (John 3:16)

First steps

Here are some suggestions for your first steps as a new member of God's family.

(i) Make a permanent note of the date.

It's your new birthday! You'll want to remember this day in the future. '*When someone becomes a Christian, he becomes a brand new person inside. He is not the same any more. A new life has begun!*' (2 Corinthians 5:17 TLB)

(ii) Tell someone what you have done.

'*For if you tell others with your own mouth that Jesus Christ is your Lord and believe in your own heart that God has raised him from the dead, you will be saved.*' (Romans 10:9 TLB)

(iii) Be baptized.

"Those who believe and are baptized will be saved." (Mark 16:16 TLB)

In the Bible, baptism means being immersed in water by a church leader. It is a way of making public your decision to belong to Jesus, just as a wedding is a way of making public

181

your decision to share your life with someone permanently. Baptism doesn't 'save' you. It's how you show Jesus you are willing to obey him, and how he shows you that your sins have been washed away and your new life with him has genuinely begun.

To be baptized you will have to find a church, if you don't already belong to one. Churches can be big or small, formal or informal, dead or alive. A good local church will welcome you into God's family and help you to grow as a child of God. Do an Internet search for 'Lively church in Marshmere-under-Water / Little Grumbling / Ambling-by-the-Sea' or wherever you live, to find what's available. If several churches are listed, ask God to guide you, and try visiting two or three of them on Sundays until you feel you have found one that could become your spiritual home. Make sure they do proper baptisms!

(iv) Ask the church leaders to pray at your baptism that God will fill you with his Holy Spirit.

Jesus said, *"...if even sinful persons like yourselves give children what they need, don't you realize that your heavenly Father will do at least as much, and give the Holy Spirit to those who ask for him?"* (Luke 11:13 TLB) It doesn't happen automatically, we have to ask!

The Holy Spirit gives us the power to live as God wants us to. '*...those who follow after the Holy Spirit find themselves doing those things that please God.*' (Romans 8:5 TLB)

(v) Find a mentor

If you already have a Christian friend, ask if he or she would be willing to meet you on a regular basis for a while, to help you to learn how to follow Jesus. If you don't have such a friend, ask if there is someone in the church who would like to help you in this way.

(vi) Talk to your heavenly Father each day.

Find a quiet place to pray and follow the TSP 'teaspoon rule':
Thank God for anything that comes to your mind.
Tell him you are *sorry* for any way you've failed him and ask him to forgive you and to help you to do better.
Ask him *please* to help you, and to help anyone else you know who is in need.

(vii) Read the Bible.

The Bible is like food for your spirit. It will enable you to grow into a strong Christian. If you don't have a Bible of your own you can download one as an app, or else you can buy an electronic or physical copy. There are different kinds of English translation, as well as translations into other languages. Search for 'Bibles for New Believers' to find the translation that would best suit you, or ask someone in the church for advice. If you have never read the Bible, you might find it helpful to start with a very short version of it, written by Philip Law: *The One Hour Bible - From Adam to Apocalypse in sixty minutes.*
In Annex 7 there is a helpful list of Bible readings suitable for new Christians.
Further help can be found in *Every Day with Jesus for New Christians*, published by the Crusade for World Revival as a small paperback and as an e-book. Ideally, set aside a time each day when you can read a passage of the Bible, think about it, and perhaps also make some notes on what you learn in a notebook. My wife and I used to read it together every morning in bed before we got up, and then we prayed about what we had read as well as anything else that was on our minds.

Enjoy your new life as a member of God's family. And please introduce yourself to me when we meet in the resurrection!

If God has spoken to you through this book, please recommend it to your friends or buy them a copy so that God can speak to them too.

A positive review on Amazon or another bookseller's website would be very much appreciated.

> *Folk hesitate to buy a book that no one else has read,*
> *But if it has a good review then they might go ahead!*

Annex 1. Egyptian chronology and the date of the Flood

The problem

The generally accepted date for the first Egyptian dynasty is earlier than the date of the Flood indicated by the Bible.

In Chapter 2, I explained how the genealogies in Genesis enable us to calculate that the Exodus took place 2679 years after creation. In the same way it can be calculated that the Flood occurred 1656 years after creation. Then in Chapter 9 I concluded that according to Biblical chronology the world was created in the year 3971 BC. So if God created the world in 3971 BC, the Flood would have occurred in 2315 BC. This means that the following year there would have been only eight people alive on the earth: Noah, his wife, their three sons and their wives. Yet according to Egyptologists Dodson and Hilton[89] the First Dynasty of Egypt is conjectured to have begun in 3150 BC, 835 years *before* the Flood!

Dating the dynasties

Although the names of some 300 Egyptian kings are known, dating them is notoriously difficult. Some surviving king lists cover many rulers but have significant gaps in their text, others provide a complete list of rulers for only a short period of Egyptian history. Some dynasties may have overlapped, with different kings ruling in different regions at the same time

---

[89] *The Complete Royal Families of Ancient Egypt.* A.Dodson & D.Hilton, Thames and Hudson, 2010.

rather than serially.[90] Since the next conjectural date after the establishment of the first dynasty in 3150 is that of the final ruler of the second dynasty (the unfortunately named Nebwyhetepimyef, 2611-2584 BC), I am of the opinion that the earlier date of 3150 BC is somewhat speculative. 2611 BC however would be exactly 300 years after the Flood.

While Dodson and Hilton's book sets out the consensus of most scholars, there are a number of alternative chronologies.

Donovan Courville in his 700-page two-volume book *The Exodus Problem and Its Ramifications: A Critical Examination of the Chronological Relationships Between Israel and the Contemporary Peoples of Antiquity*[91] concluded that Egypt was founded around 2300 BC, which would have been shortly after the Flood.

The 'New Chronology', developed by the English Egyptologist David Rohl and other researchers in the 1990s, sets the New Kingdom dates as much as 350 years later than the conventional dates.[92] Rohl asserts that the New Chronology allows him to identify some of the characters in the Hebrew Bible with people whose names appear in archaeological finds.

In summary, it is difficult but not impossible to reconcile the early history of Egypt with the chronology of the Bible.

---

[90] Prophesying about forthcoming civil warfare in Egypt, the prophet Isaiah wrote, '*city against city, kingdom against kingdom*'. (Isaiah 19:2) This supports the view that in Egypt there were multiple kingdoms and therefore multiple kings reigning contemporaneously.

[91] See the Wikipedia article on 'Donovan Courville'.

[92] *A Test of Time*. D.Rohl, Cornerstone, 2001.

Annex 2. Early Jewish and Christian teaching on the Millennium and the date of creation

Early Jewish teaching

For Jews, the most authoritative book after the Old Testament is the Talmud. The famous eleventh edition of the *Encyclopaedia Britannica*, published in 1910/11, stated:

> *The view most frequently expressed* (in the Talmud) *is that the Messianic kingdom will last for one thousand (some said two thousand) years. "In six days God created the world, on the seventh He rested. But a day of God is equal to a thousand years (Psalm 90 verse 4). Hence the world will last for six thousand years of toil and labour; then will come one thousand years of Sabbath rest for the people of God in the kingdom of the Messiah." This idea must have already been very common in the first century before Christ.*

Here are some further examples of such teaching.

The Talmudic book *Sanhedrin*, 97a-97b, states, 'The *Tanna debe Eliyyahu* (the School of Elijah) *teaches: "The world exists for six thousand years — two thousand of them tohu (void); two thousand toralv* (under the Torah, i.e. the Law); *and two thousand, the era of the Mashiach* (Messiah). *But because of our numerous iniquities many of these years have been lost."* A footnote in the Soncino Press English edition of the Talmud explains, '*Messiah will come within that (third) period. He should have come at the beginning of (it); the delay is due to our sins.*' Of course, Christians and Messianic Jews believe the Messiah did come then, just as the ancient rabbis had predicted. The problem was that Jesus was not recognized by the majority of his nation.

A similar passage is found in the *Gemara*, which is a commentary on the first and older part of the Talmud. The book *Avodah Zarah*, 9a, comments on the 'Sanhedrin' passage and then turns to mathematical calculations as to when the two thousand years of Torah should be considered to have started and when the Messiah was to have come.

Sanhedrin, 97a-97b, goes on to state, '*Rabbi Kattina said, "Six thousand years shall the world exist, and one (thousand, the seventh) it shall be haruv* (desolate), *as it is written, 'And the Lord alone shall be exalted in that day.'" (Isaiah 2.11)*'

The comment on this in the *Gemara* is, '*Rabbi Kattina said, "The world endures six thousand years and one thousand it shall be laid waste (that is, the enemies of God shall be destroyed), whereof it is said, 'The Lord alone shall be exalted in that day.'" As out of seven years every seventh* [is a] *year of remission, so out of the seven thousand years of the world, the seventh millennium shall be the millennial years of remission, that God alone may be exalted in that day.*'

Wikipedia's article on 'The Six Ages of the World' includes a further extract from *Sanhedrin* 97a: '*R. Katina also taught, "Just as the seventh year is the Shmita* (letting the land lie fallow) *year, so too does the world have one thousand years out of seven that are mushmat* (fallow), *as it is written, 'And the Lord alone shall be exalted in that day' (Isaiah 2.11); and further it is written, 'A Psalm and song for the Sabbath day' (Psalm 92.1) – meaning the day that is altogether Shabbat – and also it is said, 'For a thousand years in thy sight are but as yesterday when it is past' (Psalm 90.4)."*' 'Shabbat' is Hebrew for sabbath, which means rest.

The Wikipedia article continues with an extract from the *Zohar*, a group of Jewish books which comment on the more mystical aspects of the Torah (the five books of Moses). '*The redemption of Israel will come about through the mystic force of the letter "Vav" (which has the numerical value of six), namely, in the sixth millennium... Happy are those who will be left alive at the end of the sixth millennium to enter the Shabbat, which is the seventh millennium;*

for that is a day set apart for the Holy One on which to effect the union of new souls with old souls in the world.' (Zohar, Vayera 119a)

The same article says (in 2021) that many early and late Jewish scholars wrote on a similar theme, including the Ramban, Isaac Abarbanel, Abraham ibn Ezra, Rabbeinu Bachya, the Vilna Gaon, the Lubavitcher Rebbe, the Ramchal, Aryeh Kaplan, and Rebbetzin Esther Jungreis. It provides references to their works for anyone who wants to follow them up.

The extract from the Zohar, in writing about the union of new souls with old souls, clearly refers to a day of resurrection, something which is also taught in *Sanhedrin* 97: *'Abaye said, '[The world] will be desolate two thousand years, as it is said, 'After two days he will revive us; on the third day he will raise us up, that we may live before him.'''* The *Encyclopaedia Britannica* entry on 'Millennium', which I mentioned above, interpreted this as referring to a two thousand year 'sabbath'. This may well be a correct interpretation of Abaye's understanding of Hosea's prophecy, but I believe Hosea's prophecy meant the Lord would raise up his people two thousand years after he raised his Son Jesus from the dead. This would then be at the beginning of the seventh 'day' and would not contradict the teachings of the other rabbis who all believed the 'sabbath' would last for only one thousand years.

Finally, there is a reference in the *Book of the Secrets of Enoch*, a Jewish book compiled between about 300 BC and the middle of the first century BC. *"And I appointed the eighth day also, that the eighth day should be the first-created after my work, and that the first seven revolve in the form of the seven thousand, and at the beginning of the eighth thousand there should be a time of not-counting, endless, with neither years nor months, nor weeks nor days nor hours."* (Chapter 33:1, p.93). In other words, eternity. These words exactly match what I have been teaching in this book, for at the beginning of the 'eighth thousand' is when God will create a new earth – which will be the first newly created thing out of nothing that he has made since his work of creating the present earth.

The Jewish calendar puts the date of creation as 3760 BC. Presumably this means that the rabbis who believed the Messiah would come four thousand years after creation, expected him to come in AD 240. However it is impossible to reconcile a date of 3760 BC with the Tanakh (Old Testament) itself.

The Hebrew text of the Tanakh provides an unambiguous dating of the exodus from Egypt as about 2679 years or so after creation, as I explained in Chapter 2. 1 Kings chapter 6 says that King Solomon began to build the Temple 480 years after the Exodus, taking 13 years to complete it. This means that the Temple would have been completed 2679 + 480 + 13 = 3172 years after creation, or in 588 BC. However, it is known that the Babylonian King Nebuchadnezzar destroyed the temple in 587 BC, only a year after Solomon completed it according to the Jewish calendar! And since many kings of Israel succeeded Solomon before the temple was destroyed, the Jewish calendar cannot be reconciled with the Bible and history.

If the Greek text of the Tanakh is used, reconciliation is still harder. In this case the Jewish calendar would lead to a date of AD 385 for the completion of Solomon's temple!

It has therefore been suggested that the Jewish calendar dates not from creation but from the time that men first began to record the passing of the years, perhaps at the birth of Adam's first grandson Enosh, 235 years after creation. At that point, when Adam and Eve were still in their prime, I can well imagine their deciding it was time to start keeping a written record of the birthdays of their multitudinous offspring, as the only way to remember to give birthday presents to them all!

Furthermore, while God created Adam and Eve with a complete and perfect language in their brains (for they spoke to each other and to God, but they could not have learned to speak from their parents), it could well have taken them until Enosh's birth to invent writing and thus be able to keep written records.

If the Jewish calendar did begin with the birth of Enosh, it would yield a date of 3995 BC for creation, not so different from 3971 BC, the date I have calculated.

Early Christian teaching

The first generation of Christians believed Jesus would return within their lifetime, or at least within the lifetime of most of them, but they eventually realized that they had been mistaken. In Mark's Gospel, thought to be the earliest and written some time between AD 55 to 60, Jesus is reported as describing his future return on the clouds of heaven to raise 'the elect' from the dead. He then declared, *"Truly I say to you, this generation will not pass away before all these things take place."* (Mark 13:30)

These words are repeated exactly in the Gospels of Luke (AD 60) and Matthew (AD 60 to 65), perhaps because they used Mark's Gospel as their source, or possibly some common earlier material. I've addressed in Chapter 8 the question as to whether Jesus really meant that he would return in the lifetime of his hearers, but it does appear that the writers of the first three Gospels believed this is what he meant.

John, the author of the fourth gospel, also believed in Christ's imminent return when he wrote the book of Revelation in AD 68. He ended it with the words, *"Surely, I am coming soon!"*

Paul too believed in the imminent return of Jesus, at least when he wrote his earlier letters. In AD 51 he wrote in 1 Thessalonians 4:15-17, *'We who are alive, who are left until the coming of the Lord, shall not precede those who have fallen asleep.'* In AD 55 he was even more definite that Jesus would return in the lifetime of at least some of his readers. In 1 Corinthians 15:51,52 he wrote, *'We shall not all sleep, but we shall all be changed... at the last trumpet.'* He advised single people not to marry, if they could manage to remain single, because the appointed time had grown very short, and he wanted to spare them unnecessary burdens.

191

However, by AD 64 and AD 66/67 respectively when he wrote his two letters to Timothy, it is clear that he had realized Christ's return was not going to be as soon as he had believed. Here he was telling Timothy that bishops and deacons must be married and teach their children to be submissive; he was making arrangements for the care of widows and other elderly relatives; commanding younger widows to marry so that the church would not have to support them; and envisaging his own imminent death by speaking of the crown of righteousness which the Lord would award to himself and to all who had loved his appearing. There is pathos in those last words, for Paul had finally realized he would not be alive to see his beloved Lord Jesus return to the earth in triumph.

It was also in about AD 67 that Peter wrote his second New Testament letter. Far from talking about Christ's imminent return, Peter found himself explaining the apparent delay by saying that God wanted to give everyone possible the opportunity to repent and be saved, and that a thousand years were like only a day to God. By the time John wrote the final Gospel, probably between AD 85 and 90, he hardly mentioned the return of Jesus. Right at the end of it he even protested that Jesus had never promised to return before he himself died.

By AD 100, when the first generation of Christians had all died without witnessing the return of Christ, it appears that Christian teachers or 'apologists' were teaching instead that Christ would come back six thousand years after creation. Barnabas, writing in about AD 100; Justin Martyr (AD 100 to 165, in *Dialogue with Trypho*, 80); Irenaeus, the bishop of Lyons, (died AD 202, in *Against Heresies* 5:28:3); the Roman theologians Sextus Julius Africanus (AD 160 to 240) and Hippolytus (AD 170 to 235, in *Commentary on Daniel 4*); Victorinus, the bishop of Poetovio in modern Slovenia (died c. AD 303, in *Commentary on the Apocalypse*, 20); Methodius the bishop of Olympus in Lycia (died AD 311, in *Fragments*, 9); Lactantius, tutor of the son of the Roman Emperor Constantine (AD 250 to 325, in *The Divine Institutes*, 7:14); and

Augustine (AD 354 to 430, in *The City of God*, 20:7) all believed and taught that the current world order would end six thousand years after the creation of the world, to be followed by a thousand years of rest from strife under the rule of Christ.

As I quoted in Chapter 2, Barnabas wrote, '*As there have been two thousand years from Adam to Abraham, and two thousand from Abraham to Christ; so there will be two thousand years for the Christian era and then will come the millennium.*'

Irenaeus wrote, '*For the day of the Lord is as a thousand years; and in six days created things were completed; it is evident, therefore, that they will come to an end at the sixth thousand years.*'

Lactantius stated, '*Let the philosophers know that the six thousandth year is not yet completed; and when this number is completed, the consummation must take place.*'

In around AD 270, Victorinus wrote that '*the true and just Sabbath should be observed in the seventh millennium of years. Wherefore, to those seven days the Lord attributed to each a thousand years... Wherefore, as I have narrated, that true Sabbath will be in the seventh millenary of years, when Christ with His elect shall reign.*'

Unfortunately most or all of these early Christian teachers believed the world was created in about 5500 BC, which meant they were expecting Jesus to return in about AD 500, so once again they were destined for disappointment. The explanation for a creation date of 5500 BC is that the most widely used version of the Old Testament at that time was the 'Septuagint'. This was a translation of the Hebrew scriptures into common Greek carried out in stages from the third to the first century before Christ. It began when 72 Jewish scholars were asked by the Greek king of Egypt, Ptolemy II Philadelphus, to translate the Torah (the five books of Moses) from Biblical Hebrew into Greek for the Library of Alexandria.

In this translation the recorded ages of Adam's descendants when each of their first sons was born were greater, often 100 years greater, than their ages in the original Hebrew text. Today most translations of the Bible are based on what is known as the Hebrew 'Masoretic' text, but it wasn't until the seventh to tenth centuries of the current era that this was formerly assembled and written up. It eventually came to be regarded as more reliable than the Septuagint.

Using the Septuagint's ages, the years assigned to the reigns of Biblical kings, and various accepted dates for historical events such as the Babylonian exile, the earliest Christian teachers calculated that the world had been created around 5500 BC: Clement of Alexandria [5592 BC], Julius Africanus [5501 BC], Eusebius [5228 BC], Jerome [5199 BC], Hippolytus of Rome [5500 BC], Theophilus of Antioch [5529 BC], Sulpicius Severus [5469 BC], Panodorus of Alexandria [5493 BC], Isidore of Seville [5336 BC], Maximus the Confessor [5493 BC], George Syncellus [5492 BC] and Gregory of Tours [5500 BC].

Bede, an English monk generally known as 'the Venerable Bede', was one of the first to break away from the standard Septuagint date for the creation. In his work *De Temporibus*, completed in AD 703, he dated creation to the 18th of March 3952 BC. In 1650 James Ussher, the protestant Archbishop of Armagh and Primate of All Ireland, published a history of the Old Testament in which he deduced that the first day of creation began at nightfall on Saturday, October the 22nd, 4004 BC.

Bede and Ussher were far from the only scholars to attempt such a calculation. Other similar dates were reached by the second-century Rabbi Jose ben Halafta [3761], Martin Luther [3961], John Lightfoot [3929], the German mathematician and astronomer Johannes Kepler [3992], and even Sir Isaac Newton [c. 4000 BC]. The Wikipedia article 'Dating creation' lists a total of 26 famous people who arrived at similar dates, with an average answer of 3946 BC.

The reason Ussher's date of 4004 BC is so widely known is that from 1701 onwards his chronology of Biblical events was often incorporated into editions of the Authorized (King James) Version of the Bible, either as marginal notes or even as section headings.

The fact that everyone has come up with a slightly different answer only proves how difficult it is to know exactly when the world began, even for those who believe that the Biblical record is true and free from error.

Conclusion

Virtually all the Jewish rabbis, Christian teachers and other learned men in the Western world, at least until the seventeenth century, believed the Messiah would return six thousand years after the world was created and would then reign in peace for a further thousand years until God created the promised new earth. You could say, therefore, that all I have done in writing this book is to revert to the traditional teaching of the Christian church!

Annex 2. Early Christian and Jewish teaching on the Millennium and the date of creation

Annex 3. The truth about eternal punishment

In Chapter 7 I showed that neither the Bible as a whole, nor the ancient creeds of the church, require a belief in the everlasting punishment of evildoers and unbelievers after they die. Nevertheless, there are a few passages in the New Testament which appear to support such a belief, so I shall address them in this annex.

Unquenchable fire

In Mark chapter 9, verses 47 and 48, Jesus says, *"And if your eye causes you to sin, pluck it out; it is better for you to enter the kingdom of God with one eye than with two eyes to be thrown into hell, where their worm does not die, and the fire is not quenched."*

The Greek word translated as 'hell' is 'gehenna' (*geenna*). Gehenna was Jerusalem's principal rubbish tip, and unlike today's recycling centres nothing that was thrown into it was resurrected into something new. Jesus was simply saying, "It is better for you to enter the kingdom of God with one eye than with two eyes to be thrown on the rubbish tip…"

With regard to the undying worm and unquenchable fire, Jesus was quoting the very last verse of the book of the prophet Isaiah. God had been telling Isaiah what life would be like when Israel's enemies had finally been defeated. He concluded, *"And they shall go forth and look on the dead bodies of the men that have rebelled against me; for their worm shall not die, their fire shall not be quenched, and they shall be an abhorrence to all flesh."* (Isaiah 66:24)

The bodies of the rebellious men being consumed by worms and fire were dead bodies, not living bodies. There is no hint in this passage that the men who had rebelled against the Lord were going to live in torment for ever, rather the opposite. Isaiah's meaning was that the worms wouldn't die of indigestion and the fire wouldn't go out for lack of fuel until the dead bodies had been entirely consumed. It was unquenchable fire, so there was no hope that somehow firemen would put it out before it had completed its task of total destruction.

Similarly, in Jeremiah 17:27 the Lord declared to the ancient Jews, *"...if you do not listen to me... then will I kindle a fire in* [Jerusalem's] *gates, and it shall devour the palaces of Jerusalem and shall not be quenched."* That prophecy of Jerusalem's destruction was fulfilled when the Babylonians torched the city. Clearly, the fire they lit is not still burning today, so was the prophecy wrong? No. 'The fire shall not be quenched' never meant that the fire would burn for ever. It meant that no one would be able to quench its flames until they had completed their task of total destruction.

It was these Old Testament pictures and expressions which Jesus was recalling, in order to make his vivid point that it is better to make any sacrifice necessary to eliminate sin and enter the kingdom of God than to face the dreadful alternative of an ignominious, complete, final and permanent end to one's life, from which there could be no escape.

The sheep and the goats

In Matthew 25:46, Jesus ended his teaching on the last judgement by describing the fate of the 'goats'. *"And they will go away into eternal punishment, but the righteous into eternal life."* In the Authorized Version the fate of the goats sounds even worse: *"And these shall go away into <u>everlasting</u> punishment: but the righteous into life eternal."*

At first sight the word 'everlasting' appears to contradict the fact that the alternative to eternal life is to perish, as it says in John 3:16. How can anyone perish everlastingly? You either perish or you don't. To understand the word translated as 'everlasting', we have to go back to the Greek, the language in which this Gospel was written. *Aiōnios*, the word which is translated as 'eternal' or 'everlasting', has several possible meanings. It is the adjective from the noun *aiōn*. (The English version of this is 'aeon'.) *Aiōn* can mean 'life and breath, a human lifetime, an unbroken age, a historical age, the age or ages to come, perpetuity of time, or eternity past present and future'.[93] So *aiōnios* can mean 'everlasting', but it can equally mean 'the kind that will exist in the age to come' or even 'permanent'.

In Matthew 10:28 Jesus said that the punishment awaiting sinners will be the destruction of both their bodies and souls. In other words, it will be a final death from which there can be no further resurrection, an eternal death as distinct from a temporal death, the permanent kind of death which will exist in the age to come, not the mere physical death of the body which will later be brought back to life to face judgement. And that is why Jesus described the forthcoming punishment of the unrighteous as eternal.

Precisely the same point is made in *The New Bible Commentary Revised*[94]: '*Eternal punishment* and *eternal life* are not necessarily the same in duration. *Eternal* (Greek *aiōnios*) simply refers to the age to come and makes the point that the division is final for men's destiny.'

This explanation applies also to Paul's words in 2 Thessalonians 1:8,9, where he says that those who do not know God or obey the gospel of Jesus will suffer the punishment of eternal (final) destruction.

---

[93] *A Greek-English lexicon of the New Testament*. Grimm's Wilke's Clavis Novi Testamenti, translated, revised and enlarged by Joseph H. Thayer, fourth edition, T & T Clark, Edinburgh, 1901.

[94] *The New Bible Commentary Revised*. D.Guthrie and others. Inter-Varsity Press, Leicester, 1970, p.846.

The rich man and Lazarus

In Luke chapter 16 Jesus told a story about an unnamed rich man and a very poor man named Lazarus, who both died at about the same time. Here is part of the story:

> *"The rich man also died and was buried; and in Hades, being in torment, he lifted up his eyes, and saw Abraham far off and Lazarus in his bosom. And he called out, 'Father Abraham, have mercy upon me, and send Lazarus to dip the end of his finger in water and cool my tongue; for I am in anguish in this flame. ...send him to my father's house, for I have five brothers, so that he may warn them, lest they also come into this place of torment.' But Abraham said, 'They have Moses and the prophets; let them hear them.'"*

Luke 16:22-29

This story is rather strange.

(i) For a start, it is the only passage in the Bible which represents Hades or Sheol as a place of flames and torment. As we have seen, Job wrote, '*There the wicked cease from troubling, and there the weary are at rest. There the prisoners are at ease together.*' (Job 3:17,18) 'At ease' doesn't sound very much like torment! Other passages in the Old Testament tell us there is no knowledge there, no remembrance of God or anything else, and no speaking. (Ecclesiastes 9:10; Psalm 88:11,12) If Jesus meant this parable to be taken literally he would have been contradicting the word of God in the Old Testament. And nowhere else does Jesus himself describe Hades as a place of torment, or even warn his hearers against ending up there.

(ii) When Jesus told this parable, everybody, rich and poor alike, went in spirit to Hades at their death, even the prophet Samuel. (Job 3:19; 1 Samuel 28:3-19) So why did

Lazarus go somewhere nicer, and the rich man somewhere far nastier?

(iii) In the Bible the dead are always regarded as sleeping, i.e. unconscious, until they are resurrected on Resurrection Day or at the last judgement. (Daniel 12:2; Matthew 9:24; 1 Corinthians 15:18; 1 Thessalonians 4:13-17) Yet as soon as the rich man died he and Abraham were conversing with each other!

(iv) It suggests that Lazarus went to a place of blessing simply because he was poor.

(v) By describing the rich man as being in torment while his brothers are still alive, it suggests that judgement takes place the moment someone dies. However, the New Testament consistently says that the destiny of people who do not believe in Jesus won't be decided until the day of judgement.

(vi) It suggests that disembodied souls have eyes, fingers and tongues!

The explanation of all these anomalies is simply that it was a story Jesus made up, based on the beliefs of the Pharisees whom he was addressing. Almost every detail of this story can be found in Jewish writings, in the Talmud and other literature current at the time. For example, in the Babylonian Talmud, Book II, folio 72, 'Kiddushin', it is said of a rabbi on the day of his death, *"This day he sits in Abraham's bosom."*

Jesus told this story in terms which the Pharisees could accept, in order to show them truths which they were not accepting. The Sadducees once did exactly the same thing to Jesus. They didn't believe in any resurrection, but they told Jesus a fictional story about a woman who had seven husbands in turn, and then asked him whose wife she would be 'in the resurrection'. Just as they made up a story in terms of something they didn't personally believe, in order to get their point over to Jesus, so Jesus made up a story about the rich man and Lazarus in terms he didn't believe, in order to get his point over to the Pharisees in terms which they could accept.

Jesus told this story primarily to urge his audience to believe the teaching of Moses and the prophets, and to tell them that if they didn't do so, then even when he rose from the dead they would not believe in him. He never intended it to be a factual account of what happens in the afterlife.

Sadly this parable has been influential in shaping an understanding of life immediately after death that is contrary to the Bible's teaching, including the false doctrine of purgatory.

Revelation 14:9-11

> *"If any one worships the beast and its image, and receives a mark on his forehead or on his hand, he also shall drink the wine of God's wrath, poured unmixed into the cup of his anger, and he shall be tormented with fire and sulphur in the presence of the holy angels and in the presence of the Lamb. And the smoke of their torment goes up for ever and ever; and they have no rest, day or night, these worshippers of the beast and its image, and whoever receives the mark of its name."*
>
> Revelation 14:9-11

These verses describe the fate of people who surrender to the Antichrist during the last three and a half years before Jesus's return, not the fate of anyone who dies before this. We are told that those who worship the beast will be tormented with fire and sulphur by a wrathful God in the presence of Jesus and his angels; 'the smoke of their torment' will continue 'for ever and ever'; and that they 'have no rest, day or night'. To understand all this we first have to understand how the various words and phrases are used elsewhere in the Bible.

The Greek word *basanizō*, translated 'torment', normally means 'to vex with grievous pains of body or mind, to torment'. However, in Revelation 18:9,10,15-17 John uses the same word 'torment' to refer to the destruction of Rome.

202

(Revelation 17:1-12 makes it clear that 'Babylon' was a pseudonym for the city of Rome. If John had openly predicted the imminent destruction of Rome he could easily have been put to death as a traitor.) *'And the kings of the earth... will weep and wail over her when they see the smoke of her burning; they will stand far off, in fear of her torment... The merchants... will stand far off, in fear of her torment, weeping and mourning aloud, "Alas, alas, for the great city... In one hour all this wealth has been laid waste."'* So in Revelation the word 'torment' can refer to a relatively brief process of destruction.

In the Bible, fire and brimstone (sulphur) is a principal means of destruction used by the Lord. *'Then the Lord rained on Sodom and Gomorrah brimstone and fire from the Lord out of heaven; and he overthrew those cities, and all the valley, and all the inhabitants of the cities...'* (Genesis 19:24,25) *'On the wicked [the Lord] will rain coals of fire and brimstone...'* (Psalm 11:6) *'And the streams of Edom shall be turned into pitch, and her soil into brimstone; her land shall become burning pitch.'* (Isaiah 34:9) *'...the heads of the horses were like lions' heads, and fire and smoke and sulphur issued from their mouths. By these three plagues a third of mankind was killed, by the fire and smoke and sulphur issuing from their mouths.'* (Revelation 9:17,18) The Lord sends fire and brimstone to produce destruction and death.

The Greek word *orgē*, translated 'wrath', is used in the New Testament to mean *'God's anger at man's disobedience, obduracy (especially in resisting the gospel) and sin, which expresses itself in punishing the sinner'.*[95] An earthly ruler acts on God's behalf in punishing wrongdoers: *'...he does not bear the sword in vain; he is the servant of God to execute his wrath on the wrongdoer.'* (Romans 13:4) In the Bible any ruler who did not punish the wicked would have been regarded as a bad ruler who encouraged wrongdoing.

---

[95] *A Greek-English lexicon of the New Testament.* Grimm's Wilke's Clavis Novi Testamenti, translated, revised and enlarged by Joseph H. Thayer, fourth edition, T & T Clark, Edinburgh, 1901.

'The smoke of their torment will continue for ever' is a Biblical expression which means that the associated destruction will be permanent. It may also contain the idea that the destruction will be permanently remembered. Prophesying the forthcoming destruction of the land of Edom, Isaiah wrote, '*...its smoke shall go up for ever. From generation to generation it shall lie waste; none shall pass through it for ever and ever.*' (Isaiah 34:10,11) Clearly Edom did not burn for ever and the smoke of its burning did not go up for ever, but its *destruction* lasted for ever: it was a permanent destruction.

In Revelation 19:3 a multitude in heaven celebrates the burning of Rome (see Revelation 18:8) with the words, *"Hallelujah! The smoke from her goes up for ever and ever!"* Again, this did not literally mean that the smoke would rise for ever, for two chapters later John tells us that Rome and everything else in the present earth will pass away and God will make all things new. (Revelation 21:1,5) The heavenly multitude probably meant that the destruction of Rome would never be forgotten.

The Greek word *anapausin*, translated 'rest', means 'intermission', 'cessation', 'rest' or 'recreation'.

'Day *and* night' is a phrase used in the Bible to mean 'continuously'. *"This book of the law shall not depart from your mouth, but you shall meditate on it day and night..."* (Joshua 1:8) '*...his delight is in the law of the Lord, and on his law he meditates day and night.*' (Psalm 1:2) At the dedication of the temple Solomon prayed *"...that thy eyes may be open day and night toward this house..."* (2 Chronicles 6:20) [96] 'Day and night' always means something which happens or is done continuously. (See also Psalms 32:4; 42:3; 55:10; 88:1)

'Day *or* night' and 'day *nor* night' are phrases used in the Bible to refer to something which does *not* happen or is *not* done. '*...neither day nor night one's eyes see sleep...*' (Ecclesiastes

---

[96] Revelation 20:10 says that the devil and his associates '*will be tormented day and night for ever and ever.*' In the book of Revelation at least the phrase 'day and night' doesn't necessarily mean two 12-hour units of time in this present age. It just means continuously.

8:16) *"...neither eat nor drink for three days, night or day."* (Esther 4:16) *'It shall not be quenched night nor day...'* (Isaiah 34:10 AV. 'Nor' is the correct translation of this verse in Isaiah, not 'and' as in the RSV.)

So let's see now what these verses in Revelation chapter 14 mean.

Using the explanations I have given above, the words, *"he also shall drink the wine of God's wrath, poured unmixed into the cup of his anger, and he shall be tormented with fire and sulphur in the presence of the holy angels and in the presence of the Lamb. And the smoke of their torment goes up for ever and ever"*, mean that anyone who worships the beast will be justly, painfully and permanently destroyed by God in the presence of Jesus.

The second part, *"and they have no rest, day or night, these worshippers of the beast and its image and whoever receives the mark of its name,"* has to be correctly translated and punctuated in order to be understood. Although the RSV says 'day or night', the Greek says 'day *and* night'. As I've explained, 'day and night' always means something which happens or is done continuously, not something which doesn't happen, like not having any rest. Secondly, there was no punctuation in the original Greek text, so we have to decide from the context where one sentence ends and another begins. Although this second part begins with the word 'and', John begins at least half the sentences in this chapter with the word 'and', so it could easily be the start of another separate sentence. It would then literally be translated, '(And) they have no cessation day and night the ones worshipping the beast and its image, and whoever receives the mark of its name.'

This new sentence is now a comment on the previous sentence. It explains that God's condemnation and sentence of death on these people is because day and night, without ceasing, they worship the beast and its image. Their behaviour is the antithesis of the behaviour of the four living creatures around the throne of God in Revelation chapter 4. The four heavenly creatures never cease day and night to worship *God!*

205

'*…day and night they never cease to sing, "Holy, holy, holy, is the Lord God Almighty, who was and is and is to come!"*' (Revelation 4:8)[97]

So this second part of Revelation 14:9-11 is not about ceaseless torment, it is about the ceaseless *worship* of the beast worshippers, and it is that which justifies their death sentence.

In the bright light of the rest of Scripture, Revelation 14:9-11 cannot possibly mean that those who worship the beast will be tortured in flames for ever in the presence of the Lamb, for the following very good reasons:

- The Lamb is Jesus, and when Jesus comes to dwell on earth in the heavenly city, there will be no more crying nor pain in his presence. (Revelation 21:4,22,23)
- Once the new heaven and earth have been made, nothing and no one will be accursed any more. (Revelation 22:3)
- To those whose names are written in the book of life God has promised to wipe every tear from their eyes and replace sorrow and sighing by everlasting joy. (Revelation 21:4; Isaiah 35:10) How could the redeemed of God be free from sorrow and sighing if unbelieving members of their families – perhaps even their own children – are everlastingly burning to death in flames of choking sulphur?[98]
- As we have seen earlier, the fate of the damned is the permanent destruction of body and soul: it is not everlasting life in any form. '*The wages of sin is death.*' (Romans 6:23)

---

[97] The Greek of Revelation 4:8 says, 'They do not have respite day and night they are saying holy, holy, holy' etc. The phrase 'day and night' describes what they *are* doing, not what they are *not* doing, just as it does in other Bible passages.

[98] As I deduce in Annex 4, there will be weeks and months in the age to come, so it would not be true to argue that there is no time in eternity.

- God has said, *"Vengeance is mine; I will repay,"* (Romans 12:19; Deuteronomy 32:35; Hebrews 10:30) God said this to stop people taking vengeance into their own hands, by promising he would deal with wrongdoers himself. In 2 Thessalonians 1:5-9 Paul does indeed state that the Lord Jesus will inflict *'vengeance upon those who do not know God and upon those who do not obey the gospel of our Lord Jesus'*, but he immediately explains what form that vengeance will take: *'They shall suffer the punishment of eternal destruction.'* The Greek words *olethron aiōnion* mean permanent ruin, destruction or death. That is the vengeance which God will inflict on the disobedient, through his Son Jesus.

- *"...all his ways are justice... just and right is he."* (Deuteronomy 32:4) God himself laid down a rule that justice must be *equitable*: 'an eye for an eye and a tooth for a tooth'. (See Leviticus 24:17-20) How then could he torment for ever someone who has been forced into worshipping an idol for no more than three and a half years as the only way to buy food for his children? Or why should the only people to be tormented for ever be those who worship the Antichrist's image, when the Bible specifies no such torment for people who throughout the ages have committed genocide, torture and crimes against humanity?

- God's anger against sinners will *not* last for ever. *'He will not always chide, nor will he keep his anger for ever.'* (Psalm 103:9)

- God is merciful. *"Be merciful, even as your Father is merciful."* (Luke 6:36) Everlasting torture would by definition be unmerciful.

Revelation 20:9,10

Another New Testament passage about torment is in Revelation chapter 20. Two verses describe the fate of the human armies of the Antichrist who will assemble to attack Jerusalem at the end of Christ's thousand-year reign, and the fate of the Antichrist, the false prophet and the devil.

And they marched up over the broad earth and surrounded the camp of the saints and the beloved city; but fire came down from heaven and consumed them, and the devil who had deceived them was thrown into the lake of fire and sulphur where the beast and the false prophet were, and they will be tormented day and night for ever and ever.

Revelation 20:9,10

The most obvious meaning of these verses from the Revised Standard Version is that the human armies of the Antichrist, together with the Antichrist, the false prophet and the devil, will be tormented for ever in a lake of fire and sulphur. This presents two further problems.

Firstly, verse 9 says the human armies will be consumed by fire. The Greek word translated 'consume', *katefagen*, means 'to consume by eating, to eat up, to devour; or to utterly consume or destroy by fire'. That can only mean the end of them. This contradicts verse 10, which seems to say they will then be tormented day and night for ever.

Happily, there is a simple solution to this first problem. As I said, the Greek text itself doesn't have any punctuation, and John often starts a sentence in Revelation with the word 'and'. So without changing any words, the two verses above should be punctuated as two separate sentences like this: '*And they marched up over the broad earth and surrounded the camp of the saints and the beloved city; but fire came down from heaven and consumed them. And the devil who had deceived them was thrown into the lake of fire and sulphur where the beast and the false prophet were, and they* (i.e. the devil and the beast and the false prophet) *will be tormented day and night for ever and ever.*' That is how these verses are punctuated in the Authorized Version, which in this case is correct. The devil, the beast and the false prophet will be perpetually tormented, but the human supporters of the Antichrist will be destroyed. However, there is a more serious problem in verse 10. If the devil, the beast and the false prophet are to be tormented for ever, that can only mean they will exist for ever. Yet the letter to the Hebrews tells us that Jesus took on our human nature, '...*that through death he might destroy him who has the power of death, that is, the devil.*' (Hebrews 2:14) Similarly Paul wrote in 1 Corinthians 15:24 that when Jesus delivers the kingdom to God the Father at the end, it will be '...*after destroying every rule and every authority and power,*' by which he meant the devil and all his angels. So whether Jesus is going to destroy the devil or destroy the devil and all his angels, the devil cannot continue to live for ever, as Revelation 20:10 seems to suggest.

Moreover, Paul wrote in 2 Thessalonians 2:8 that the beast (the Antichrist) will be destroyed too. '...*the Lord Jesus will slay him with the breath of his mouth and destroy him by his appearing and his coming.*'

So how can Revelation 20:10 be true when it implies that the devil, the beast and the false prophet will live for ever? How can God unite *all things* in heaven and earth in Christ (Ephesians 1:10) if those three continue to exist?

As we saw earlier, the phrase 'the smoke of their torment goes up for ever and ever' is not intended in the Bible to be interpreted literally, except perhaps in the sense that the memory of it will endure for ever. So when Revelation says that the devil, the beast and the false prophet will be tormented for ever and ever, is that intended to be understood literally or not?

John Wesley adopted two principles in interpreting the Bible. (i) '*It is a stated rule in interpreting scripture never to depart from the plain, literal sense, unless it implies an absurdity,*' and (ii) '*The general rule of interpreting scripture is this: the literal sense of every text is to be taken, if it be not contrary to some other texts. But in that case, the obscure text is to be interpreted by those which speak more plainly.*'[99] He

---

[99] From a letter written by Wesley to Samuel Furly.

mentioned both principles together in his sermon 'A Call to Backsliders': '*It does not appear that we have any reason to depart from the literal meaning* [of Hebrews 6.4] *as it neither implies any absurdity, nor contradicts any other scriptures.*'[100]

If Revelation 20:10 were interpreted literally it would contradict several other scriptures, so by Wesley's wise rule it should not be interpreted in this way. Instead, '*The obscure text is to be interpreted by those which speak more plainly.*'

To start with, there are several instances in the Bible where the phrase translated 'for ever and ever' is not intended literally, or at least, not as we understand those words. We've already seen this in Isaiah 34:10 and Revelation 19:3.

David concluded Psalm 23 with the words, '*Surely goodness and mercy shall follow me all the days of my life; and I shall dwell in the house of the Lord for ever.*' In the style of Hebrew poetry, the Psalms frequently say the same thing twice in different ways. In Psalm 23 the words 'for ever' are parallel to 'all the days of my life': so 'for ever' is another way of saying 'all the days of my life'. In the Revised Standard Version there is actually a footnote to the words 'for ever'. It says, '*Or as long as I live*'.

Again, in Psalm 145 David twice declared that he would bless God 'for ever and ever', the exact phrase that John used in Revelation. But once again David meant that he intended to go on blessing God *as long as he lived*. For he said precisely that in Psalm 63:4: "*I will bless thee as long as I live.*" He did *not* believe that he would continue to bless or praise God after he died, for he wrote, '*In death there is no remembrance of thee; in Sheol who can give thee praise? Will the dust praise thee?* (Psalm 6:5; 30:9)

In reality David will get his wish to praise God for ever in eternity, but what he actually meant was that he would continue to bless God *until he died*.

Just as David meant by blessing God 'for ever and ever' that he would do so until he died, so John meant by 'for ever and ever' in Revelation 20:10 that the devil and his two

---

[100] *A Call to Backsliders*. Sermon 86, I (4), 1778.

collaborators will be continuously tormented until they die: finally, completely and for ever. When that has happened, death itself will be destroyed (Revelation 20:14; 21:4) and all things that then exist will finally be united in Christ. (Ephesians 1:10)

That is the only possible interpretation of this verse consistent with other New Testament scriptures.

Annex 3. The truth about eternal punishment

Annex 4. A new heaven or new heavens?

All things new

In Revelation chapter 21 and verse 1 we read, '*Then I saw a new heaven and a new earth,*' and in verse 5, '*...He who sat upon the throne said, "Behold, I make all things new."*' Did the Lord mean 'all things' literally? What exactly is he going to make again?

- The word 'heaven' could mean everything apart from the earth, or just the earth's atmosphere.
- The Greek word translated 'new' can mean 'brand new', 'new and better', or even 'of a new unprecedented kind'.
- Presumably 'all things' doesn't include God himself, the holy angels, people who will have already been made new through resurrection to eternal life, nor those who will be condemned to final death.

Therefore 'behold, I make all things new' could mean one of three possibilities:

- God is going to replace everything by a totally new earth, and that is all. There will be a new earth and its atmosphere, but no sun, moon or stars, and no day and night.
- God is going to remake everything. There will be a new and better earth, a new sun and moon, new planets and stars, and perhaps even new space and time.

- God is going to remake only the earth, which has been corrupted as a result of sin, i.e. the earth, its atmosphere and the world of nature, but nothing more.

(i) God will replace everything with a new earth, and there will be nothing beyond it

This is the most extreme possibility. There will be neither sun, moon, planets or stars in the age to come, but just a new earth. Revelation 21:23-25 says, '*And the city has no need of sun or moon to shine upon it, for the glory of God is its light, and its lamp is the Lamb. …there shall be no night there…*' Similarly Revelation 22:5 says, '*And night shall be no more; they need no light of lamp or sun, for the Lord God will be their light…*'

If there is to be no sun, moon or night, the world will be totally different from how it is now. Isaiah 60:19,20 appears to support this idea. '*The sun shall be no more your light by day, nor for brightness shall the moon give light to you by night; but the Lord will be your everlasting light, and your God will be your glory. Your sun shall no more go down, nor your moon withdraw itself; for the Lord will be your everlasting light, and your days of mourning shall be ended.*' It looks very much as though John was quoting from these two verses.

In further support of the idea that there will be no night, Zechariah 14:5-7 says, '*Then the Lord your God will come, and all the holy ones with him. On that day… there shall be continuous day (it is known to the Lord), not day and not night, for at evening time there shall be light.*'

The problem is that all this appears to contradict many other verses in scripture. For example Isaiah 66:22,23 says, "*For as the new heavens and the new earth which I will make shall remain before me, says that Lord; so shall your descendants and your name remain. From new moon to new moon, and from sabbath to sabbath, all flesh shall come to worship before me, says the Lord.*" Isaiah foresaw the continuing existence of a moon, as well as of a sun, because in those days the months were set by the moon and the hours of the Sabbath were set by sunrise and sunset. And if there is to be sunrise and sunset, there will also be day and night.

There will still be seasons, for the passage in Zechariah 14:8 goes on to say, '*On that day living waters shall flow out from Jerusalem... it shall continue in summer as in winter,*' and Revelation 22:2 speaks of twelve months in a year, even in the heavenly city. Furthermore, Isaiah says that when God creates new heavens and a new earth people will '*...plant vineyards and eat their fruit*' (Isaiah 65:17,21), and Micah says that '*...they shall sit every man under his vine and under his fig tree...*' (Micah 4:4) It is hard to envisage summer and winter months and natural growing seasons unless the earth continues to orbit the sun on an inclined axis. And if it orbits the sun it must also rotate, otherwise one face will be too hot to support life and the other face too cold. And if it rotates there will still be days and nights.

Finally, without days and nights there cannot be weeks, and without weeks there cannot be a weekly Sabbath. Yet God said that the observance of the Sabbath every week was to be a perpetual covenant for ever. (Exodus 31:16,17) We are back to life more or less as we know it, at least with the earth on an inclined axis orbiting the sun, and the moon orbiting the earth.

So what is the explanation of the verses in Isaiah and Revelation chapter 21 which suggest there won't be any sun or moon? Well, they do not specifically say this. They say that the presence of the Lord will bring so much light that the light of the sun and moon will not be *needed*. And in Revelation this light is said to be in the holy city, not throughout the earth. So it is the people in the city who will have no need of sun or moon and who will not experience darkness at night, not the earth as a whole.

When Zechariah prophesied, '*On that day... there shall be continuous day (it is known to the Lord), not day and not night,*' he was most likely referring to the actual 24-hour day of Christ's return. Just as God halted the earth's rotation for about a day to give Joshua time to completely defeat the Amorites (Joshua 10:12-14) so he might delay the onset of night on the day Jesus

215

returns to give him time to take over the government of the world.

The only reason I can think of to support the idea that God will replace everything with something totally different is that natural stars, including the sun, could not last for eternity. Perhaps the explanation lies in continuous creation. No doubt the final answer lies in one of the many future ages yet to come, which even the Bible does not describe. A lot can happen in our first 5 billion years!

(ii) God will remake everything that currently exists

When the Bible writers looked up into the sky at night they didn't see space as we know it to be. They knew what God had told them, but they were not omniscient. So to their eyes the heavens looked like a kind of canopy stretched out over the earth.[101] Genesis Chapter 1 says that the sun, moon and stars and birds all occupy 'the firmament of the heavens'. So it must have seemed obvious to the writers of the Bible that if a bird could fall out of the firmament then in theory the stars could too.

Hence, when Isaiah wrote, '*All the host of heaven shall rot away, and the skies roll up like a scroll. All their host shall fall, as leaves fall from the vine, like leaves falling from the fig tree*' (Isaiah 34:4), he was picturing the sun, moon and stars falling out of the sky above us and landing on the ground. Of course, such a passage might be interpreted as poetic or symbolical language, but when the same prophet reported God's words, *"For behold, I create new heavens and a new earth,"* (Isaiah 65:17) he would have understood this to include the sun, moon and stars, because these were an essential part of the heavens. The writers of the Bible would have found it difficult to conceive how God might recreate the

---

[101] Psalm 104:2 says that God has 'stretched out the heavens like a tent,' and Isaiah 40:22 says that God 'stretches out the heavens like a curtain, and spreads them like a tent to dwell in.'

earth and sky without recreating everything in them at the same time, including the sun, moon and stars.

Similarly, when in Revelation 21 John saw a new heaven and earth and God said, *"Behold, I make all things new,"* John too would have understood 'all things' to include the sun, the moon and all the stars. This seems to mean that there will still be a sun, moon and stars, but they will be new ones.

One reason God might want to make *everything* new is because somehow it has all been corrupted through sin. Although everything was 'very good' when God first made it (Genesis 1:31) Job said, *"The stars are not pure in* [God's] *sight".* (Job 25:5 AV) If that is literally true, it suggests that the stars too may have to be remade.

(iii) God will renew only the earth and its atmosphere

Nevertheless there are many other reasons for believing it will be only the earth and its atmosphere that God is going to recreate. In his letter to the Romans Paul wrote:

> *...the creation waits with eager longing for the revealing of the sons of God; for the creation was subjected to futility, not of its own will but by the will of him who subjected it in hope; because the creation itself will be set free from its bondage to decay and obtain the glorious liberty of the children of God. We know that the whole creation has been groaning in travail together until now; and not only the creation, but we ourselves... as we wait for... the redemption of our bodies.*
>
> Romans 8:19-23

The word translated 'futility' can mean 'weakness'. In the world of nature it corresponds to the weakness in our physical bodies, which will be 'sown in weakness and raised in power'. (1 Corinthians 15:43) The word translated 'decay' generally means 'perishing'. In the world of nature it corresponds to our perishable physical bodies, which will be 'sown perishable but raised imperishable'. (1 Corinthians 15:42)

In these verses Paul was thinking about the consequences of Adam's sin in the natural world. Just as decay and death entered human bodies as a result of sin, so the world of nature was altered, not only by the introduction of thorns and thistles, but by disease, degeneration and death. Even without our help, species have continually been dying out. So by 'the whole creation' Paul almost certainly meant the living but perishing world of nature, not the entire universe. The Living Bible translation makes this clear: '*For on that day thorns and thistles, sin, death and decay... will all disappear, and the world around us will share in the glorious freedom from sin which God's children enjoy. For we know that even the things of nature, like animals and plants, suffer in sickness and death as they await this great event.*' (Romans 8:20-22 TLB)

In this passage Paul was not assigning to the world of nature any idea of moral decay, only physical decay. Apart from a literal reading of the words in Job about the stars not being pure, there is no suggestion in the Bible that God cursed the sun or the moon or anything as a result of man's sin, except life on earth (Genesis 3:17,18) and the physical changes to the earth which took place as a result of the Flood. Therefore it is only the earth and its atmosphere which need to be replaced.

2 Peter 3:6,7 draws a close analogy between the forthcoming destruction of the earth by fire and the previous destruction of the earth by a flood. '*...the world that then existed was deluged with water and perished. But by the same word the heavens and earth that now exist have been stored up for fire, being kept until the day of judgement and destruction of ungodly men.*'

When Peter wrote 'the world that then existed' he was referring only to the earth and its atmosphere. So when he went on to say that by the same word the present heavens and earth will be destroyed by fire he was almost certainly referring again only to the earth and its atmosphere. Peter connected both events with the destruction of the ungodly, so in both cases it is only the earth where the ungodly have lived that needs to be destroyed. Since the planet cannot be totally destroyed by fire without also destroying its atmosphere, that too will have to be replaced.

In Psalm 89:35-37 the Lord made a promise so serious that he backed it up by swearing, even though Jesus said we should never swear! Here's what he said. *"Once for all I have sworn by my holiness; I will not lie to David. His line shall endure for ever, his throne as long as the sun before me. Like the moon it shall be established for ever; it shall stand firm while the skies endure."* God would never have used those words in a most solemn oath if he knew that one day he was going to destroy the present sun, moon and skies.

Psalm 119:89 says, *'For ever, O Lord, thy word is firmly fixed in the heavens.'* The Bible tells us that God named the stars. (Psalm 147:4) There is philological evidence[102] that the oldest names for the stars and their constellations spelt out in every language the story of creation and redemption from start to finish. Examples are Virgo the Virgin Mary, Leo the Lion of Judah, and Libra the scales of God's judgement. That's why Psalm 19:1-4 says, *'The heavens are telling the glory of God; and the firmament proclaims his handiwork... There is no speech, nor are there words; their voice is not heard; yet their voice goes out through all the earth, and their words to the end of the world.'* If God has fixed his word for ever in the existing stars and constellations he will hardly destroy them all and remake them again in exactly the same positions as before!

So I believe that God will not remake the stars, sun or moon, and that they will continue to exist as they are. I am supported in this by Professor J. Richard Middleton. In his scholarly work, *A New Heaven and a New Earth* [103], he concludes that God will remake only the earth and its atmosphere.

---

[102] See *The Heavens Declare* by W.D.Banks, Impact Books Inc., Family Reading Centre, Kent, UK, ISBN 0-089228-101-4; and *The Witness of the Stars* by E.W.Bullinger, reprinted by Kregel Publications, Grand Rapids, Michigan, ISBN 0-8254-2245-0.

[103] *A New Heaven and a New Earth* . J.R.Middleton, Baker Publishing Group, December 2014,

Annex 4. A new heaven or new heavens?

Annex 5. Where will believers spend eternity?

A big question

This annex answers the question, "If we believe in Jesus, shall we spend eternity on earth or in heaven?"

For many Christians the answer is obvious: it will be in heaven. That's certainly the answer given by many traditional hymns. Before my sisters and I went to sleep our mother used to sing a hymn which ended: '*Take me when I die to heaven, happy there with thee to dwell*'. Similarly, the Christmas carol 'Once in Royal David's City', which starts off every Christmas Eve carol service at King's College, Cambridge, ends with the words:

Not in that poor lowly stable with the oxen standing by
We shall see him, but in heaven set at God's right hand on high,
When like stars his children crowned, all in white shall wait around.
Cecil Frances Alexander

The trouble is that if I had to wait around for ever, even with a crown on my head, I'd die of boredom. And for the average non-believer who doesn't particularly desire to see Jesus anyway, telling him he can have eternal life in heaven in the presence of Jesus and his angels is simply a turn-off. In fact, I am sure the rather nebulous image of eternal life which most Christians have is a principal reason that we don't share the gospel more enthusiastically. How can we hope to excite anyone about something if, to be honest, it doesn't excite us very much?

I was once at a church luncheon club where an elderly man was complaining that his body was wearing out.

"Never mind," I said. "If you trust in Jesus you can live for ever."

"I don't want to live for ever," he replied.

Strangely enough the Bible itself doesn't seem to agree with traditional church teaching on this subject. Almost without exception it teaches that the eternal destiny of believers will not be in heaven but on earth, on earth with the resurrected Lord Jesus Christ. For example, we are to pray that God's kingdom will come *on earth*. (Matthew 6:10) The Lord will become king over all *the earth*. (Zechariah 14:9) The saints from all nations will reign *on earth*, Revelation tells us. In a vision of heaven John heard angelic beings worshipping Jesus with this song:

> *"Worthy art thou to take the scroll and to open its seals, for thou wast slain and by thy blood didst ransom men for God from every tribe and tongue and people and nation, and hast made them a kingdom and priests to our God, and they shall reign on earth."*
>
> Revelation 5:9,10

So do such scriptures describe in some symbolical way how things are supposed to be now, or are they a literal description of how things will be in the life to come? Let's have a closer look at what the Bible teaches about God's plans for our future.

The kingdom of God

In John's Gospel the good news is mainly about eternal life, but in the other three Gospels, and to some extent in the book of Acts, the good news is mainly about the kingdom of God:

And Jesus went about all the cities and villages, teaching in their synagogues and preaching the gospel (good news) *of the kingdom...*

Matthew 9:35

Jesus came into Galilee, preaching the gospel of God, and saying, "The time is fulfilled, and the kingdom of God is at hand..."

Mark 1:14,15

When you pray, say... "Thy kingdom come."

Luke 11:2

[Jesus] presented himself alive after his passion by many proofs, appearing to them during forty days, and speaking of the kingdom of God.

Acts 1:3

Jesus based all his teaching on the Old Testament, which he said he had come to fulfil. *"Think not that I have come to abolish the law and the prophets; I have come not to abolish them but to fulfil them."* (Matthew 5:17) All his audience were Jews, and they would have understood from the Old Testament what he meant by the kingdom of God. The Old Testament taught that God would send a king, a descendant of King David, who would rule the earth with justice for ever on the throne of his famous ancestor.

There shall come forth a shoot from the stump of Jesse (King David's father), *and a branch shall grow out of his roots. And the Spirit of the Lord shall rest upon him, the spirit of wisdom and understanding, the spirit of counsel and might, the spirit of knowledge and the fear of the Lord. ...with righteousness he shall judge the poor, and decide with equity for the meek of the earth; and he shall smite the earth with the rod of his mouth, and with the breath of his lips he shall slay the wicked.*

Isaiah 11:1-4

223

For to us a child is born, to us a son is given; and the government will be upon his shoulder, and his name will be called "Wonderful Counsellor, Mighty God, Everlasting Father, Prince of Peace." Of the increase of his government and of peace there will be no end, upon the throne of David, and over his kingdom, to establish it, and to uphold it with justice and with righteousness from this time forth and for evermore.

Isaiah 9:6,7

But you, O Bethlehem Ephrathah, who are little to be among the clans of Judah, from you shall come forth for me one who is to be ruler in Israel, whose origin is from of old, from ancient days. ...he shall be great to the ends of the earth.

Micah 5:2,4

The prophets realized that if the coming descendant of King David was to reign for ever over the earth he would have to be more than human. His origin would be 'from ancient days' (a description normally reserved for God – see Daniel 7:9); he would have to be an 'everlasting Father' (again, a description previously applied only to God – see Deuteronomy 33:27 and Malachi 2:10); in fact he would somehow have to be the 'Mighty God' himself! Obviously these were all prophecies of Jesus, who was both the Son of Man and the Son of God. But what's important here is that they all foretold that Jesus's everlasting reign would be *on the earth*. And Jesus said he had come to fulfil all that the prophets had foretold.

A new earth

The old Jewish prophets had two dilemmas. First, if the coming king was to rule for ever he would have to be more than human. Second, if he was to rule over the earth for ever, then something revolutionary had to happen to the earth. For they were realistic about the present earth's condition: it could not last for ever. '*Of old thou didst lay the foundation of the earth, and the heavens are the work of thy hands. They will perish, but thou dost endure; they will all wear out like a garment.'* (Psalm 102:25,26) *"...the heavens will vanish like smoke, the earth will wear out like a garment..."* (Isaiah 51:6)

We can see the earth wearing out right now, in the alarming loss of topsoil and the increasing desertification of once fertile lands; the disappearance of tropical rainforests and vital sources of fresh water like Lake Chad in western Africa; the pollution of the air, oceans and outer space by industrial waste products and human garbage; the fast diminishing natural resources of oil, gas, copper, rare earths and other elements that are essential for contemporary life; and the continuing loss of species in the animal, plant and other kingdoms.

Climate change – whether or not human activity is its principal cause – is a reality which is also threatening life as we know it.

However, the Lord told the prophets not to worry. Just as he had made this earth long ago, so he planned to make a new one, even better than the one we have now. *"...the earth will wear out like a garment, and they who dwell in it will die like gnats; but my salvation will be for ever, and my deliverance will never be ended."* (Isaiah 51:6) *"For behold, I create new heavens and a new earth."* (Isaiah 65:17) In the New Testament Peter wrote, '*...according to his promise we wait for new heavens and a new earth in which righteousness dwells.*' (2 Peter 3:13) And John was given a vision of this new earth: *'Then I saw a new heaven and a new earth; for the first heaven and the first earth had passed away, and the sea was no more.'* (Revelation 21:1) The Bible consistently tells us that God is going to make an Earth Mark 2. And what would be the point of that if no one is going to live in it?

The present earth has acquired many defects since God first made it, when it was 'very good'. (Genesis 1:31) Thorns and thistles have appeared. Mountains have risen up resulting in earthquakes, volcanic eruptions and avalanches; oceans have spread out producing storms, floods and tsunamis. Some regions have become too hot or dry for comfort, while others

225

are too cold or wet; animals and plants suffer from diseases and compete against each other for survival; too much sun causes skin cancer and too little produces vitamin D deficiency. But God has promised to put everything right by starting again, and this time the earth he creates will not be spoilt as a result of mankind's sin.

The wilderness and the dry land shall be glad, the desert shall rejoice and blossom...

Isaiah 35:1

Instead of the thorn shall come up the cypress; instead of the brier shall come up the myrtle...

Isaiah 55:13

The wolf shall dwell with the lamb, and the leopard shall lie down with the kid, and the calf and the lion and the fatling together, and a little child shall lead them... They shall not hurt or destroy in all my holy mountain; for the earth shall be full of the knowledge of the Lord as the waters cover the sea.

Isaiah 11:6,9

There shall no more be anything accursed...

Revelation 22:3

"Then I saw a new heaven and a new earth, for the first heaven and the earth had passed away... God himself will be with them; he will wipe away every tear from their eyes, and death shall be no more, neither shall there be mourning nor crying nor pain any more, for the former things have passed away."

Revelation 21:1-4

In the Authorized Version's literal translation of Matthew 19:28, Jesus tells his disciples, *"Verily, I say unto you, that ye which have followed me, in the regeneration when the Son of man shall sit in the throne of his glory, ye also shall sit upon twelve thrones, judging the twelve*

226

tribes of Israel." According to my vast Greek-English lexicon[104], the Greek word *paliggenesia*, which is translated as 'regeneration', means *'recreation, or the restoration of a thing to its pristine state.'*

Again, in the Authorized Version of Acts 3:21, Peter declares that heaven must receive Jesus *'...until the times of restitution of all things, which God hath spoken by the mouth of all his holy prophets since the world began.'* According to the lexicon, the words translated as the 'restitution of all things' mean *'the restoration not only of the true theocracy* (rule by God) *but also of the more perfect state of even physical things which existed before the fall.'*

Thus, the Bible unambiguously declares that the new earth which God will make will be just like the present earth was before Adam and Eve fell into sin. Thorns and thistles will no longer be the bane of gardeners and farmers. Species of animals and plants which perished in the flood or have disappeared in more recent years will be restored. [105] Woolly mammoths, Pacific Island Reed-warblers, and even the duck-billed platypus will be back!

People will inhabit the new earth

If God is going to take the trouble of making a brand new earth fit for humans, it's obvious that human beings are going to live in it. Otherwise, what would be the point of making it? Since death will be no more, those who live in it will not die. And if they are not going to die, they will have to be people who have been granted eternal life, either through their faith in Christ while they were alive, or else at the last judgement in response

---

[104] A Greek-English lexicon of the New Testament. Grimm's Wilke's Clavis Novi Testamenti, translated, revised and enlarged by Joseph H. Thayer, fourth edition, T & T Clark, Edinburgh, 1901.

[105] I do not personally believe that the fiercer flesh-eating dinosaurs will be restored. I believe they were a corruption of some of God's original animals, just as Genesis 6.1-4 and related Jewish writings tell us that giants were a corrupted version of human beings.

to how they lived without any knowledge of him. In other words, only the saved will inhabit the new earth. And that is pretty well what the Bible says: '*Outside are the dogs and sorcerers and fornicators and murderers and idolaters, and every one who loves and practises falsehood.*' (Revelation 22:15)

The saved will have been resurrected from death in physical bodies that no longer have any defects. '*Then the eyes of the blind shall be opened, and the ears of the deaf unstopped; then shall the lame man leap like a hart, and the tongue of the dumb sing for joy.*' (Isaiah 35:5,6) When Jesus healed the blind, deaf, dumb and lame, he was giving people a foretaste of his kingdom to come, in which no one will be disabled or sick.

These resurrected bodies will be real bodies, just like Jesus Christ's resurrection body. '*…the Lord Jesus Christ, who will change our lowly body to be like his glorious body…*' (Philippians 3:20,21)

On the evening Jesus rose from the dead, he told his astonished disciples, "*…a spirit has not flesh and bones as you see that I have.*" (Luke 24:39) In his resurrection body Jesus ate fish and bread; he looked forward to eating another Passover meal when he returned; and he looked forward to drinking some fresh ('new') grape juice with them. (Luke 24:42; John 21:9,15; Luke 22:14-18) People won't need physical food or drink in heaven, which is why Jesus said he wouldn't eat a Passover or drink again of the fruit of the vine until he returned in his resurrection body to establish his kingdom.

And it's a resurrection body like his body that we shall have if we believe in him. We shall have a body designed to eat earthly food and drink earthly drink, in other words *a body designed to live on the earth.*

'*The heavens are the Lord's heavens, but the earth he has given to the sons of men.*' (Psalm 115:16) The Bible clearly states that everyone who is saved through faith in Christ and is granted a place in his kingdom will live on the wonderful new earth that God has promised.

- The meek will live on the earth. (Matthew 5:5)
- Jesus's original apostles and the saved people of Israel will live on the recreated earth. (Matthew 19:28)
- People from every people group, language and nation who have been saved by the blood of Jesus will live on the earth. (Revelation 5:9,10)

So we shall not go up to the heavenly city: instead the heavenly city will come down to us. We shall not dwell for ever with God: instead he will dwell for ever with us, in the person of Jesus Christ the king.

> *And I saw the holy city, new Jerusalem, coming down out of heaven from God, prepared as a bride adorned for her husband; and I heard a loud voice from the throne saying, "Behold, the dwelling of God is with men. He will dwell with them, and they shall be his people, and God himself will be with them."*
>
> Revelation 21:2,3

But doesn't the Bible say…?

Nevertheless, some Christians believe Paul's letter to the Ephesians tells a different story. Ephesians 1:20 says that Christ is currently seated at the right hand of God in heavenly places. Ephesians 2:4-7 then says:

> *…God, who is rich in mercy, out of the great love with which he loved us, even when we were dead through our trespasses, made us alive together with Christ (by grace you have been saved), and raised us up with him, and made us sit with him in the heavenly places in Christ Jesus, that in the coming ages he might show the immeasurable riches of his grace in kindness toward us in Christ Jesus.*
>
> Ephesians 2:4-7

Some people interpret these verses to mean that the saved will spend the coming ages seated with Christ in heavenly places rather than earthly ones. Some who hold this view also teach that the Bible verses referring to a future life on the earth refer only to Jewish believers and perhaps also to some of the first Gentile believers to whom Paul wrote in his earlier letters.

First I'll explain what's wrong with the idea that Jewish and Gentile believers will be treated differently. And then I'll explain what Paul actually meant.

The idea that Jewish and Gentile believers will be treated differently contradicts everything Paul wrote in the rest of Ephesians chapter 2. In Christ, he wrote, Jews and Gentiles have been made one: they are fellow citizens, joined together into a holy temple in the Lord. How can any of this be true if Jewish believers are going to live on the earth while Gentile believers live in heaven?

In Ephesians chapter 4 Paul went even further. '*There is one body and one Spirit, just as you were called to the one hope that belongs to your call...*' How can Jewish and Gentile believers have one and the same hope if some of them hope to live on the earth and the others hope to live in heaven? Or how can they be one body if it is split in two?

In Galatians 3:28,29 Paul told his readers, '*There is neither Jew nor Greek, there is neither slave nor free, there is neither male nor female; for you are all one in Christ Jesus. And if you are Christ's, then you are Abraham's offspring, heirs according to the promise.*' In other words God makes no distinction between Jews and non-Jews who believe in Jesus Christ, any more than he distinguishes between slave and free, male and female.

There were Jewish believers in the church at Ephesus to which Paul was writing. (See Acts 19:1) So when he wrote that God 'made us sit with him in the heavenly places in Christ Jesus', the 'us' must have included Jewish readers as well as the Gentile ones. If this really meant that the destiny of believers is to live for ever in heaven, it must include Jewish Christians too.

As we saw earlier, the Bible clearly teaches that the Lord Jesus will return to the earth to reign. '*On that day his feet shall stand on the Mount of Olives which lies before Jerusalem on the east... Then the Lord your God will come, and all the holy ones with him. ... And the Lord will become king over all the earth...*' (Zechariah 14:4,5,9) If Jesus is going to reign on the earth in the age to come, how can Gentile believers remain seated with him in heaven?

The belief that Gentile Christians will be privileged to spend eternity in heavenly places with Christ, while Peter and Paul and the rest of Christ's *Jewish* apostles will have to stay down here on the earth can only appear to be racist. I would be most uncomfortable with the idea that as a Gentile believer I shall have a more privileged position than Jesus's first apostles.

Revelation 5:9,10 says that Jesus has ransomed men 'from *every* tribe and tongue and people and nation', i.e. both Jews and Gentiles. He has 'made them a kingdom' and 'they shall reign *on earth*', it says. That is about the future ('they shall reign') and it means that in the future all resurrected believers in Jesus will live on the earth.

As believers in Jesus Christ we all share in one, single, glorious hope, whether we are Jews or Gentiles, male or female, rich or poor. Guaranteed by the promises of Jesus and by the reality of his own resurrection from the dead, we shall live with him in a new earth. He will rule over a worldwide kingdom in which sin and all its horrible consequences will be replaced by unity, love, truth, justice, peace, and unimaginable joy to the end of eternity. What a glorious hope we have!

So what *did* Paul mean by this verse in Ephesians 2:6? For a start he wasn't talking about the future. He didn't say God *will* raise us up with Christ and seat us with him in heavenly places: he said that God has done this already. God '*raised us up with him, and made us sit with him...*' In Ephesians 2:1,2 Paul wrote, '*And you he made alive, when you were dead through the trespasses and sins in which you once walked...*' That was about something God had already done for the believers in Ephesus. So in verses 4 to 6 Paul reiterated what God *had done* for them, and then he expanded it: '*God... made us alive together with Christ... and raised us up with him, and made us sit with him in the heavenly places...*' Those are all things that God has already done. They are a present fact. Believers in Christ are spiritually alive now, and in the same way they are seated by faith with Christ in heavenly places right now! That's so exciting, if you are a believer!

What does that actually mean? I understand it to mean that we can share in Christ's authority and victory over the evil one, here and now! *"All authority in heaven and on earth has been given to me,"* Jesus told his original apostles. (Matthew 28:18) But he didn't keep this spiritual authority to himself: he delegated it to them. *"...I have given you authority to tread upon serpents and scorpions, and over all the power of the enemy..."* (Luke 10:19) Paul applied this to all the believers in Ephesus, and by implication to us: '*...we are not contending against flesh and blood, but against... the spiritual hosts of wickedness in the heavenly places.*' (Ephesians 6:12) The only way we can contend against the evil hosts who inhabit heavenly places is to be seated in those same heavenly places with Christ here and now by faith.

Then Paul went on to state what God *would* do in the coming ages. '*...that in the coming ages he might show the immeasurable riches of his grace in kindness toward us in Christ Jesus.*' (Ephesians 2:7) Having spoken about the amazing privileges God has granted to believers in this age, he goes on to tell us that in the ages to come God will treat us with absolutely immeasurable grace and kindness. And that grace and kindness will include restoring all believers to everlasting life in the paradise that Adam and Eve lost, back here in a new earth, an earth which will once again be perfect in every detail. What an awesome hope we have in Jesus Christ!

Annex 6. Jewish feasts and their fulfilment in Jesus Christ

The principal Jewish feasts

In Chapter 9, I described the amazing correspondence between the Jewish feasts which are prescribed in the Old Testament and the life of Jesus Christ – both his past earthly life and his promised return to the earth. In this annex I show this in more detail.

Figure A.1 shows the dates of the principal annual Jewish feasts. As you can see, the Jewish calendar differs from the Gregorian calendar that the rest of the world uses.[106] In the Jewish calendar each month begins with a new moon, so the months are only 28 or 29 days long, and every two or three years a thirteenth month has to be inserted to restore the seasons to their proper place. Passover is celebrated in Nisan, which is in March or April, and the Jewish New Year formally begins with the Festival of Trumpets on the first day of Tishri.

---

[106] The Gregorian calendar was introduced under Pope Gregory XIII in 1582 to replace the previous Julian calendar. The Julian calendar did not synchronize properly with the earth's rotation about the sun, with the result that Easter was being celebrated too late in the year. At the time of the correction ten days had to be lost. Personally, I think they should have lost twenty days to make January 1st the shortest day of the year. Then from New Year's Day onwards the days would have grown progressively longer. They could also have taken the opportunity to make the months more equal in length by increasing the number of days in February to 30 and reducing the length of two of the 31-day months to 30. Perhaps when the Beast of Revelation takes over the world, he will follow my advice! See Daniel 7:25.

You can read more about these festivals in chapter 23 of Leviticus, the third book of the Bible.

Moses commanded the people of Israel to observe these festivals, following instructions he had received from the Lord on Mount Sinai. It's important to understand that both the details and the dates were set by the Lord.

Figure A.1: The principal Jewish feasts

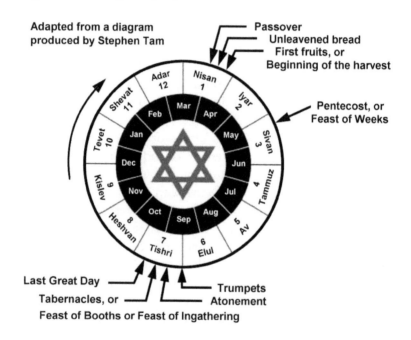

Table A.1 shows how wonderfully the first four festivals in the spring, starting with the Passover, foretold events in the life of Jesus when he was first here; and how the second four festivals in the autumn, starting with the festival of trumpets, correspond to the coming events at the time of his return.

Table A.1: Jewish festivals and their fulfilment in the life of
Jesus Christ

Spring Festivals	Description and Purpose	Fulfilment in Christ
Passover (Pesach) Leviticus 23:5	A communal meal involving various symbolical foods and the retelling of the Exodus story. It originally centred around a whole roast lamb. It is to recall Israel's deliverance from slavery in Egypt on the night when the blood of a lamb protected the Hebrew people from the angel of death.	Jesus died as a sacrificial lamb at Passover time to deliver us from slavery to Satan and death. *'Christ, our paschal* (Passover) *lamb, has been sacrificed.'* (1 Corinthians 5:7) See also Isaiah chapter 53.
Unleavened bread (Chag HaMatzot) Leviticus 23:6-8	Originally a week of eating unleavened bread, beginning on the day after the Passover, it was to remind Israel that in their haste to leave Egypt there was not time to	Jesus called himself 'the bread of life'. A typical matzah or unleavened loaf is: striped (*'…with his stripes we are healed.'* Isaiah 53:5); pierced (*'…when they look on him whom they have pierced, they shall mourn…'* Zechariah

	make proper bread. Nowadays unleavened bread is eaten on Passover Day and the following day. Unleavened bread speaks of purity of life. Every trace of yeast is first removed from the house.	12:10); and pure ('*He committed no sin; no guile was found on his lips.*' (1 Peter 2:22).
Beginning of harvest, or First Fruits (Reishit Katzir) Leviticus 23:10-14	The Israelites were told to bring to the priest a sheaf of green barley on the second day of the week of unleavened bread, which began and ended with a sabbath. It was a thank offering to the Lord for the first fruit of the new year's planting.	Jesus rose from the dead on this day of First Fruits. Passover Day was Thursday evening to Friday evening; the Sabbath and the first day of unleavened bread was Friday evening to Saturday evening; and the Feast of First Fruits, the second day of unleavened bread and the first day of the Jewish week was Saturday evening to Sunday evening. It was on the morning of this day that Jesus rose from the

		dead. *'Now after the Sabbath, toward the dawn of the first day of the week, Mary Magdalene and the other Mary went to see the sepulchre.'* (Matthew 28:1). *'…Christ has been raised from the dead, the first fruits of those who have fallen asleep.'* (1 Corinthians 15:20)
Pentecost, or the Feast of Weeks (Shavuot) Leviticus 23:15-22	Seven weeks after the Feast of First Fruits came the celebration of the wheat harvest at Pentecost. Every Israelite had to bring two loaves of bread made from wheat flour to the priests as a thank offering.	It was on the day of Pentecost that the power of the Holy Spirit miraculously filled the first disciples of Jesus of Nazareth. That same morning they led another three thousand people to believe in Jesus as the Messiah. Jesus said, *"…unless a grain of wheat falls into the earth and dies, it remains alone; but if it dies, it bears much fruit."* (John 12:24) The first harvest of souls resulting from Christ's death and

237

		resurrection took place on the very day the wheat harvest was celebrated.
Autumn Festivals	**Description and Purpose**	**Fulfilment in Christ**
The Feast of Trumpets (Rosh Hashanah or Yom Teruah) Leviticus 23:24 This is considered in Judaism to be or to represent the first of three special days of judgement.	The first day of the seventh month was to be observed as a sabbath, proclaimed by a blast of trumpets. It was to be a day of memorial or remembrance, but God did not specify in Leviticus what was to be remembered, perhaps because it hadn't yet happened!	As I explained in Chapter 5, it is very likely that Resurrection Day for believers in Christ will take place on the Feast of Trumpets. In a sense, that day will also be a day of judgement for the rest of the world, when they realize they should have believed in Jesus Christ after all.
The Day of Atonement (Yom Kippur) Leviticus 23:27,28 & 16:1-34 Ten days after the Feast of Trumpets, the Day of Atonement is considered in	This was the one day of the year when the high priest was permitted to enter the holiest place in the tabernacle or temple. He had to confess all the	I believe that the Day of Atonement, which will follow the disappearance of Christians on Resurrection Day, will be a day for true repentance on the part of many Jews who remain behind.

Judaism to be or to represent the second of three days of judgement for those who on Rosh Hashanah were on the borderline of righteousness and unrighteousness. The intervening ten days are to give them an opportunity to repent and amend their lives.	sins of the people and make atonement for them with some serious animal sacrifices. Today it remains a day of solemn reflection and repentance for religious Jews.	On that day those who truly love Yahweh will finally realize that Jesus (Yeshua ben Yosef) was and is the Messiah (Yeshua ben David, the Mashiach). They will put their faith in him and in his sacrificial death for salvation, instead of in their own efforts to keep God's laws. '*...a hardening has come upon part of Israel, until the full number of the Gentiles come in, and* [then] *all Israel will be saved...*' (Romans 11:25,26)
The Feast of Booths or Tabernacles (Sukkot) Leviticus 23:33-36,40-43 This week begins five days after the Day of Atonement.	This was celebrated – and still is – by a week of feasting and sleeping out in shelters made of branches and palm fronds or sticks and leaves or in tents, in memory of the forty years that the Hebrews sojourned in	For Christians, the Feast of Booths can remind us that this present world is only our temporary home. Our permanent home will be in the kingdom of God under the rule of Jesus Christ, when sin and death will be gone for ever and God restores the

	tents in the wilderness. It is a time for the people of Israel to look back on their deliverance from Egypt and to look forward to life in the promised kingdom of God. It is also a celebration of the fruit harvest.	earth to its original perfection. As the final harvest festival of the year, it also symbolizes Jesus's picture of the angels gathering in God's elect '...*from one end of heaven to the other.*' (Matthew 24:31)
The Last Great Day (Hoshana Rabbah) Leviticus 23:35,36,39-43; John 7:37 According to the Jewish 'Midrash', the seventh day of the Feast of Booths is or represents the day when God issues his final judgement.	Jews call the seventh day of the Feast of Booths 'Hoshana Rabbah', meaning 'Great Supplication'. This is probably the day referred to in the Gospel of John as the last great day of the feast, when Jesus prophesied that those who believed in him would be filled with the Holy Spirit. A popular view of this day is that it is the day when	Because Hoshana Rabbah is associated in Judaism with God's pronouncement of judgement on the lives of his people, and because it comes at the end of the seven-day Feast of Booths, it prefigures the final day of judgement, the one which will come at the end of the seven 'days' or millennia of this present earth's existence. '*Then I saw a great white throne and him who sat upon it... And*

240

	God decides how the rest of the new year will turn out.	*I saw the dead, great and small, standing before the throne, and books were opened. ... And the dead were judged by what was written in the books, by what they had done.'* (Revelation 20:11-15) On that day everyone who has ever lived and who has not already been raised to eternal life as a believer in Christ will be judged by Jesus Christ. (John 5:22; Matthew 25:31-46) Then will follow not one new year on this earth, but endless years on a new earth under the kingship of Jesus, Yeshua ben David.

Hanukkah and the birth of Jesus

There remains another significant event in the life of our Saviour: his birth! In Chapter 9, I mentioned Kenneth Doig's conclusion that Jesus was born on or about December 25th in the year 5 BC. So did Jesus's birth coincide with a Jewish feast too? I think you can guess the answer...

241

Some people argue that Jesus could not have been born in winter because the Bible tells us that there were sheep out on the hills on the night that Jesus was born. Well, sheep graze in winter even in the far north-east of Scotland, where it must be far colder than it is in Israel. Furthermore, the most common breed of sheep in the Middle East is the hardy Awassi, and December is the heart of the lambing season for Awassis.[107] During lambing shepherds have to keep a close watch on their sheep, not so much to protect them from thieves, as to look out for any first-time ewes ('shearlings') who may be in trouble giving birth. In North Yorkshire shepherds call it 'looking the sheep'.

So when the Bible tells us that there were shepherds out on the Bethlehem hillside 'looking the sheep' that night, it almost certainly fixes the date of Jesus's birth in December. And what could have been a more appropriate time for Jesus, the Lamb of God, to be born than in the heart of the lambing season![108]

Others say that Gabriel's appearance to Mary 'in the sixth month' (Luke 1:26) doesn't support a December birth date, assuming that she conceived Jesus at time of the angel's visit. But it does support it! To start with, the Greek text and a comparison with similar wording in the Old Testament make it clear that Luke was referring to the sixth calendar month, not the sixth month of Elizabeth's pregnancy. Luke, a non-Jew

---

[107] www.sciencedirect.com/topics/agricultural-and-biological-sciences/awassi, viewed February 2021.

[108] Some people believe that Jesus was born on the Feast of Tabernacles in September, because John 1:14 says that the Word became flesh and 'tabernacled' among us. But by that logic, all Christians must have been born again on the Day of Atonement, because in the Authorized Version of Romans 5:11 it says that in Jesus we have 'atonement'. 'To tabernacle' means to inhabit a temporary dwelling, like a tent. A tabernacle is a tent. In 2 Corinthians 5:1 Paul likens our temporary mortal bodies to tents, using the same Greek word 'tabernacle' as John did. So when John wrote that Jesus came to 'tabernacle' among us he simply meant that the Word became flesh by temporarily dwelling among us in a human body just like ours. He was saying nothing about the date of Jesus's birth.

writing to another non-Jew (Luke 1:3) would almost certainly have been referring to the sixth month of the ancient Macedonian calendar. This was the calendar in general use at that time among all non-Jewish people in that part of the world. [109] The sixth month was termed Xanthikos, which corresponded approximately to our month of March. [110] According to the historian Kenneth Doig, Xanthikos in the year 5 BC ran from March 10th to April 7th, with March 25th roughly in the middle of it.[111] In other words, Luke tells us that Gabriel's visit to Mary came just nine months before Jesus was born, further evidence in support of a December birth!

But back to Hanukkah. The annual Jewish Feast of Hanukkah, or Chanukah, celebrates the return of the victorious Maccabees to Jerusalem after they had defeated the Greeks. They found only enough sacred oil in the ruined temple to light one candle for one day, but miraculously it went on burning for eight days and nights while they prepared more.

During each festival, which therefore lasts eight nights, a nine-branched menorah with eight coloured candles and one white one is lit every night in remembrance of the victory and the subsequent events. The white candle is lit on the first night: it is known as the 'shamash' or 'servant', and it is used to light the others on successive nights.

In Hebrew 'hanukkah' means 'to dedicate'. The feast is referred to as the Feast of Dedication or the Festival of Lights. So if Jesus's birth took place at the time of a corresponding Jewish feast, as every other major event in his life did or will do, Hanukkah is surely the one. Isaiah described the coming saviour as *the servant* of the Lord (Isaiah 52:13); Joseph and Mary *dedicated* Jesus to the Lord in the temple according to the law for the dedication of the first-born (Exodus 13:2,12); and

---

[109] There are references to the Macedonian calendar month of Xanthikos in the second book of Maccabees, chapter 11.

[110] See *Ancient Macedonian calendar* on Wikipedia, viewed November 2021.

[111] *New Testament Chronology*. K.F.Doig, Edwin Mellen Press, 1990.

Jesus absolutely fulfilled the prophetic promises that he would be *a light* to the nations. (Isaiah 49:6)

So when does Hanukkah take place? It begins on the 25th day of Kislev in the Jewish calendar, which can be at the end of November or on almost any date in December in our calendar. An interactive calendar on the website of *The Church of God Study Forum* confirms that Kislev 25, the first day of the Feast of Dedication, was on December 25th in the year 5 BC.[112] There was a strong tradition in the early church, recorded in writing by several of the early church fathers, that Jesus was indeed born on December 25th, in other words, on the first day of Hannukah.

John alluded to the birth of Jesus by writing, '*The true light that enlightens every many was coming into the world.*' (John 1:9) How perfect, then, that Jesus was born on the first day of Hanukkah, the Festival of Lights. Furthermore, he would have been circumcised on the final eighth day of the festival.

Hanukkah is surely the Jewish feast that God brought about to be a prophetic celebration of his Son's birth!

Purim – the final major Jewish feast

Purim recalls and celebrates how Queen Esther risked her life to save the entire Jewish race from death during the exile in Babylon. The story is told in the book of Esther. It's the only book in the Bible that doesn't mention God!

Christian preachers sometimes liken the courageous Esther to Jesus; her wise uncle Mordecai to the Holy Spirit; the proud and wicked Haman to Satan; and the mighty King Ahasuerus to God the Father, who eventually sentenced Haman to death. In this way, Purim prefigures the collaboration of the Holy Spirit with Jesus to defeat Satan and bring salvation to all the people of God. Is it possible, just possible then, that Purim too has something to do with the life of Jesus? For there is one more

---

[112] www.cgsf.org/dbeattie/calendar/?roman=-4

significant event in the life of Jesus that I haven't yet mentioned...

Purim is celebrated on the 14th and 15th days of the Jewish month of Adar. (See Esther 9:20-22) In 5 BC[113] these days fell on March 23rd and 24th, almost exactly nine months before Jesus was born. So it is entirely possible that Mary conceived Jesus, not only in the sixth month of Xanthikos, but at the Jewish festival of Purim!

---

[113] www.cgsf.org/dbeattie/calendar/?roman=-4

Annex 7. Fifty-day Bible reading plan

Reproduced by permission of Shoreline Community Church, Monterey, California.

By now you must have realized that a reference like 'Luke 4:14-44' means the book of Luke, chapter 4, verses 14 to 44. All Bibles have an index to the various books at the front.

The Story of the Christian Faith (New Testament)

Day 1. Luke chapters 1 & 2: The birth of Jesus
Day 2. John 1:1-18: The identity of Jesus
Day 3. Luke 4:14-44: Jesus begins his ministry
Day 4. Matthew 5 & 6: The core of Jesus's teachings
Day 5. John 3: God's love for the world
Day 6. John 5: Jesus's miracles and authority
Day 7. John 11: Jesus's power over death
Day 8. John 15: The Christian life defined
Day 9. Matthew 26 & 27: The arrest and crucifixion of Jesus
Day 10. John 20 & Luke 24: The resurrection of Jesus and his ascension
Day 11. Acts 2: The coming of the Holy Spirit
Day 12. Acts 9:1-19: The conversion of Saul and his ministry
Day 13. Acts 26: Paul's defence of the Christian faith
Day 14. Romans 3: Justification by faith alone
Day 15. Romans 7 & 8: The battle with sin, and life in the Spirit
Day 16. 1 Corinthians 13, Ephesians 5: The way of love
Day 17. 1 Corinthians 15: The power of the resurrection
Day 18. Galatians 5, Ephesians 4: Freedom and unity in Christ
Day 19. Ephesians 6: The whole armour of God

Day 20. Philippians 1:18 to 2:18: Christ's example
Day 21. Colossians 3:1-17: Putting on the new self
Day 22. Hebrews 4:14 to 5:10: Jesus the great high priest
Day 23. James 1 & 1 Peter 1: Pure religion
Day 24. 1 John 4:7-21: God is love
Day 25. Revelation 21 & 22: The new heaven and earth

Old Testament survey

Day 26. Genesis 1:1 to 3:19: The creation and fall of
humanity
Day 27. Genesis 12; 28:10-15; 32:22-28: God calls a people
Day 28. Genesis 37; 39 to 46: The story of Joseph
Day 29. Exodus 1 to 6: The call of Moses
Day 30. Exodus 7 to 14: Moses and Pharaoh
Day 31. Exodus 19:1 to 20:20: The Ten Commandments
Day 32. Deuteronomy 6:1 to 7:26; 11:13-21: Obedience
Day 33. Judges 1:1 to 2:19: Cycles of disobedience in God's
people
Day 34. 1 Samuel 7 to 9; 15 to 17: The fall of Saul and rise of
David
Day 35. 2 Samuel 5; 7 to 9; 11 & 12: Tales of David's life
Day 36. 1 Kings 2 & 3; 6; 11: Solomon's reign
Day 37. 1 Kings 11:9 to 14:31: The dividing of the kingdom
Day 38. 1 Kings 17 to 19; 2 Kings 2 & 4: The prophets
Elijah and Elisha
Day 39. Job 1 & 2; 38 to 42: How the righteous respond to
hard times
Day 40. Psalms 1; 23; 139: Psalms that enrich your soul
Day 41. Psalms 6; 22; 38; 51: Psalms for the suffering and
sinful
Day 42. Proverbs 3; 5; 7; 16; 31: Wisdom for everyday life
Day 43. Jeremiah 11 &12; 31:31-40: The covenant broken
Day 44. Jeremiah 23:1-6; Isaiah 9:6,7; 53:1-12: Jesus the
promised king
Day 45. Jonah 1 to 4: The story of Jonah
Day 46. Daniel 1 to 3: Exile in Babylon
Day 47. Daniel 4 to 6: The life of Daniel

Day 48. Nehemiah 1 & 2; 4 & 5; 8 & 9: The rebuilding of
          Jerusalem
Day 49. Esther 1 to 8: The story of Esther
Day 50. Malachi 1 to 4: Final words of the Old Testament

Annex 7. Fifty-day Bible reading plan

Other books by Arnold V Page

This book will also be available in Spanish in the summer of 2022.

La Fecha del Regreso de Cristo
ISBN: 978-1-91612-139-3 (paperback)
ISBN: 978-1-91612-134-8 (Epub)
ASIN: (Kindle)

God, Science and the Bible – Genuine Science Confirms the Bible's Amazing Message

URLink Print & Media, LLC, 2020.
ISBN: 978-1-64753-299-4 (paperback)
ISBN: 978-1-64753-300-7 (Epub)
ASIN: B086P9VJ4Z (Kindle)

According to the Bible, God created the universe and life as we know it in six literal days, only a few thousand years ago. And according to the Bible, everyone who receives his Son Jesus Christ as Lord and Saviour will one day live for ever in a recreated earth, totally free from hunger, disease, suffering and death, just as things were before human sin spoilt things. But how can such ideas be reconciled with mainstream science, which believes the universe to be 13.8 billion years old, and life to be the result of random mutations rather than divine design? What evidence is there that God even exists? Bible teacher and scientist Arnold V Page tackles these questions with original and powerful logic in a readable book which will alter your entire world view!

This is a brilliant book and definitely one I will recommend to my friends. God, Science and the Bible asks and answers the questions we have all wondered about but maybe never found the answer to. This book was fascinating. I couldn't put it down.

Helen Lawrence, Amazon reviewer

Twenty-first Century Nutrition and Family Health

New Generation Publishing, 2015.
ISBN: 978-1-78507-177-5
ASIN: B00SRDI34M
Available from www.booksforlife.today.

This important book explains what is wrong with current recommendations for healthy eating and provides clear guidance on a genuinely healthy diet and lifestyle. It is supported by references to over 500 peer-reviewed scientific papers and similar publications. The author's wife was taken off thirteen years of medication for Type 2 diabetes when the recommended diet corrected her blood sugar level. Having adopted both the diet and the recommended exercise regime, the author at the age of 70 climbed all sixteen peaks in Snowdonia over 3000 feet high in 24 hours.

I'm very impressed. Brilliant!

Dr David Walton, MBBS

Unearthly Passion – a novel for New Adults by Vincy Page

Books for Life Today, 2020.
ISBN 978-1-91612-130-0 (Paperback)
ASIN B08BW872H7 (Kindle)
ISBN 978-1-91612-131-7 (Nook)
Published as an audiobook by Spoken Realms in 2020.
ASIN B08DYGN7RX (Amazon)
ISBN 978-1-66478-294-5 (Barnes & Noble and others)

Unwanted and unloved as a child, Natalie Parsons longs to escape from the moral restraints of her foster family and embark on a life of boozing and floozing at Edinburgh University. Her geophysics course finds her rebelling against the idea that the universe created itself, and that her life therefore has no purpose. Longing for love and a sense of identity, she drifts ever deeper into drink, debt and depravity, until she hits a rock which sinks her in a life-threatening depression. Rescue comes through a friend who claims to know God, producing a dilemma that only a miracle can solve.

I loved the protagonist, Natalie Parsons. Her experiences with her foster parents, religion, sex, and drugs were relevant and eerily similar to mine, an African American man. I found this fascinating.
Ray Simmons, ReadersFavorite.com

This is a great book for those getting ready to leave home and head for university. It makes you think about what really matters when pressures come from every angle.
Will Sampson, Amazon reviewer

I only wish that every pastor, parent, teacher, social worker and indeed anyone interested in truth and morality, as I am, would read this excellent book.
Rev. Gregory Hargrove, JP

Uplifting through its powerful lessons.
Edith Wairimu, ReadersFavorite.com

Tell me about the Holy Spirit. - How to be filled with love, joy, peace and power, and extend the Kingdom of God.

Books for Life Today, 2021.
ISBN: 978-1-91612-135-5 (paperback)
ISBN: 978-1-91612-136-2 (Epub)
ASIN: B09F25G24X (Kindle)

- How can I be filled with the love, joy and peace which characterized the lives of the first Christians?
- How can I be bold and effective in sharing the gospel with others?
- How can I as a church leader open up our worship to the presence and power of the Holy Spirit, so that lives are changed and God can be seen to be at work among us?
- And what's all this about speaking in tongues?

With powerful personal illustrations author Arnold V Page unlocks the Bible's teaching on the promised gift of the Holy Spirit for all who believe in Jesus Christ as Saviour and Lord.

This book is a must read for the sceptic but also for those who believe that they have received the Holy Spirit and yet lack the full experience as evidenced in the Acts of the Apostles. So many claim to have received the Holy Spirit, yet lack any real evidence. This book will help them to find what they are searching for.

Rev. David Hathaway D.D.
President Eurovision Mission to Europe

If you are hungry for more of God, more of His power, presence and presents, this is the resource you need.

Leki Sanusi, Head,
Redeemed Christian Church of God Mission, UK

This is the best book on the Holy Spirit I have ever read. Brilliant!
Rev. Gregory Hargrove, JP

About the author

Rev Arnold V Page BSc BD MIWSc served God as a Methodist minister for thirteen years, and as the pastor of an Evangelical Free Church for a further twelve years. His passions are to proclaim the reality of God as creator and to introduce people to Jesus as Lord so that they can share in his promise of resurrection to everlasting life in a re-created earth to come.

He says, "My goals in writing *The Date of Christ's Return* were to share my long-held belief – and the largely forgotten belief of almost all Christian and Jewish teachers down the centuries – that the Bible does tell us when the promised Messiah will come; and to encourage every reader not only to commit their lives to Jesus Christ as Lord but to lead others to do the same while there is still time."

Page founded and directed the charity ChileforChrist.org, and he managed to fit in additional successful careers as a structural research engineer, a professional software developer, and the managing director of a domestic cleaning company!

He is an accomplished speaker, and is always willing to consider requests to speak on the subjects covered by this book or others he has written. (See www.booksforlife.today.) Email brief details and a telephone number to info@booksforlife.today.